Thirty
CLASSIC BOAT DESIGNS

Thirty
CLASSIC BOAT DESIGNS
The Best of the Good Boats

Roger C. Taylor

 International Marine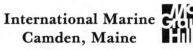
Camden, Maine

International Marine/
Ragged Mountain Press

A Division of The McGraw·Hill Companies

Copyright © 1992 International Marine®, a division of the
McGraw-Hill Companies.

Library of Congress Cataloging-in-Publication Data

Taylor, Roger C.
    Thirty classic boat designs : the best of the good boats / Roger
C. Taylor.
       p.   cm.
    Includes bibliographical references and index.
    ISBN 0-87742-329-6
    1. Sailboats. 2. Sailing ships.   I. Title. II. Title: 30
classic boat designs.
    VM331.T394 1992
    623.8'223 — dc20   92-24455
                                                      CIP

Questions regarding the content of this book should be
addressed to:

International Marine
P.O. Box 220
Camden, Maine
207-236-4837

Questions regarding the ordering of this book should be
addressed to:

The McGraw-Hill Companies
Customer Service Department
P.O. Box 547
Blacklick, OH 43004
Retail customers: 1-800-822-8158
Bookstores: 1-800-722-4726

Thirty Classic Boat Designs is printed on acid-free paper.

10 9 8 7 6 5 4 3

To Kathleen Elizabeth Carney
Shipmate, Editor, Wife

Contents

Introduction

For some fifteen years, I had the pleasure of writing about boat designs I like and then publishing the writing. I called my choices "good boats," and they appeared in a series of books called Good Boats, More Good Boats, Still More Good Boats, and then, striking my flag, The Fourth Book of Good Boats.

The term "good boat," as I used it, could apply only to a design for a boat that is handsome and able, and also interesting. I didn't want to contribute to publicity for ugly, unseaworthy, or boring boats, which always seem, somehow, to be in the majority. That kind, I call "lousy boats."

These criteria are subjective; one sailor's beauty is another's beast. I used to wonder whether readers would like my choices, as the plans of the precious boats I'd dreamed over for years, or maybe even sailed, roared through the printing press. Reactions have varied from readers writing letters accusing me of being an old timer captivated by gaff vangs and the like (both charges are true) to a few sailors building boats for themselves to one or another of my favorite designs.

All of the good-boats books are out of print, and they are not readily obtainable from dealers in used books. This is a dangerous situation, for the promoters of lousy boats keep on churning out their literature. It is only right that sailors should have some good boats to choose from if they wish. So, International Marine and I agree that it is time to revisit my 148 good boats and make the best of them available again.

It has been instructive to look back and inspect the fleet. Each still passes the test for a good boat, but today some of the boats seem more relevant than others. I have selected thirty designs to rejuvenate.

I settled on three criteria, at least one of which had to be met for a design to be considered "best": First, that a boat has been built as a result of its design being dusted off and published; second, that the design provoked interest when published, shown by a fair number of inquiries and comments; and third, that I, myself, keep referring back to the design as an aid to daydreaming.

I know of a half-dozen boats that have been built apparently as a direct result of the owners discovering a design in my books. They are the Fundulus (two boats), Chapter 8; the Gloucesterman, Chapter 11; the Calypso, Chapter 14; the Hand double-ended schooner, Chapter 19; and the Susan (I claim at least half a boat, but there are probably more.), Chapter 22. It brings a great feeling of satisfaction to be the "godfather," as one of these owners called me, of a fine, new vessel, built to a good, old design.

It is also satisfying to get letters from sailors who like my choices. Most of the letters ask for more information about the design, which can sometimes be supplied, usually in the form of the address of the designer, or the name and address of his heir or the institution holding his plans. Some of the letters correct errors of fact that have stowed away in my writing. It's always good to have these rooted out and now, having reached the haven of republication, to send them packing. The good boat that produced by far the greatest volume of what the politicians call "positive mail" was the pocket cruiser designed by Arthur Robb that appears in Chapter 5. Evidently many of us like the concept of the tiny vessel that has everything and that can put to sea in a hurry and stay out as long as her crew wants.

Not the least of the reasons I wrote and published the good-boats books was so I'd have many of my favorite vessels at hand in nicely bound form, ready to get underway at the first hankering to "get to sea as soon as I can," as Ishmael said. Like many sailors, I suspect, I've tried out hundreds and hundreds of designs on imaginary trips. My visualized voyages *must outnumber my real ones by at least ten to one. These cruises are great fun. I always handle the boat smartly, and I never get scared, wet, or cold. Moreover, an imaginary voyage is a great way to test a good boat. If my daydreaming is at all realistic, I'll discover her faults: Maybe she tries to broach when driven hard off the wind; maybe she has no handy sail combination in a strong breeze; maybe there is no place in the cabin to sit to leeward on the starboard tack. The first fault would be enough to recategorize the design from good boat to lousy boat. The second might be correctable by such simple editing—allowable with a good boat—as adding more and deeper reefs in the mainsail. I might deal with the third by ripping out an unworkable head compartment and replacing it with a comfortable settee.*

The older I get, the smaller the boat I like to dream about. I used to think nothing of putting to sea in a great brigantine, with all her complexities of rig, deck houses, small craft for tenders, lavish accommodations, and big crew requirements, but now I much prefer the simplicity of a 25-footer with two or three sails, nothing more complicated on deck or below than can be taken in at a single glance of my mind's eye, and the ability to go single-handed or double-handed. I seem to concentrate more and more of my imagination on the nice motion of a little vessel in the small seas to be found near the land.

As I write this, my most active and persistent imaginary voyage is a winter cruise in the Nimbus, *the tiny schooner in Chapter 26. Due to circumstances beyond my control, I couldn't leave Maine until my 60th birthday, November 18th. Perhaps a bit late in the season to try to get south down the East Coast in a little boat with no "power" but a pair of*

sweeps. While you can never change the actual weather occurring at the time of a dream cruise—at least my rules for this cruise don't allow such shenanigans—one of the beauties of visualized winter sailing is that you do get to pretend that your foul-weather gear never leaks and that the stove never goes out. This trip is an experiment to see, given the actual weather this winter, just how far I can get in the little schooner before being halted (if indeed I am halted) by ice or by a long spell when it is just too cold or too blustery to sail. I won't go out in more than a fresh breeze or if it's much below 40 degrees Fahrenheit. Just so you don't get the impression that I'm a hard case, I've been making port every night and have been sleeping ashore, whenever possible, in warm hostelries. (Money is no object on these trips.) It's now December 13th, so I've been out just shy of a month. The weather is forcing me to take a second lay day in Oyster Bay, Long Island, which is farther along than I expected to be. Yesterday, it was too calm to get anywhere, and today it's blowing a strong breeze right on the nose. I'd love to get down to Annapolis before winter stops me cold. Well, you get the idea. I've selected for this book boats I like to dream about.

I hope the best of the good boats will appeal to you. Perhaps you will find here a design to build. Or maybe some of these designs will simply strike a sailorly chord in you. I hope you will take at least a few of them on your own imaginary voyages. See you out there.

Oh, by the way—keep those postcards and letters coming. If International Marine has to forward enough of them, they might be convinced of the pressing need for "The Fifth Book of Good Boats."

Roger C. Taylor
Rockland, Maine
Spring 1992

Chapter 1

Chapelle Sharpies

The first paragraph of the chapter on sharpies, referring to the type as an ideal depression boat, is all too timely as this is written. It is true that the flat-bottomed sharpie is relatively cheap for what she can do: sail fast and take her crew far from the madding (and deeper-draft) crowd.

Since writing this chapter about sharpies, I've had the experience of cruising south of Cape Cod in a 34-footer that drew less than six inches, a Shearwater, designed by Phil Bolger and built by Edey and Duff. On previous trips into Katama Bay on Martha's Vineyard, I'd had to anchor well short of its intriguing east end, whose empty beaches are protected from most visiting cruising boats by extensive sand flats. In the ultra-shoal-draft sharpie, I could go anywhere the sun reflected off water.

I flew right to the end of Katama Bay, running wing-and-wing before a fresh breeze. The tide was up over the flats just enough for the skimmer to clear them. It seemed too shallow to

round up to anchor, so I decided to make a flying moor. I'd drop an anchor off the stern as she smoked across the sand and, by checking and finally holding the anchor rode, would bring her smartly to a halt just off the beach with the sails still wung out full of wind.

Oh my, but didn't that anchor line whizz out. With my mind full of a vision of the sharpie rocketing right up over the beach into the breakers beyond, I just did manage to check her way and get her stopped. When I looked down, I had, out of 200 feet of anchor rode, less than a fathom left. Looking back, I could just make out the lazy fluke of the anchor sticking up out of the water.

That night, I got up in the wee hours to catch the tide and had one of the most dramatic sails of my life, a soft reach back across the bay with the sandy bottom slipping away under the boat, eerily visible in bright moonlight. Ah, the delights of the sharpie.

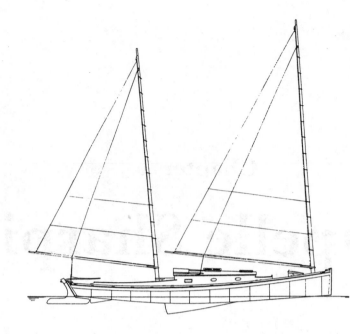

In the depths of the Great Depression, Howard I. Chapelle introduced a series of articles in *Yachting* magazine on workboats that he considered suitable for pleasure use with these words: "In these days of depleted bankrolls, 'cheap' yachts are a matter of importance to most of us." While the bankroll is merely a historical curiosity to many, we could certainly understand and agree with Chapelle's statement today if we substituted some such phrase as "purchasing power" for "bankrolls."

Chapelle's series was an admirable one, covering such craft as catboats, Friendship sloops, pinkies, Bahama sharpshooters, Gloucester sloop boats, fishing schooners, and pilot schooners. But he began with the simplest craft of all, the New Haven sharpie, a type developed in the late 1850s from the flat-bottomed sailing skiff. The New Haven sharpie, built to serve the Long Island Sound oyster fishery, is probably the thoroughbred of the type. But sharpies also came into use on the Chesapeake Bay, up and down the Carolina Sounds, and in the waters of Florida, the West Indies, and the Great Lakes. These boats fished, carried mail and cargo, went sponging, and even did a bit of smuggling here and there.

A significant modification to the sharpie was introduced in 1878, when Thomas Clapham, building sharpies at Roslyn, Long Island, New York, gave his boats a little deadrise in the bow and stern, though he left the bottom flat. The resulting partially vee-bottomed sharpies, used

mostly as pleasure boats, were known as Roslyn or Nonpareil sharpies.

One of the basic rules in building a sharpie was that the width of the bottom should be one-sixth of the length on deck. The boats were built with from 3½ to four inches of flare per foot of depth amidships, with less flare if speed was a primary consideration, and more flare if seaworthiness was a key objective. Sharpies were always light-displacement craft, with low freeboard and strong sheer. It was thought that with the boat floating with her normal weight aboard, the heel of the stem should be just out of the water. (This rule was not followed from the Chesapeake Bay south; Bay watermen always built their skiffs and sharpies so they would float with the heel of the stem just underwater.) The sharpie always had a long, flat run. She has a light rig with a low center of effort.

The sharpie is an extremely simple type of craft, yet one that will give excellent performance with intelligent use. A Pentagon systems analyst would describe a sharpie as "very cost effective." A builder of sharpies of a century ago would have found the phrase meaningless, but he understood the principle involved. It was simply to develop a craft that could accomplish more work per dollar expended on her than could any other.

The "intelligent use" part simply has to do with the fact that the sharpie lacks ultimate stability. She cannot be driven but must be

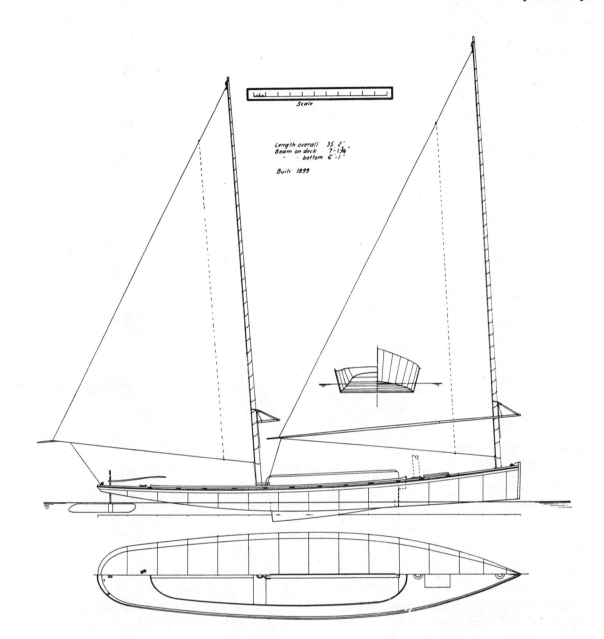

Length overall   35' 2"
Beam on deck   7'-1¾"
    "   bottom   6'-1"

Built 1899

Lester Rowe's sharpie of 1899 was considered by Howard Chapelle to be a fine example of the type. (*Yachting*, May, 1932)

shortened down in a breeze. Her rig is designed very much with her stability problem in mind. The masts are unstayed and are very flexible, so that they will bend to the gusts and spill wind out of the sails. They are not strong enough to exert enough force to tip the boat over; they will break before she capsizes.

Being flat-bottomed, sharpies pound more than most boats do, but as they heel, the pounding is reduced. A sharpie is not the ideal boat for a long, hard thrash to windward, nor for lying at anchor in a small chop. The former problem can

be avoided by not using the boat on a schedule that demands getting somewhere on a given day regardless of wind or weather. The second problem usually can be solved by using the sharpie's advantage of shoal draft to slip into smooth water close to shore or snuggle right up onto a protected beach.

Of course the sharpie depends on her centerboard for lateral resistance and maneuverability. She may have one long board of about one-third the length of the boat, or two shorter boards, one forward and one aft. Her lee chine also

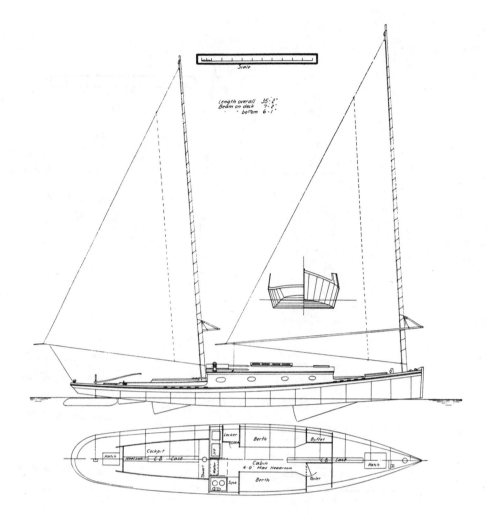

Length overall 35·2"
Beam on deck   7·2"
  " bottom   6·1"

Chapelle designed this sharpie
yacht to follow closely the model
of the Rowe sharpie. The sides of
her house extend to the rail.
(*Yachting*, May, 1932)

provides considerable lateral resistance, and she
can work to windward and maneuver with surprisingly little board lowered when necessary.

The sharpie's centerboard trunk or trunks lend
strength to her backbone, which typically consists
of a log keelson made up of three two-by-eights
on edge. As traditionally built, she had wide side
planks, usually three or four strakes to a side, of
1½-inch white pine. Her bottom was always cross-
planked, usually with 1½-inch yellow pine. The
bottom planks were fastened both to the sides
and to a chine log. A sheer clamp was used, and
instead of frames she had cleats running between
it and the chine log.

The sharpie rig is very simple, with few parts,
all easily made, and little in the way of gadgets.
The sails are reefed vertically, with a brail or laceline used to hold the unwanted bunt to the mast.
Some sharpie sails have a vertical batten at the
reefing line, thus using the same reefing principle

developed by the Chinese, but rotated ninety
degrees. With sprits extending the clews of the
sails, it is desirable to have the masts rotate when
the boat is put on the other tack, so some
builders have installed mating brass plates on the
mast heel and mast step.

The first sharpie plan shown is that of a thirty-
five-footer built by Lester Rowe in 1899. Howard
Chapelle, who drew the plans, felt that this was a
very fine example of the type, and I certainly
agree with him. Every line is a fine, fair sweep;
she would probably look like a sissy if it weren't
for her bold plumb bow. Her length on deck is
35 feet 2 inches, her beam is 7 feet 2 inches, and
her draft is one foot.

The second sharpie shown is a yacht designed
by Chapelle based closely on the Rowe thirty-
five-footer. The dimensions of the two craft are
nearly identical, but Chapelle has deepened the
stern a bit and increased displacement slightly to

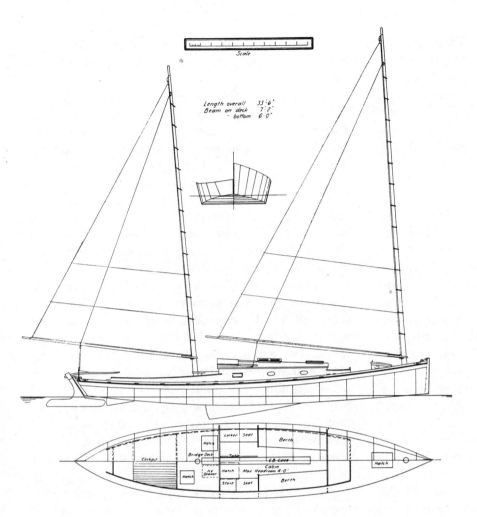

Length overall 33'6"
Beam on deck 7'2"
" bottom 6'0"

Left: Chapelle designed this double-ended sharpie after Ralph M. Munroe's able *Egret.* He retained traditional sharpie construction for simplicity. (*Yachting,* May, 1932)

Below: The *Wood Duck,* built in 1932 to Chapelle's design for a 33½-foot, double-ended sharpie by Ralph H. Wiley for Glenn Stewart. She was modified with a raked stem, a high house, and a 16-hp. outboard motor. (*Yachting*)

take the weight of the house. Under the house, this boat has four feet of headroom, the maximum obtainable in a sharpie of this length without spoiling her. To get full headroom, you would have to go to a sharpie forty-five feet long. Chapelle felt the minimum length for a cabin sharpie along these lines would be twenty-eight feet.

When most people look at sharpie plans such as these, they say, "Isn't she beautiful!" Then they promptly start making changes, such as deepening the hull a bit, giving her a little more beam, giving her considerably more freeboard, adding a few inches of height to the house, and making everything a little heavier all around. If such thoughts are put on paper and built into a boat, the resulting craft is never a sharpie and is often a disappointment.

Chapelle wrote: "It should be remembered that most boat types are developed by means of trial and error, over a period of years, hence modification must be made only after considerable study of the type. In the sharpie this is markedly true; seventy years of continuous evolution cannot be disregarded with impunity." It can also be added that nearly all modifications to the sharpie increase her cost.

The third sharpie shown is a 33½-foot double-

ender that Chapelle designed based on Ralph M. Munroe's *Egret*. She would be cheaper to build than a round-stern sharpie, and Chapelle kept her just as simple as possible in every respect. She would, in my opinion, make an admirable coastwise cruising and exploring vessel for the single-hander, for two people, or for a couple with a child.

This sharpie is 33 feet 6 inches long on deck, with a waterline length of 31 feet 3 inches, a beam on deck of 7 feet 2 inches, beam on the bottom 6 feet, and a draft of 10 inches. Her sail area is 434 square feet.

Her hull is sleek, fair, and simple. In fact, she is deceptively simple. The designer of a flat-bottomed craft has few lines to work with, and if the boat is to be handsome and able, sheer and chine must have their perfect double curvature.

I like the tandem centerboard idea for sharpies and feel the second board would be worth its extra cost in this boat. Two boards help both balance and steering and are a bit less in the way below. They give the boat such versatility. For example, if she were sailing around her anchor too much in a shifty breeze, dropping the forward board would quiet her down considerably. On this boat, the skeg might be deepened slightly to give the balanced rudder a bit more protection.

On the double-ender, the sprits have given way to booms. But her rig is still very simple, consisting in its entirety of two masts, two booms, two halyards, two topping lifts, and two sheets. I'd add lazy jacks, in the belief that being able to haul the sails right down (using the bitter end of the halyard as a downhaul) with the booms broad off without the sails thrashing around in wind and water would be a blessing in a boat like this and well worth the extra strings. The masts have a strong taper, from 6½ inches to 1½ inches in diameter, to give them that vital flexibility.

A sharpie needs to be sailed fairly free when on the wind. You have to concentrate on footing rather than on pointing. She won't eat up to weather, but she'll fly along and won't take overly long to reach an objective to windward. Off the wind, she can be really fast. Due to her

moderate sail area, she's not a particularly good ghoster, but she's light enough to be rowed in a calm.

The sharpie's foresail can always be kept full off the wind, either with the wind far enough forward to fill it to leeward or, if the wind is too far aft for that, wung out on the windward side. The absence of standing rigging allows the boom to be squared right off so the sail won't jibe.

All her gear can be kept very simple and light, and she is a very easy boat to sail. For instance, her anchors do not need to be very heavy, a feature that might endear her to sailors over, say, the age of eighty.

On deck, the coaming extended forward from the house keeps gear from getting adrift over the side and would also be a nice place to sit and watch her go when she is running off at high speed. For a rainy day at anchor, a tent over the after end of the foreboom might be a good idea: it would allow the main hatch to stay open and provide a place for standing and stretching and looking across the harbor—so your eyes can refocus when you go back to your book on the transom below. This boat also has about four feet of headroom.

The centerboard trunk looks very much in the way, until you remember that the boat is narrow enough so that you can lean across the trunk and simply remove from the shelf whatever you want from the other side of the boat. She has considerable storage space in the forepeak and under the bridge-deck.

In a boat like this sharpie, you cruise with the weather, avoiding long, rough beats and exposed anchorages. You use your wits and get very close to the weather and the water. Just imagine poking her bow up onto a sheltered beach or into the mud bank of a wild salt marsh. Think of the places she could go. With a boat like this in mind, you can pull out a thoroughly familiar chart and find a whole new cruising experience involving shallow water. Why, in this sharpie a man could hide from the revenue boys for months without leaving the eastern shore of Chesapeake Bay—unless, of course, they cheated and went to aerial spotting.

Chapter 2

The *Presto*

When I win the lottery, one of the first things I'm going to do is get somebody to build me a replica of the Presto. *Then I'm going to sail her in harm's way to determine once and for all whether Commodore Ralph M. Munroe was the designer of a remarkably seaworthy type of shoal-draft boat or a spinner of tall yarns. (I'll tow a stout peapod to come home in should the latter possibility prove true.)*

The yarn about sailing the Presto *in rough water quoted in this chapter involves witnesses, so it can't be too tall. One thing that surprises me, though, about this and other tales of derring-do by the* Presto *and her similar successors is that there is never any talk of shortening sail. On my* Presto, *when it breezes up, I'm going to reef, until she shows me an unexpected power to carry sail. And even then, I doubt she'll need driving to make respectable speed.*

In correspondence with Captain Robert Beebe, who drew the Presto's *lines, L. Francis Herreshoff wrote, ". . . her sections are so much lacking in stability that she would have to reduce her sail very greatly in any kind of a breeze." In his own design for a shoal-draft cruiser, the* Meadow Lark, *Herreshoff stuck much closer to the true sharpie, rounding bottom and sides just slightly and retaining a chine.*

There's a third possibility: Maybe the Commodore was, like Joshua Slocum, a superlative seaman who could make any vessel do his bidding, come what may. Building and sailing a new Presto *is going to be an interesting experiment; I hope my lucky number comes up soon.*

I mentioned the Egret *as a successor to the* Presto, *and two correspondents, David Keith and Kenneth P. Latham, both pointed out that the* Egret *(designed the year after the* Presto*) was not a* Presto *type, but rather a sharpie with a flat bottom and hard chines, and with less draft than a* Presto *boat. Jon Wilson, the editor of* WoodenBoat *magazine, who has done as much recent research on Munroe as anyone, confirmed this. Please strike the* Egret *from the list of the* Presto's *successors.*

Since writing about the Presto, *I have seen one of her successors that I mentioned, the* Micco, *a ketch seven feet longer than the* Presto *and with a clipper bow. Sadly, she is disintegrating in an open shed in the south Florida climate, laid up at The Barnacle, the Commodore's wonderful house on the waterfront at Coconut Grove. The* Micco *says something for the seaworthiness of the type, for she raced to Bermuda in 1924 at age thirty-three (and came in second in her class of four, and seventh in a fleet of fourteen). My pilgrimage to The Barnacle, now a state historic site, was most satisfying. The house is charming and unique; the boathouse, fascinating; and the view of Biscayne Bay can take you back (with a little imagination) to a Florida before high rises and high-powered speedboats, back to the scene in the last photograph in the chapter.*

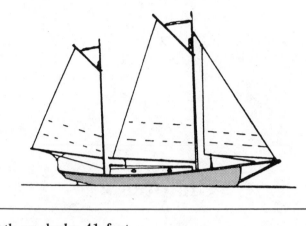

Length on deck: 41 feet
Length on waterline: 35 feet 6 inches
Beam: 10 feet 6 inches on deck; 9 feet 1 inch at waterline
Draft: 2 feet 6 inches
Sail area: 878 square feet
Designer: Ralph M. Munroe

The double-barreled myth that the coast of Maine consists solely of deep-water harbors and coves, while the Chesapeake Bay contains only shallow creeks and sand flats, is gradually being—um—eroded. There are plenty of deep anchorages in Chesapeake Bay and plenty of gunkholes along the Maine coast where only the shoalest craft can go. It was a Maine tidal cove that reminded me of the shallow *Presto*.

We were cruising in a small schooner drawing six feet and anchored in Winter Harbor, that deep, narrow fjord that cuts straight into the east side of Vinalhaven Island. Part of the crew, returning from a high-tide dinghy reconnoiter, reported the most beautiful hidden cove they had ever seen. We all rowed in through a narrow entrance between high, tree-covered ledges and agreed, when we saw a huge, wild, secluded harbor, that it was indeed a rare and exquisite spot. Someone asked, "Can we bring the schooner in?"

The answer had to be no. We might have squeezed her in then at high water, but life aboard would not have been pleasant six hours later, for the place nearly dries out. I wished we were in a boat like the *Presto*, for then we could have holed up in there perfectly comfortably for as long as we cared to.

"Ah," you may say, "but surely the schooner, with her eminently seaworthy hull, is a better all-around boat for the rough-and-tumble coast of Maine?" Perhaps, but that raises another myth: that all truly shoal-draft boats are unseaworthy.

Commodore Ralph M. Munroe—wanting a boat that could sail in the shallow waters of Biscayne Bay, yet would be seaworthy enough to sail anywhere on the Atlantic coast—decided to design a boat that he thought would be an improvement on the sharpie, a type whose performance had greatly impressed him. He said the sharpie type provided "the greatest accomplishment for least cost."

So in 1885, Commodore Munroe designed the *Presto*, and a comparison of her lines with those of the New Haven sharpie built by Lester Rowe, described in the preceding chapter, will show the changes he made. (The Rowe sharpie was not built until 1899, but she is an excellent example of the basic sharpie type Commodore Munroe knew.) He made the *Presto* a bit wider and gave her considerably more flare in the topsides. He increased the depth of hull somewhat, gave her bottom a little deadrise, and rounded the bilges. Most important, he added considerable inside ballast, 4½ tons of iron. Her dimensions worked out to: length on deck, 41 feet; length on the

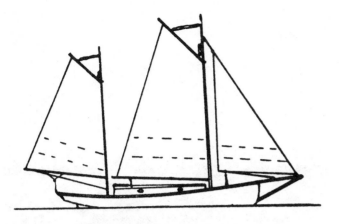

The *Presto*'s sail plan indicates a simple ketch rig with self-tending headsail. She has preventer backstays, but no fixed shrouds. (Reprinted, by permission, from *The Good Little Ship*, by Vincent Gilpin, 3rd ed., 1975; drawn by Capt. Robert P. Beebe, U.S. Navy, Retired)

waterline, 35 feet 6 inches; beam, 10 feet 6 inches on deck and 9 feet 1 inch at the waterline; draft with the board up, 2 feet 6 inches; depth amidships, 4 feet 3 inches. Her centerboard was 11 feet long by 4 feet deep.

That Commodore Munroe was satisfied with the *Presto* is shown by the fact that he designed a number of other similar boats in later years, all with the same basic hull form, though in the later models he did increase the beam slightly to make

the boats foot a little faster when on the wind. Some of the *Presto*'s successors were the *Egret*, the *Wabun*, the *Micco*, and the *Utilis*.

To answer the obvious question and start working on that myth, Commodore Munroe can be quoted: "None of them were ever capsized to my knowledge." In fact, all of these boats performed very well up and down the Atlantic coast for years, including getting caught out in northers in the Gulf Stream.

Commodore Munroe often told his favorite story about the way the *Presto* could sail:

Not long after her trial trip I invited several friends to see another international race. The day came in with a rainy southeaster and, none of my guests appearing, I started in *Presto* under full sail, with a small boy for crew, and worked out across the bar to Gedney's Channel sea buoy, with wind and sea increasing all the time. We had seen the yacht fleet lying in the Horseshoe with no sign of getting under way, and I was about squaring off for home when a large tug with the N.Y.Y.C. burgee headed our way. We hove to and waited, still under full sail and quite comfortable, while the tug was laboring hard, completely disappearing in clouds of spray every few seconds. As she approached I drew away the jib, and passed close aboard. There was no one on deck, but abreast of us a pilot-house window was dropped a bit and someone waved a handkerchief. She soon turned and ran for the Hook, and we followed.

Next morning I had a note from my old friend Louis Bayard, then Secretary of the Seawanhaka-Corinthian Yacht Club, saying: "I waved to you from the *Britannia* yesterday outside the bar. You were apparently enjoying a pleasant sail; it was quite the contrary aboard the tug.

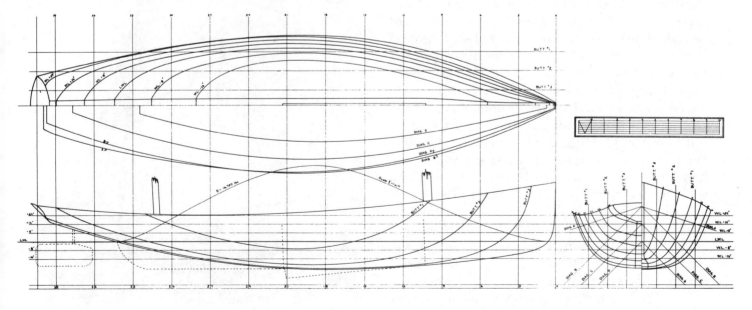

The lines of the *Presto* show a modified sharpie drawing 30″ on a waterline length of 35′6″. (Reprinted, by permission, from *The Good Little Ship*, by Vincent Gilpin, 3rd ed., 1975; drawn by Capt. Robert P. Beebe, U.S. Navy, Retired)

Left: The *Presto* on a nice reach in Great Kills, on the outer shore of Staten Island, N.Y. (*The Commodore's Story* by Ralph Middleton Munroe and Vincent Gilpin)

Right: She goes on by, displaying her fine form for the camera. (*The Commodore's Story* by Ralph Middleton Munroe and Vincent Gilpin)

A. Cary Smith, Phil Ellsworth, and others on board, were much interested in the performance of *Presto*, and Smith laid a wager that I was mistaken in the 30-inch draft and other dimensions I gave him, saying no such craft could possibly carry her sail and make such good weather of it. When can you lay her on the beach and let us measure her?" I made the appointment, they all came, and after a pleasant discussion the bet was paid to Bayard.

So the *Presto* was a great performer. It must be remembered, though, that she was always expertly handled. She would be found wanting in stability at angles of heel greater than ninety degrees. For this reason, I don't believe she could be called the ideal ocean cruiser, but I do feel that in view of her proven performance and the fact that vessels that sail coastwise have every opportunity of avoiding the worst weather, she would make an ideal coastal cruising boat. This is not to make any apologies for her behavior in rough water. Her light displacement would allow her to rise to the seas, nor would she trip on her keel when driven bodily to leeward by a breaking sea. Her flare and weight of inside ballast would give her sufficient initial stability. I should say, though, that if I were to meet that ultimate wave I hope never to meet, I'd rather not be in the *Presto*. (My first choice, actually, would be a deeply submerged, nuclear-powered submarine.)

The *Presto*'s hollow entrance must have been approved by Nathanael G. Herreshoff, that good friend of Commodore Munroe's and great utilizer

of concave waterlines in the bow. While I'm talking about the shape of the bow, I might as

Slipping along in a light air, her yard-and-sprit topsail doing its work (*Yachting*, November, 1926).

Four of the modified sharpies designed by Commodore Munroe photographed by him at Biscayne Bay: the *Egret* is in the foreground getting her bottom scrubbed; anchored off are the *Nethla, Nicketti,* and *Presto,* from left to right. (*Yachting,* June, 1937)

well discuss pounding, that old sharpie nemesis. The man who scorns flat-bottomed boats says you can never get them to stop pounding, while the defender of the flat-bottomed faith will remind you that any boat will pound, given a certain angle of heel and a certain wave shape. (I can verify that even the most beautiful concave flaring bow Nat Herreshoff ever created is capable of hitting a sea just wrong on rare occasions.) Here again, it is instructive to compare the *Presto*'s lines with those of the Lester Rowe New Haven sharpie. See how Commodore Munroe did away with the troublesome flat triangular bottom up forward by rounding back and deepening the forefoot slightly and giving the bow sections considerable deadrise. I doubt pounding was a problem in the *Presto.*

The main advantages of a centerboard in a boat are apparent, but there are ancillary advantages that may not be immediately obvious. In shoal but friendly waters, the centerboard makes an ideal sounding machine. Under similar conditions, it can also be used as a brake or a temporary anchor.

The *Presto*'s balanced rudder certainly made for most sensitive and responsive steering. One wonders, though, if its shoalness might mean some loss of steering control when a big sea ran up under her quarter.

The *Presto*'s ketch rig was a simple one. Vincent Gilpin, Commodore Munroe's great friend and student, quotes his mentor as saying,

"I would cheerfully sit up all night to cut out one superfluous rope from a sail plan." The *Presto* had no permanent shrouds but did have preventer backstays that could be brought aft and set up in a strong breeze.

The *Presto*'s working sail area was 878 square feet, broken down into a mainsail of 412 square feet, a mizzen of 266 square feet, and a jib of 200 square feet. Her topsail (see photo) added an additional 274 square feet up where it would do the most good in a light air. Her mainmast stood 35 feet above the deck, and her mizzen 29 feet 6 inches. The length of the bowsprit outboard was 9 feet.

Her jib and mizzen were loose-footed, yet self-tending. The topsail was set on a club and sprit and was sheeted from the middle of the foot. It could be swung out on the opposite side from the mainsail when running before the wind.

It would be wonderful to see the *Presto* centerboarder rejuvenated. She'd make an admirable cruising boat for any coastline. Just imagine the fun of ghosting her into a totally secluded cove running way up into the middle of some Maine island and knowing that you could lie there in perfect comfort at low tide with your anchor in plain view out ahead. Then you'd watch the tide come back, gradually filling every nook and cranny and sending her afloat again. Yes, there is a place for the sharpie on the coast of Maine, nor would she fail to make a good account of herself on the Chesapeake Bay.

Chapter 3

The *Brownie*

When Peter Wickwire, of Beaufort, South Carolina, saw the plans of the yawl Brownie in Good Boats, he made an exquisite half model of the boat I grew up in and sent it to me as a gift. This was in 1982; I've gratefully admired his handiwork — and that of the boat's designer, Sam Crocker — every day for a decade. Getting that model from her generous carver is the nicest thing that has happened to me as a result of writing about good boats.

I learned more about the design of the Brownie and about her sisterships from S. Sturgis Crocker, Sam's son, through publishing his book, Sam Crocker's Boats: A Design Catalog. Crocker made the design freelancing at home; at the time he was working in the office of John G. Alden. The Brownie was built in 1925, not 1931, as I had thought. Her original name was Caronia. She was on her fourth owner by 1932, when my father bought her, and it was the fourth owner who renamed her Brownie.

Brownie was an elfin name that suited the Taylor tradition; Uncle Fred's boat was the Goblin. In fact, by the greatest coincidence, the 30-foot, keel-and-centerboard, gaff-rigged sloop my father had before the Brownie was also named Brownie. So the name on the new boat stuck. The sloop was then referred to as "the old Brownie," and the new boat was called "the yawl Brownie."

The yawl Brownie had seven sisterships. Rigs, cabinhouses, and cabin arrangements varied. Among the rigs, there was a single-headsail gaff yawl, a single-headsail gaff sloop, a double-headsail gaff sloop, and a single-headsail Marconi yawl, as well as the Brownie's double-headsail gaff yawl rig. In the Marconi yawl, the mast was moved forward, which allowed a longer cabinhouse, and it was given rectangular, Herreshoff-type windows. This boat had transom berths in the main cabin and an enclosed head forward. Two of the sisters were owned by famous people, Frank Vining Smith, the marine artist, and Murray Peterson, designer of good boats (see chapters 9 and 22).

I received a listing from a yacht broker for one of the sisters. He referred to my description of the design and even attached a photocopy of her plans from Good Boats. I might have been tempted, but she wasn't the Brownie, and I think the Brownie's rig, house, and layout are the best of them all. When Uncle Fred's Goblin reappeared after a long hiatus, and I had the chance to bring her back into the family, I did so, but that is another story.

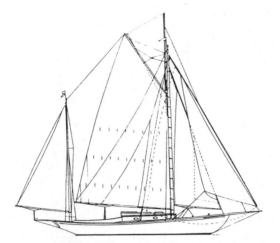

Length on deck: 31 feet 11 inches
Length on waterline: 23 feet 6 inches
Beam: 8 feet 6 inches
Draft: 5 feet 6 inches
Sail area: 590 square feet
Displacement: 5½ tons
Designer: S. S. Crocker, Jr.

A couple of years ago, when I was prowling the waterfront in Newport, Rhode Island, I saw a boat that gave me a real start. The little yawl looked somehow so completely familiar, yet at the same time so strange and small lying at the end of a float just beyond the usual lineup of stock plastic sloops.

It took me quite a few seconds of gawking to realize that here was a sistership of the yawl my father had owned during my growing-up years. I used to think of the *Brownie* as a very big boat indeed, and not having seen her in a couple of decades, it gave me a funny feeling to look over all the once so thoroughly familiar features of the boat, seemingly in miniature.

About four boats were built to the design, a creation of S. S. Crocker, Jr. Pop always said she was the best boat Sam Crocker ever turned out, and I have to agree with him. The *Brownie* was built by Goudy and Stevens at East Boothbay, Maine, in 1925. She is 31 feet 11 inches long on deck, with a waterline length of 23 feet 6 inches, a beam of 8 feet 6 inches, and a draft of 5 feet 6 inches. Her displacement is about 5½ tons and she carries 590 square feet of working sail area.

She has a sweet set of lines; hauled out on the railway we built for her on the Rhode Island bank of the Pawcatuck River, she was always pretty to look at.

We did all our own work on the yawl; everybody in the family knew every inch of the boat inside and out. I liked varnish work best myself, that is, until Pop discovered a holiday where I'd just been brushing. After one or two of those revelations, you made sure you had the light reflecting off the spar just right as you brushed, so you could see those little suggestions of bare spots and go back over them quickly.

Every seam below the waterline was red-leaded and puttied. She looked nice that way, with all the lines of her planks accentuated, but then somehow even better with the fresh copper paint on.

But all that took place after the bottom was sanded smooth. I remember uncles, who had boats of their own, coming around and feeling the yawl's bottom. They'd always say how smooth it was, but I never knew whether our bottom was really smoother than theirs or not. I guess Pop knew.

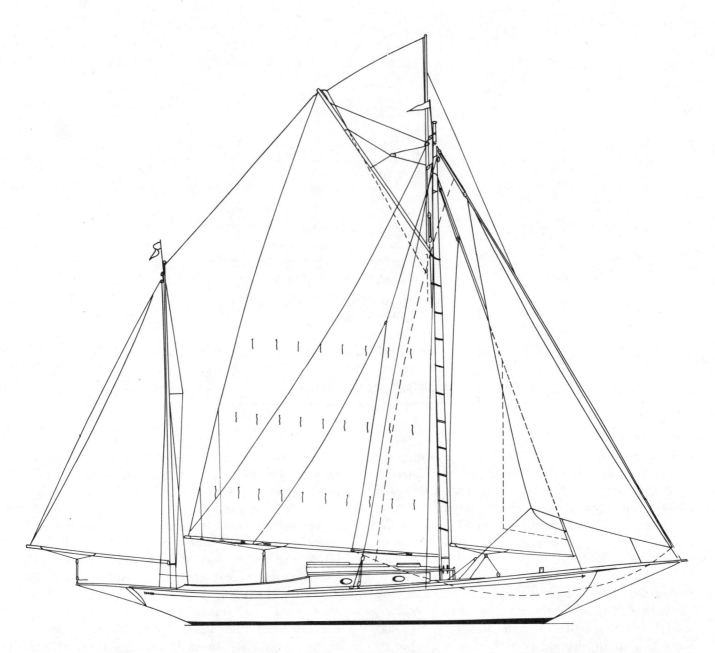

The *Brownie*'s sail plan is most versatile for cruising, and with nearly 600 square feet of working area, setting kites is more for fun than necessity.

I hated sanding the canvas-covered deck. Where the paint was chipped, you had to feather the edges, which meant bearing down hard. But you weren't to dig into the canvas on any account. This created a dilemma. You'd be working away and not getting anywhere, so you'd bear down impatiently and have a near miss with the canvas, so then you'd let up again and not get anywhere with the feathering. Pop never seemed to recognize this problem.

Of course, the great reward for all our toil was launching day, followed by rigging her up and going sailing. Launching was always quite an excitement, because to get from our railway across the River to the dredged channel and hence to the mooring, you had to thread your way through the so-called old channel, which included dodging some oyster beds. This could only be done at the top of a spring tide and took some tricky piloting. It was done in daylight, of

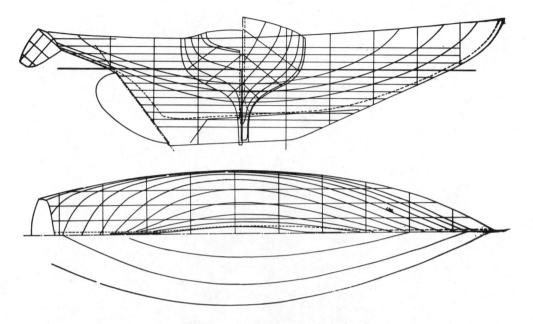

Her lines show an almost dainty hull, yet one with plenty of power and ability.

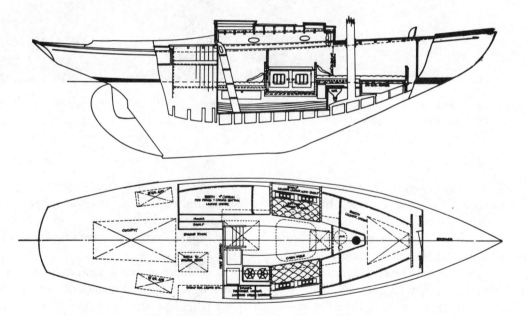

She could house three people comfortably, but cruising with two was real luxury; each one had his own seat at the table and you could keep junk in the quarterberth.

course, whenever possible, but I remember a couple of times when Pop buoyed the oyster beds and lashed lanterns to the buoys so he could hit the top of the tide after dark. To us, that put Pop way ahead of Columbus.

We had some fine cruising in the little yawl.

The *Brownie* would sail. A good friend of mine used to say that watching my father sailing this boat was a maddening experience: "He just sits there and sails by everybody."

The yawl goes especially well to windward, for she has enough ballast low enough to really stand

Pop leaving Block Island, Rhode Island, with a couple of his cronies. This is a rare photograph, for it shows Great Salt Pond in something less than a gale. (Photo by Edward Cabot)

up to her sail, enough lateral resistance to go where she looks, and a low enough hull and house so as not to have too much windage.

The heavy, low, iron keel gives her her only fault; she has a rather quick roll at times.

Her wide transom gives her extra bearing when heeled and also plenty of room on deck to handle the mizzen. In fact, there is room to stow a dinghy aft, as shown in the photo, and we used the mizzen boom as a boat derrick.

Her big rudder makes her maneuverable in light going and relatively easy to steer off the wind in a strong breeze and rough sea. The shape of the propeller aperture seems very practical and is a Crocker trademark. She has a two-bladed, feathering wheel.

The *Brownie* has a generous sail plan without having to resort to kites. One day in Block Island Sound we sailed right past the famous yawl *Dorade*, in light going, with both boats under working sail. The *Dorade* needed her big overlapping headsails to get her going, and had she had them set, she certainly would have turned the tables on us.

The little yawl is heavy for her length; she has to carry sail to do well to windward in a breeze, but she has the power to do it. The rig is excellent for cruising, with many combinations of sail possible for different conditions.

Going to windward in a fresh-to-strong breeze, we would take the forestaysail and mizzen off her. She balanced better under mainsail and jib than she did under main and staysail, carrying a bit too much weather helm with the latter combination.

Staysail and mizzen was the standard rig for squalls. It was handy to be able to take the mainsail off and still have the boat be well balanced.

Running off the wind in a breeze, we used to let her go under mainsail alone. Pop sort of liked that; he'd been brought up in catboats.

One nice thing you could do with this boat due to her generous mizzen was to back her down in a straight line with just the mizzen set. That trick let us get underway under sail from a tight berth more than once.

Both main halyards were rigged on the port side, so you could grip them together and hoist the mainsail singlehanded. This rig makes good sense with a small gaff sail.

A most useful piece of rigging was a downhaul on the jib, so you could pull the sail right down its stay and hold the head down without having to go out on the bowsprit until you were ready to furl up.

Now it can be revealed whence came my great love of vangs. We had a vang on the mainsail running from the end of the gaff through a single block at the mizzen masthead and down to a cleat on the mizzenmast in easy reach of the helmsman. By adjusting the vang, you could really control the shape of the mainsail beautifully. It kept all the sag out of the gaff when going to windward, and also kept the gaff off the lee rigging when running with the boom well squared off.

One time when we were setting the mainsail, powering slowly into a head sea, the slack vang managed to cast a beautiful half-hitch over the top of the mizzenmast. The next fifteen minutes produced a good lesson in seamanship—to say nothing of quite a little new terminology. It all went to show that engines and sails don't mix too well; the vang probably couldn't have performed so diabolically without the engine pushing the boat right to windward into the head sea.

The *Brownie*'s mainsail had reef points as shown in the sail plan. One time we were beating up Narragansett Bay in the late fall, and since the northwester had some plenty heavy gusts, we just had the triple-reefed mainsail and the staysail on her. Pop said he thought the close-reefed main was a "modest little sail," which it certainly was. But it suited the yawl just right that day.

One of our favorite sails was a big balloon forestaysail. We'd often carry it reaching and pole it out when running. The English used to like this sail a lot; it was the handiest light sail we ever had for cruising.

The house on this boat was short and narrow, leaving plenty of room to work on deck. We never thought of lifelines, but I don't remember anybody ever falling overboard. The rule was simply to hang on and not fall overboard. I guess we were more afraid of what Pop would say about it than we were of drowning.

The cabin was hardly palatial, but it was big enough for a father to teach his son to play cribbage during a four-day layover at Duck Island Roads forced by a miserable spell of weather. The layout was designed for three people, which is probably enough to have on board when cruising in a boat this size for any length of time. The small seats in the cabin are not often seen today. They worked out very well. You can't design a seat that's really right for sleeping, nor a bunk that's really good for sitting. In this boat, the bunks were bunks and the seats were seats.

The head, I must say, was a miserable arrangement. It could only be used when the whole cabin was cleared. It would have been better to have had a bucket in the engine room.

The separate engine room under the wide bridge deck gave relatively good access to the engine and kept that piece of machinery and all that went with it properly separated from the nicer features of life afloat. The yawl had a little Redwing that you started by rolling the flywheel with your foot while standing in the engine-room hatch. It ran so smoothly you could hardly hear it. But when the Redwing finally packed up, it just sat there as ballast for a number of years and we sailed her without power, which worked out fine, for she was always smart and easy to handle.

The *Brownie* was a great boat to grow up in, and when you sailed around the coast in her with Pop, you learned a lot about how to do things on the water. Pop sold her in the fall of 1948, after what turned out to be his last sail. In a way, it seemed right that they both should go at about the same time, because you couldn't really think of the one without thinking of the other.

Chapter 4

The *Cresset*

Eight years after they had designed and built the Cresset, *the Urry brothers wrote an article for* Yachting *about a square rig they had worked up for her. I discovered the article recently, while looking for something else. Their square rig looks to be an excellent arrangement for any fore-and-aft-rigged cruising boat.*

They wanted a rig for running in moderate weather that would give more area than mainsail and topsail, though not as much as those sails and the spinnaker. The objective was to avoid the mental wear and tear provided by "The Imminence of the Jibe." They had to be able to strike the rig, and without going aloft, and they wanted nothing that would impair the Cresset's *windward performance.*

The sail area the Urrys wanted would have required a yard 32 feet long, unwieldy in a 40-foot boat. Instead, they adapted a square rig that Commander E. G. Martin had used in the big, French pilot cutter Jolie Brise, *consisting of two separate, small yards, one on each side of the mast. On the* Cresset, *each yard was a light, manageable, 14-foot spar, and the whole rig, with all fittings and running gear, weighed less than 50 pounds.*

Martin had fixed the inboard ends of his yards to fittings high on the mast, but the Urrys put the inboard ends of their yards into fittings that slid up and down the cap shrouds, controlled by an endless hoist-downhaul. A pair of lifts and guys supported the outboard ends of the yards.

The Cresset's *squaresail was to have a head the shape of a truncated pyramid, and the relatively short truncation was to have a club that would be hoisted on the forestaysail halyard. The design greatly reduced the strain on the yards and added area at the head of the sail. Douglas Urry pointed out that the Dutch set such squaresails hundreds of years ago. A triangular raffee could be set above the squaresail.*

As it turned out, the Urrys had so much fun using their yards to hold out the clews of all manner of triangular sails, big and small, set right side up or upside down, that they never made the squaresail and raffee. They said they would have if they had been able to take a long cruise in the boat. They even used the yards in place of the spinnaker pole, which went ashore. There was talk of three spinnaker jibes in 75 seconds using the new gear. When not in use, the yards stowed up and down the shrouds or were lowered to shoulder height and swung forward, their outboard ends lashed to the bowsprit shrouds, to form liferails.

Designed for cruising, the Cresset *had an enviable racing record. From 1929 to 1935, she took twenty-one firsts and seconds. "I have never considered myself a racing man by temperament," Douglas Urry wrote, "but this sort of thing will break out in spots."*

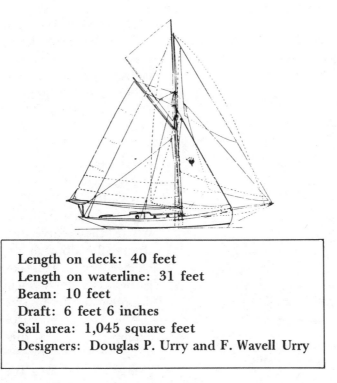

Length on deck: 40 feet
Length on waterline: 31 feet
Beam: 10 feet
Draft: 6 feet 6 inches
Sail area: 1,045 square feet
Designers: Douglas P. Urry and F. Wavell Urry

The traditional gaff-rigged cutter, with her five working sails, plumb bow, and long, fine counter, makes a handsome vessel indeed.

The *Cresset* seems well named, for she does light the way when it comes to cutter design, in my opinion. She's the handsomest cutter I know of.

This pretty boat is another creation of the Urry brothers, who created the Cogge ketch designs described in Chapter 10.

The distant heritage of the *Cresset* is perhaps in the English pilot cutters, but she is really pure Urry. Those two gentlemen certainly knew the art of forming a shapely hull and putting in a good-looking, wholesome rig. The English look of a short overhang forward and a long one aft appears out of balance to some American eyes, but the form does seem to produce a boat that somehow looks both able and delicate. And the long bowsprit helps balance her up.

Some of the plumb-bowed cutters were so fine forward that they lacked buoyancy in the bow and tended to pitch rather heavily in a head sea. I recall seeing the old *Nebula*, near the end of her long career, working into just a moderate seaway and burying her bow in every sea right down to the rail. The *Cresset* might be a bit "pitchy" too,

but this would not be excessive, for she has some fullness in her forward sections.

Her lines look sweet and fair throughout. She has a bit of hollow in the waterlines forward, quite hard bilges for stiffness, and a handsome tumblehome to her midsection that gives her an able look—and rightly so, for it would tend to keep the lee rail out of the water.

In the best cutter tradition, the *Cresset* has plenty of draft, and a hull that should foot well to windward and go where she looks. Her long, straight run flowing into the counter should give her a good turn of speed, yet the counter is steeved up high enough so that there shouldn't be too much danger of being pooped in a following sea. Her generous rudder and moderately cutaway forefoot should make her highly maneuverable, even in a light air.

The *Cresset*'s length on deck is 40 feet; she is 31 feet long on the waterline, with a beam of 10 feet and a draft of 6 feet 6 inches.

The Urry brothers worked out her design in a year of spare time in 1926 and 1927. She was built by George F. Askew in 1928 and 1929, with the Urrys doing the interior work and the spars and rigging. They also designed and built a nine-foot dinghy for her.

The *Cresset*'s traditional cutter rig is well proportioned, efficient, and versatile. (*Yachting*, July, 1930)

The *Cresset* is planked with British Columbia yellow cedar on oak frames. Her stem- and stern-posts are Australian gum. Cypress was also used in the boat. Her trim is teak.

Her keel is 10 inches by 20 inches; the frames are 1½ inches molded, 2¼ inches sided on 9-inch centers. The frames were put in on 4½-inch centers for four feet in the way of the mast. Her floors are 2½ inches sided and 10 inches deep. Her planking is 1⅜ inches and the deck is 1½ inches.

An unusual feature of her construction is an extra set of U-shaped frames running from bilge stringer to bilge stringer in a single piece down across the floors. These are the same size as the regular frames and are bolted in as sister frames. Where they curve down across the top of the floors, the floors have been cut out in an arc to receive them. This construction would keep the garboards from wringing, and it has the effect of doubling the frame size below the waterline.

The *Cresset*'s cutter rig is certainly a fine example of what this rig should and can look like. With her five working sails set, she has plenty of sail area for light going; there are big, light headsails that can be set in addition. Yet, when shortened down to her close-reefed main-sail, reefed forestaysail, and a spitfire jib, her rig would be snug indeed. I'd like to see a third deep reef available in the mainsail and a tiny jib that could replace the working jib. Some of the sail plans of English cutters show as many as four

Her lines show a hull a sailor could enjoy looking at for a long time. (*Yachting*, July, 1930)

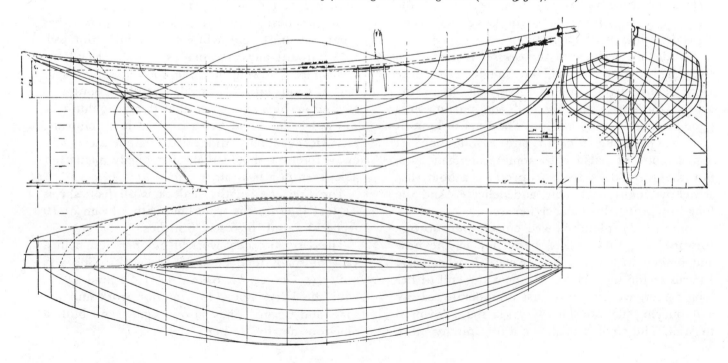

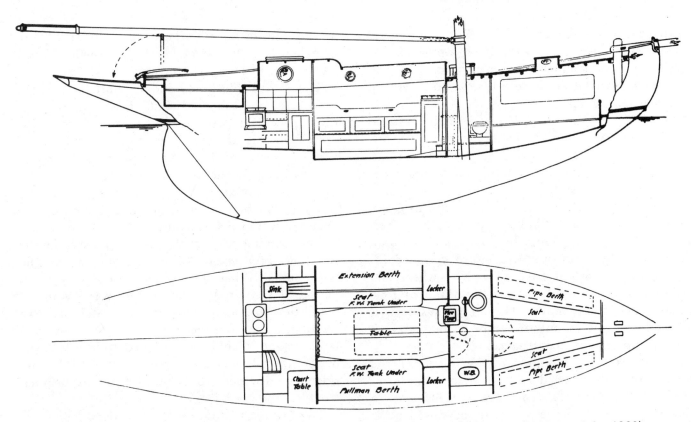

She has a common arrangement plan but with some well-thought-out modifications. (*Yachting*, July, 1930)

small jibs of varying sizes, all smaller than the working jib.

The English practice was to reef spars as well as sails in heavy going. Their topmasts could be lowered and housed right alongside the lower mast, and their bowsprits could be run in on deck. When these spars were heavy and the vessel tended to dive into a head sea, it was undoubtedly necessary to reduce the pitching moment by bringing in these spars. It would not be so in the *Cresset.* Incidentally, one advantage of the separate topmast is that if it should carry away, it leaves the lower part of the rig intact.

The *Cresset*'s sail area of 1,045 square feet is divided up as follows: mainsail, 500; forestaysail, 140; jib, 145; main topsail, 145; and jib topsail, 115.

Her mainsail is nicely shaped for efficiency. The clew is far enough abaft the peak for the sail to set nice and flat for windward work; that is, with the sheet trimmed in hard, the pull aft on the leech would keep the gaff from sagging off to leeward. Her jackyard topsail certainly reaches up where the wind blows; its head is about fifty-five feet above the water.

That balloon forestaysail can be poled out for a heavy-weather spinnaker that is under good control and easy to jibe over. Her big spinnaker would be double-luffed today, for ease in jibing. With a modern spinnaker set on this boat, she'd

The *Cresset* working to windward in a light air. (She also happens to be crossing the finish line to win the first race she entered, one of many victories.) (*Yachting*, July, 1930)

just have to go like a scared cat. But there would be no horsing around with those topmast backstays with the spinnaker set in any breeze at all. A few seconds' delay in setting up could result in a fair-sized lash-up.

The *Cresset* was bored for a shaft, but no engine was installed, at least for the first few seasons. It was found that a dinghy with an outboard, lashed alongside as a tug, could shove her along at an honest three knots in a calm. I used to see Martin Kattenhorn use this tactic to get in and out of the harbor in his engineless forty-four-foot schooner, *Surprise*, when there was no wind. It worked fine. An outboard motor designed for the purpose with a large, low-pitch wheel and reduction gear would improve this kind of towboat work considerably. The great advantage is that the engine is out of the boat for increased safety and ease of maintenance.

In a sort of premonition of the doghouse, the Urry brothers widened and heightened the after end of the *Cresset*'s cabin house. This was to allow the floor of the galley to be raised so it could be wider, and also to give plenty of light and air to the galley. The companionway is off-center, so traffic flows past the cook rather than colliding with him, and there is a skylight in the house adjacent to the companionway. Quoting the designers: "To paraphrase a well-known saying, some skylights leak all the time and all skylights leak some of the time, so the placing of the sink directly under the skylight is the crowning master stroke of this design."

The full-width head is a good arrangement. While its use may temporarily restrict traffic fore and aft, its transformation from the usual torture chamber into a respectable compartment is well worth that little inconvenience.

The short cabin house ending abaft the mast is, of course, old-fashioned. But, in my opinion, the deck space gained around the mast and forward is more valuable than full headroom in the head and fo'c's'le. The headroom under the beams at the mast step in the head is five feet.

In cool climates, the open fireplace in the cabin would be a wonderful thing; hopefully, its chimney would take the chill off the "throne."

Upon seeing my article on the *Cresset* in the *National Fisherman*, John F. Dore of Seattle wrote me, "I had the *Cresset* for a very short period of time in Vancouver. She was a witch in light airs and a strong, reliable vessel in dirty weather. The former owner, a Standard Oil tanker skipper, told me he layed to in a full gale under staysail alone for three days and made considerable distance to windward without much trouble."

The *Cresset* is now owned by Gerry Palmer of Vancouver, who has had her since 1957. He reports that her rig was changed to Marconi in about 1938. He wrote me, "In twelve to fifteen knots [wind strength] she can just about hold a new C & C 35 to windward."

All in all, the *Cresset* is a fine example of the cutter type. She might well be worth emulating today. She wouldn't be cheap to build, for she is a fancy vessel; no doubt she would be more expensive than some of her modern counterparts. It would be a joy to sail her, because she would always do well for herself under any conditions.

The *Cresset* is still going strong, now with a Marconi rig, under the ownership of Gerry Palmer of Vancouver. (Gerry Palmer)

Chapter 5

A Twenty-Three-Foot Sloop

The little, seagoing, cruising sloop designed by Arthur Robb brought a lot of mail, as I mentioned in the Introduction. Dozens of sailors wrote me when they saw her plans, and the letters kept coming for years.

The messages had three common themes: I like the boat; I want to build her; where can I get large-scale plans? I tried to find the answer to the question, but Robb had died, and I couldn't locate anyone who knew what had become of his plans.

In such a situation, my advice is to take the small-scale plans in the book to the naval architect of your choice and ask him or her to make a design from them. This procedure avoids the distortion that might occur from simply enlarging the plans. It enables you to get expert advice on the inevitable questions you will have about the design. Considering the Robb sloop, for instance, you might wonder about the short-ness of her rig. Will she do reasonably well in light weather,

or will she be a dog? If she needs more sail for your use, how best to enlarge her rig? Utilizing a naval architect will also give you an expert sounding board for the modifications to the design you may want. And it will verify the work of the original designer, perhaps even catching an error here or there. The naval architect's fee will doubtless be a very small percentage of the total cost of the vessel. This procedure only applies, of course, if you can't find the original large-scale plans. And when people admire your boat, don't forget to give credit to the original designer, as well as to your naval architect.

I'd like to think there is a fleet of Robb 23-footers happily sailing the world's oceans, but if any of my correspondents built a boat to the design, I have yet to hear of it. Come to think of it, I have no evidence that the design, apparently made on speculation early in Robb's career, was ever more than a dream ship. What a pity.

Length on deck: 23 feet 1 inch
Length on waterline: 18 feet
Beam: 7 feet
Draft: 4 feet 2 inches
Sail area: 285 square feet
Displacement: 5,789 pounds
Designer: Arthur C. Robb

Bill Thon, an artist of note who makes his home in Port Clyde, Maine, told me one time that one of the things he really enjoys about having his little Friendship sloop, the *Echo*, on a mooring right off his dock is that when he feels like it, he can just go out on board, duck down into the snug cuddy, make himself a cup of coffee, stretch out on the transom, and think about things.

The diminutive cruising sloop shown in this chapter strikes me as just that kind of boat. Of course she, like Bill Thon's *Echo*, can provide her owner much more than a momentary retreat from the world. If need be, she can provide him a permanent home and take him to any part of the world in which he might want to become involved, as long as it is washed by a bit of water. At any rate, whether at sea or at anchor, there is something like the perfection of a jewel in a small, fully found boat that has all the basic characteristics and abilities of far larger vessels.

Such craft used to be called tabloid cruisers. The term was borrowed from the world of journalism, and, of course, it indicated something that was half the normal size.

This able-looking tabloid cruiser was designed by Arthur C. Robb in 1933. The requirements were for the minimum size boat in which two people could cruise extensively. She had to be able to survive a gale offshore, and she had to be able to carry her dinghy on deck.

Robb drew a well-balanced little hull with a nice sheer line. The little sloop has a handsome look to her, despite the necessity to give her quite a lot of freeboard for her length. Her lines are a bit finer than those of many such tabloid cruisers, especially at the entrance, and she should sail reasonably well for a boat only eighteen feet on the waterline that has to be able to carry full cruising gear and survive heavy weather at sea. The sloop has quite an easy turn to her bilge, yet with her low outside ballast, she should be quite stiff.

Her hull is very buoyant, and she might have a rather tiring motion in a short, steep sea. But if a small cruising boat is to be safe in rough water, she has to be plenty corky, and you just have to hang onto your teeth.

This tabloid cruiser is 23 feet 1 inch long on deck, with a waterline length of 18 feet, a beam of 7 feet, and a draft of 4 feet 2 inches. The

designer gives her displacement as 5,789 pounds, of which 2,100 pounds is in outside ballast.

Her mainsail has 166 square feet, the staysail, 78 square feet, and the jib, 41 square feet, for a total working sail area of 285 square feet. As to construction, the frames are specified as 2¼ inches square, taking 1⅛-inch planking. To make her easier to build, the garboard was kept flat rather than drawn hollow.

Arthur Robb specified iron rather than lead for the outside ballast on the keel because of its relatively greater strength and rigidity.

The rig is very snug, perhaps even too snug. What might be wanted would be a light-weather rig in which a larger gaff mainsail might be set with the gaff jaws coming just below the forestay and lower shrouds. The permanent backstay would have to be unrigged and runners set up to the masthead. She could even carry a small club topsail! To go with the increased sail area aft, you'd want a portable bowsprit to take a good-size overlapping jib. The jibstay could be set up to the end of this bowsprit with a tackle. Such a rig would give considerably more sail area and get

Above: The sloop's sail plan looks a trifle modest for light weather. (*Yachting*, July, 1933)   **Below:** Despite a waterline length of only 18 feet, Arthur Robb's sloop has a handsome and corky hull that would be stiff, dry, and able. (*Yachting*, July, 1933)

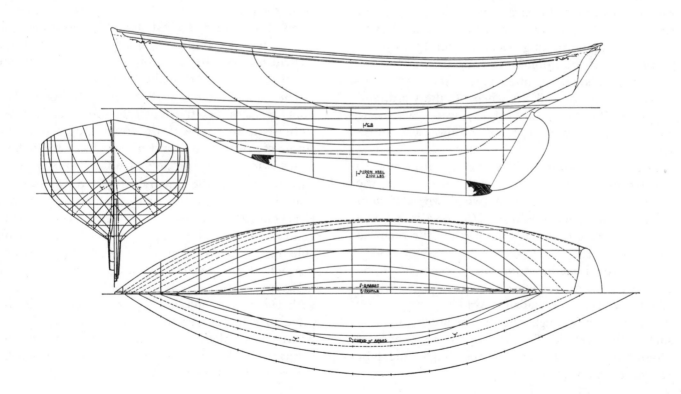

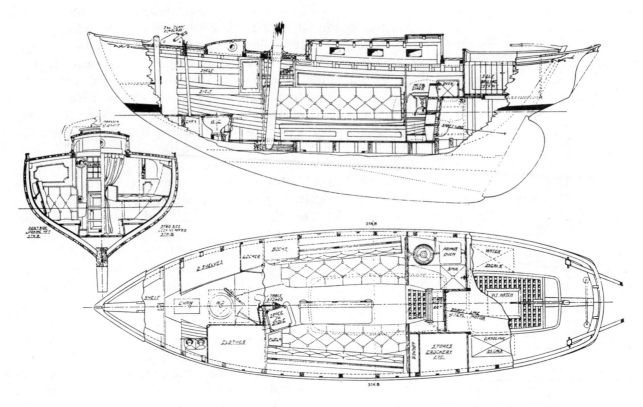

The arrangement of her little cabin is very well thought out. (*Yachting*, July, 1933)

the boat along better in light going, yet the big sails could quickly be struck if it breezed on, and she'd be right back to the snug sail plan shown, with the upper running backstays set up together to the end of the boomkin.

The sloop's raking mast makes the spar easier to stay, gives the sail lift when off the wind, and keeps the boom up out of the water when she rolls when running. The raked mast also looks well.

Mr. Robb wrote: "The rig is arranged to balance under reduced sail. With one reef in, the jib would be stowed. With two down, a smaller stays'l on a boom would be used, or a reef taken in the working one. With three reefs, the mainsail should suffice."

This little boat has room to work on deck, all too rare a feature in many small cruising boats. (While you are visualizing walking around on deck, note how high the lightboards appear in such a tiny vessel.) The deck plan was conceived around the requirement that the dinghy must be carried on board.

Robb wrote: "What most small boat men do with their tenders in a bad sea, I would like to know, for towing under such conditions is impossible." There is enough to think about when running a small boat off before a big sea without worrying about the tender turning battering ram.

The sloop's dinghy is seven feet long. The upper part of her transom folds down against her stern seat, so she will fit down snugly over the companionway hatch and not obstruct the helmsman's view. The sloop's trunk cabin is very narrow so that the dinghy will fit down over it, again with the visibility of the helmsman in mind. Headroom below has been sacrificed for the ability to carry the dinghy on deck and still be able to see where you're going all the time—not just when you bestir yourself to stand up. Few designers of modern boats would argue verbally with the sailor's maxim, "Eternal vigilance is the price of safety," yet time and again they defy it when they place high structures between the helmsman's eyes and the water through which he will soon direct his vessel.

But I preach. Back on board our nice little sloop, note that the running backstay makes a fine hoist-out for the dinghy, especially with a longer tackle on it.

The cockpit coaming is separated from the cabin house. This would allow a folding hood over just the cockpit, if wanted. There is a breakwater at the aft end of the house to turn water running aft on deck out over the rail. The cockpit itself is small and self-bailing, so it is no liability to the vessel. It's the kind of cockpit you can snuggle down into on a rough, cold day. It has no room for seats, other than the helmsman's at the after end, but there would be no reason not to keep a folding canvas armchair at hand. Now there would be solid comfort!

Down in the cabin, the boat has sitting headroom under the side decks and enough headroom under the narrow house to permit one to stand up briefly to move about or put pants on.

The transoms are seats, and the bunks fold down over them. When the bunks are folded down, they come nearly to the centerline, as can be seen in the inboard sectional drawing. Not bad sleeping arrangements, I say. The bunks could be joined to form a double or kept separate, but in any case, you have the great luxury of being able to sit up in bed and look out the cabin window to see who is making all the hullabaloo across the harbor. At sea, you'd likely use the port bunk for whoever's off watch, leaving a clear passage forward on the starboard side.

The head is up in the eyes of her, where it belongs in a little boat.

The top half of the companionway steps folds down against the bottom half to form a seat for the cook. With the ladder thus temporarily removed, the cook has some protection from the deck gang (probably a gang of one) tumbling below.

There is space abaft the cabin steps for an engine with an off-center shaft.

This little tabloid cruiser would certainly make an admirable singlehander. Or, with two aboard, standing watch-and-watch in such a perfect little vessel would be close to luxury.

Chapter 6

The *Andrillot* and the Vertues

Whenever a sailor asks my advice about the best boat in which to sail around the world singlehanded — many of us seem to have that dream now and again — I suggest considering a Vertue. The Vertue class, directly descended from the Andrillot, has increased to more than 200 boats. Vertues have been built all over the world — of wood, steel, or fiberglass. At any given time, a few of these boats are available, and their small size makes them inexpensive craft for deepwater voyaging. The Vertue is a good choice for a crew of one or two.

The Andrillot and her relatives were included in the recent book, Laurent Giles and His Yacht Designs, by Adrian Lee and Ruby Philpott. One design in the book seemed to me to be an ancestor of the Andrillot: the Lymington L Class, a 23-foot daysailer and weekend cruiser, Giles' Design No. 8, drawn five years before the Andrillot. The design was a size smaller than the Andrillot, with a similar hull form. The boats of the L Class gained a reputation for being able and dry.

Lee and Philpott wrote of notable cruises in the Andrillot and in a Vertue by one of Giles' partners, Humphrey Barton. He and his wife, Jessie, borrowed the Andrillot and cruised down Channel to Cornwall, visited the Scilly Islands, crossed the Channel to Brittany, and returned to England's south

coast, sailing 855 miles and calling at 22 ports in 23 days. "She certainly did go," Humphrey Barton wrote. With Kevin O'Riordan, Barton crossed the North Atlantic from the Lizard to Sandy Hook in the Vertue XXXV. Barton wrote: "I honestly believe that she is the best designed, built and equipped small oceangoing cruising yacht that has been produced. Her ability to stand up to bad weather, her remarkably high performance under sail [averaging 3.38 knots across the Atlantic, 23 days of it to windward, three times reduced to a bare pole], and the comfort of her accommodations are outstanding."

Of all the cruising feats of Vertues mentioned by Lee and Philpott, the most remarkable is Bill Nance's passage from Auckland to Buenos Aires, round Cape Horn, in the Cardinal Vertue, during which he sailed nearly 6,500 miles in 53 days, at 122.5 miles per day, or 5.1 knots — some going for a boat 21½ feet on the waterline.

The Andrillot and her offspring are well loved. The last sentence in the chapter is still true, except that the Andrillot has returned to Lymington, where she was designed. Tim Stevenson has restored her and given her a Bermudan rig. And the Wanderer III is also still going strong, having been rebuilt recently by Thies Matzen, who is taking her on her fourth circumnavigation.

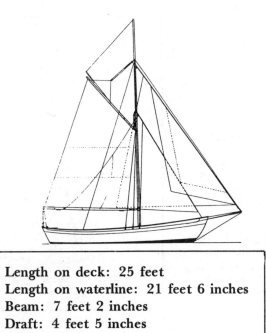

Length on deck: 25 feet
Length on waterline: 21 feet 6 inches
Beam: 7 feet 2 inches
Draft: 4 feet 5 inches
Sail area: 366 square feet
Displacement: 4¼ tons
Designer: John Laurent Giles

R. A. Kinnersly of Guernsey came to John Laurent Giles, the great British naval architect, in 1936 with the request that he design a small cruising boat in which Kinnersly and his wife could set forth from their Channel Isle and cross the often-boisterous waters that separated them from their favorite anchorages. The 25-foot cutter *Andrillot* was the result. She was built by A. H. Moody and Son of Bursledon, up the River Hamble off Southampton Water.

The *Andrillot*'s waterline length is 21 feet 6 inches, her beam is 7 feet 2 inches, and she has a draft of 4 feet 5 inches. Her displacement is 4¼ tons, and her sail area is 366 square feet.

Some years after he had designed the *Andrillot*, Jack Giles wrote that she was "shaped to maintain the general outward character of the pilot-fishing boat, but having the benefit of the concentrated thought on the design of seagoing yachts that the activities of the Royal Ocean Racing Club had by then fostered. The result was a straightforward little boat with a modest forward overhang, full displacement, outside ballast, moderate beam, and a reasonably cut-away profile."

Though she does bear a very general resemblance to such traditional English craft as, for example, the Itchen Ferry smacks, many of which were built at the village of that name on the River Itchen (up Southampton Water from the Hamble), the *Andrillot* does have some marked differences. The nearly plumb bow of this sample ancestor has been given more overhang, and the deep forefoot has been cut away. The transom has been given both rake and tumblehome. The *Andrillot* is a narrower, deeper, heavier boat than were the Itchen Ferry craft, for she is to work out in the Channel rather than in the more protected waters of the Solent, and so she must inherit these basic characteristics from other deepwater ancestors, such as the Bristol Channel pilot boats. But here again there are differences, for the garboards have been well hollowed out to give the *Andrillot* a lighter, more responsive hull than the pilot cutters had.

As to rig, the *Andrillot*'s mast has been stepped quite far aft compared to most traditional English cutters, giving her a relatively small mainsail and relatively large forestaysail. Rather than having a separate topmast, she has a tall pole mast. Her

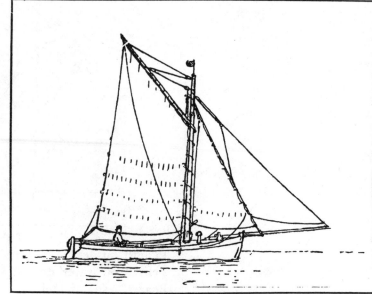

Right: One of the ancestors of the *Andrillot* is probably the Itchen Ferry smack, many of which plied the waters near where the *Andrillot* was designed and built. (Drawing by R.C. Leslie, *Thoughts on Yachts and Yachting* by Uffa Fox. Reproduced by kind permission of the Executors of Uffa Fox Deceased.)

Below: Though the *Andrillot*'s sail area is quite generous, none of her four working sails is large. (*Racing, Cruising and Design* by Uffa Fox. Reproduced by kind permission of the Executors of Uffa Fox Deceased.)

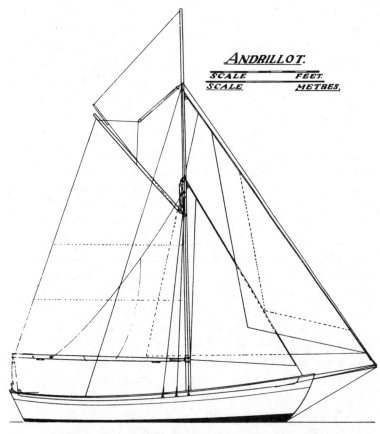

ANDRILLOT.
SCALE   FEET.
SCALE   METRES.

Hiscock. She was a foot shorter than the *Andrillot*, but she had seven inches more draft and carried 129 square feet more sail. The Hiscocks sailed the *Wanderer II* from England to the Azores and back in 1950. With later owners, she went out to Tahiti and returned singlehanded to Victoria, British Columbia.

In 1952, the Hiscocks had built for them the *Wanderer III*, a thirty-foot version of this design rigged as a Marconi sloop. They sailed this craft over 100,000 miles, including two circumnavigations.

Soon after the *Andrillot* and the *Wanderer II* were built, Jack Giles turned out a design for a forty-six-footer of this same type. This was Roger Pinckney's *Dyarchy*.

Because of the great success of the *Andrillot* and her followers, the firm of J. Laurent Giles and Partners used her design as the basis for a twenty-five-foot cruising class that they developed soon after World War II. There seemed to be demand for greater accommodation, so by 1949 this class had increased freeboard amidships, giving less sheer than the *Andrillot* had. The modest little cabin house had grown until it extended well forward of the mast, was higher, and had sprouted a doghouse at its after end. (The lee window of one of these doghouses was smashed in when the boat took a knockdown on an Atlantic crossing.)

bowsprit is rather short and well steeved by comparison with older English cutters, and the jib topsail has been eliminated.

Later in 1936, a near sister to the *Andrillot* was built by Napier at Poole in Dorset. This was the *Wanderer II*, and her first owner was Eric

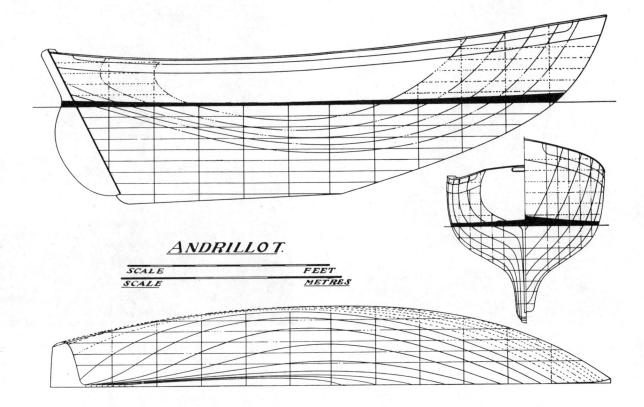

ANDRILLOT.

SCALE   FEET

SCALE   METRES

Above: Her lines show a handsome hull with plenty of lateral resistance for weatherliness and plenty of buoyancy for seaworthiness. (*Racing, Cruising and Design* by Uffa Fox. Reproduced by kind permission of the Executors of Uffa Fox Deceased.)

Below: Her cabin is snug and comfortable, but where do you sit when the boat is on the starboard tack? (*Racing, Cruising and Design* by Uffa Fox. Reproduced by kind permission of the Executors of Uffa Fox Deceased.)

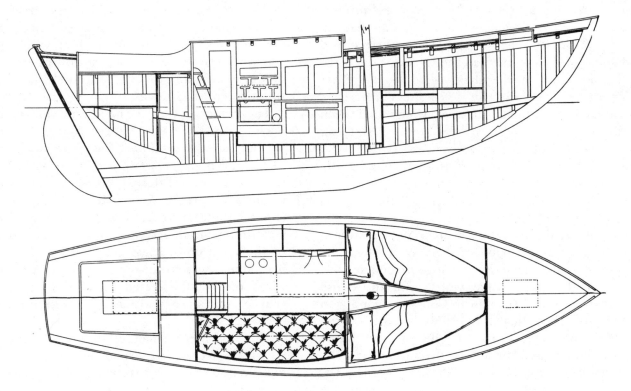

Eric Hiscock's *Wanderer II*, a near sister to the *Andrillot*. (*Voyaging Under Sail* by Eric Hiscock, Oxford University Press)

The *Wanderer II* at Honolulu just before she was sailed singlehanded to Victoria, B.C. (*Sea Quest* by Charles A. Borden, Macrae-Smith)

This class was named the Vertue class, after Michael B. Vertue, the honorary librarian of the Little Ship Club. The Vertue class boats had the same waterline length and beam as the *Andrillot*, were three inches longer on deck, and had an inch more draft. Their modest Marconi rig spread 68 square feet less sail than the *Andrillot*'s gaff rig.

In his book on the class, called *Vertue*, Peter Woolass reported that by 1972 the Vertue class numbered 128 boats, five of which had been built by their owners. Woolass records sixty-six major ocean passages made by Vertues. In 1927, Michael Vertue presented a trophy to the Little Ship Club, and this became known as the Vertue Cup. It was to be given annually for the best log of a cruise of at least a week made under the Club burgee during the year preceding the award. The award was not only for the way in which the cruise was described in the log, of course, but also for the competence with which the cruise was carried out. The Vertue Cup was twice won' by Vertue-class boats, in 1950 by the *Vertue XXXV*, in which Humphrey Barton and Kevin O'Riordan crossed the Atlantic from east to west, and in 1960 by *Cardinal Vertue*, in which Dr.

David Lewis finished third in that year's singlehanded transatlantic race.

Jack Giles said that in all his later versions of the *Andrillot* he didn't change the basic lines, because he couldn't improve on them. He has certainly created a handsome hull with an able and weatherly look. It is not surprising that many of the boats built to this basic design have made so much cruising history.

The *Andrillot*'s rig is handsome and practical. Such a small boat should certainly be a one-master, yet the *Andrillot* has four working sails set from her one mast to use in various combinations to meet different weathers. Her topsail would probably be stowed first as it breezed on, and then the staysail. Next you would probably reef the mainsail, reset the staysail, and either go to the small jib or leave the bowsprit bare of sail. She could use a storm forestaysail in combination with the double-reefed mainsail for a hard chance. Her deep reefs are most appropriate to her small size.

The *Andrillot*'s small cabin house allows only about 4½ feet of headroom in the cabin. I find that limitation less frustrating than the feeling you

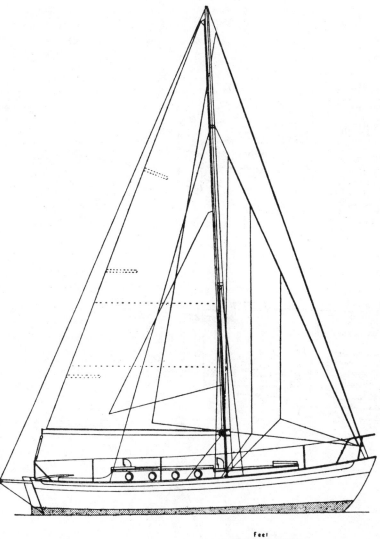

Left: The *Wanderer III* has a sail area of 423 square feet in her mainsail and working jib. (*Around the World in Wanderer III* by Eric Hiscock, Oxford University Press)

Below: The *Wanderer III* is 30′4″ long on deck, with a waterline length of 26′5″, a beam of 8′5″, and a draft of 5′. She displaces 8 tons and has a lead keel weighing 3½ tons. (*Around the World in Wanderer III* by Eric Hiscock, Oxford University Press)

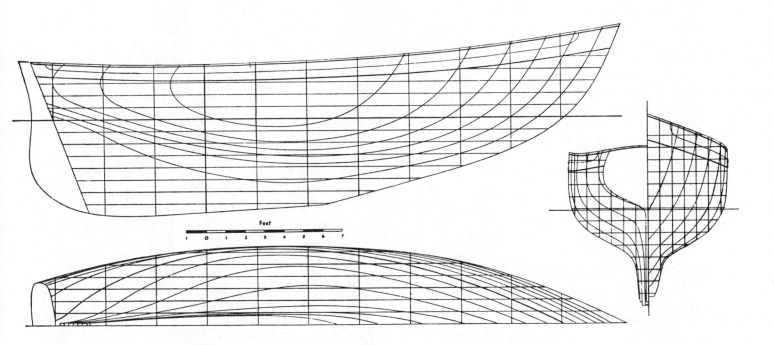

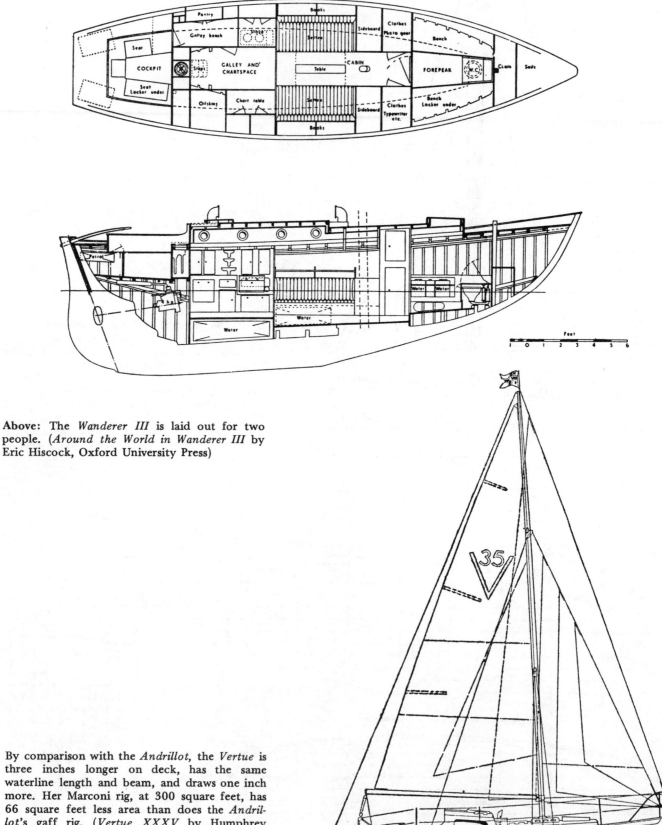

Above: The *Wanderer III* is laid out for two people. (*Around the World in Wanderer III* by Eric Hiscock, Oxford University Press)

By comparison with the *Andrillot*, the *Vertue* is three inches longer on deck, has the same waterline length and beam, and draws one inch more. Her Marconi rig, at 300 square feet, has 66 square feet less area than does the *Andrillot*'s gaff rig. (*Vertue XXXV* by Humphrey Barton)

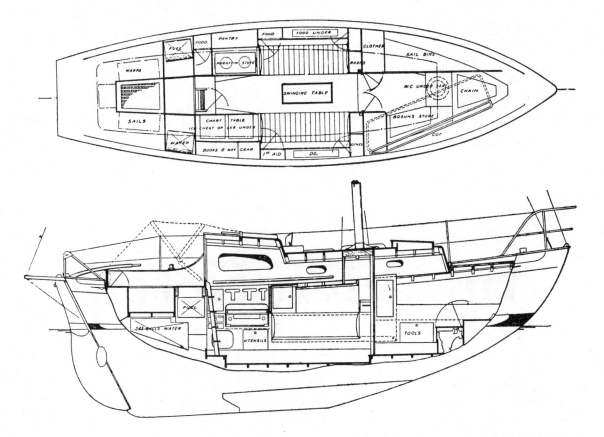

The *Vertue* has a good arrangement for two or three people. (*Vertue XXXV* by Humphrey Barton)

get—on a boat whose large cabin house blanks out your view of rail and deck—that you can't really sense her shape as she moves through the water. The *Andrillot* would be a constant joy to watch go, but at the helm of the Vertue, you would always be trying to imagine the full sense of her motion, since you wouldn't be able to see her whole shape on deck.

The *Andrillot*'s cockpit floor is a bit low for a self-draining cockpit, but this fault has been corrected in the Vertue. On both craft, the rudder could be unshipped relatively easily for inspection, cleaning, painting, or repair, a great advantage to the cruiser who would be self-sufficient.

I would prefer the arrangement plan of the Vertue to that of the *Andrillot*. The basic problem in the *Andrillot*'s cabin is that there is no place to sit comfortably when the boat is on the starboard tack.

The *Andrillot* is a fine design for a small cruising boat, in my opinion. The successful exploits of the Vertues have proven the worth of her design. But perhaps the happiest fact about the *Andrillot* is that she is still sailing on the beautiful coast of Cornwall.

Chapter 7

An Alden Ketch

This little vessel appeals to me greatly; I just love her bow. That bow is John G. Alden at his best.

The most vivid words I know to describe such a bow were written by Edgar J. March, chronicler of the working boats of Britain. He would call the bow of this ketch "sea-fendy." I like to dream of sailing this boat in rough water, her bow fending off the seas.

John Ruskin wrote at some length on the subject in his essay, "The Bow of a Boat." Sailors are fortunate that the great critic and historian of buildings turned his discerning eye seaward. Here is what he saw:

One object there is which I never pass without the renewed wonder of childhood, and that is the bow of a boat. . . . The sum of Navigation is in that. You may magnify it or decorate it as you will: you do not add to the wonder of it. Lengthen it into hatchet-like edge of iron, strengthen it with complex tracery of ribs of oak, carve it and gild it till a column of light moves beneath it on the sea, you have made no more of it than it was at first. That rude simplicity of bent plank, that can breast its way through the death that is in the deep sea, has in it the soul of shipping. Beyond this we may have more work, more men, more money; we cannot have more miracle.

. . . I know nothing else which man does, which is perfect, but that. All his other doings have some sign of weakness, affectation, or ignorance in them. They are over-finished or under-finished; they do not quite answer their end, or they show a mean vanity in answering it too well. But the boat's bow is naively perfect; complete without an effort. . . . It is a simple work, but it will keep out water.

. . . that bow of the boat is the gift of another world. Without it, what prison wall would be so strong as that "white and wailing fringe" of sea? . . . The nails that fasten together the planks of the boat's bow are the rivets of the fellowship of the world. Their iron does more than lead lightning out of heaven, it leads love round the earth.

I think Ruskin would have found the bow of the Alden ketch inspiring. I know I do.

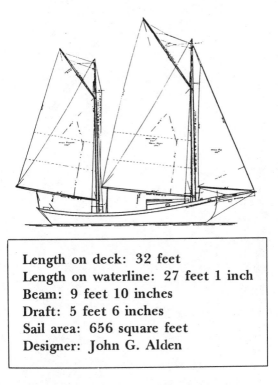

Length on deck: 32 feet
Length on waterline: 27 feet 1 inch
Beam: 9 feet 10 inches
Draft: 5 feet 6 inches
Sail area: 656 square feet
Designer: John G. Alden

Did you ever hanker after a little sailing vessel that would really be well suited for a variety of tasks—from hauling driftwood scrounged off an island beach with a good little skiff, to being mother ship for a dory with a longline trawl, to being a Good Samaritan salvage vessel for boats in trouble, to being a diving tender, to taking care of a fleet of small sailboats? I think this able-looking ketch, designed by John G. Alden in 1911, would fill the bill. She is a workmanlike cruising boat, in my opinion.

The ketch was built at Sandusky, Ohio, for Captain Richard McKean. He wanted a boat for whitefishing in Lake Superior, and the boat was designed to carry up to 5,000 pounds of fish. McKean had fished out of Gloucester, and he specified a Gloucester fishing schooner type of hull, but he wanted her rigged like a local Great Lakes ketch.

He got a wholesome hull. The diagonals are sweet and fair, showing a nice model. She is stiff and able and could be driven quite hard, including lugging sail to windward in a breeze. She also is handy and maneuverable, with her forefoot considerably cut away and a big rudder well aft. It's true she might be a bit "pitchy" (as the old-timer would say of a boat he thought would

hobby horse in a head sea), judging by the steep rise of her forebody buttocks and with the weight of her mainmast so far forward. She was built on 2-inch by 1½-inch frames and planked with 1¼-inch oak. All her ballast was carried inside.

She certainly has plenty of deck space, a great joy in a boat. She can easily carry a dory or peapod on deck, and the main boom makes a handy boat derrick. She has a seven-inch rail all around. The foredeck is as cramped as that of a catboat, of course, but the working anchor can be kept out of the way slung under the bowsprit. If her tasks require some complicated ground tackle work, this should be done over the stern. Her heavy anchor can be stowed in the bottom of the hold for ballast and can be handled easily by the main boom. A boat like this, which cries out to be used in all manner of challenging situations, ought to have a 100-pound, old-fashioned anchor on board, so the master knows he can keep her where he wants her under almost any adverse conditions.

The ketch has no power, but if absolutely necessary, an engine could be installed amidships with the wheel in an aperture on the centerline, but with the motor placed off-center just enough

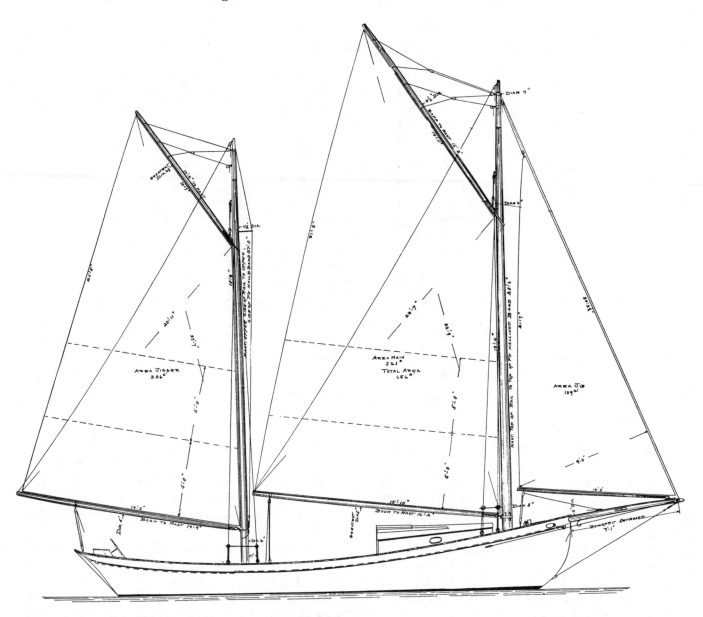

The sail plan of the Alden fishing ketch shows a practical rig that would balance well under mainsail alone and sail like a reefed catboat. Or, under jib and reefed mizzen, she would handle nicely in heavy going. (*Rudder* Magazine, © 1911, Fawcett Publications, Inc.)

so the shaft would clear the mizzenmast. With this arrangement, the motor would be positioned to port of the centerline to counteract the twist of the right-hand-turning propeller.

With the engine to port and the propeller on the centerline, the boat would tend to turn to the right. The right-hand-turning propeller, turning clockwise when viewed from aft, would tend to walk her stern to the right, thus turning the boat to the left. The reason for the slight turning force applied to the boat by the direction of rotation of the propeller is that the propeller's

blades give more push in the deeper water at the bottom of their swing than they do in the shallower water at the top of their swing. The push to the right imparted to the stern by a given blade at the bottom of its swing is a bit more than the push to the left imparted to the stern by the same blade at the top of its swing.

The quarters for two may look snug, but it should be remembered that whatever space there is can be devoted entirely to living. With so much stowage space aft, there is no reason why any boat gear, spares, or staples should ever find their

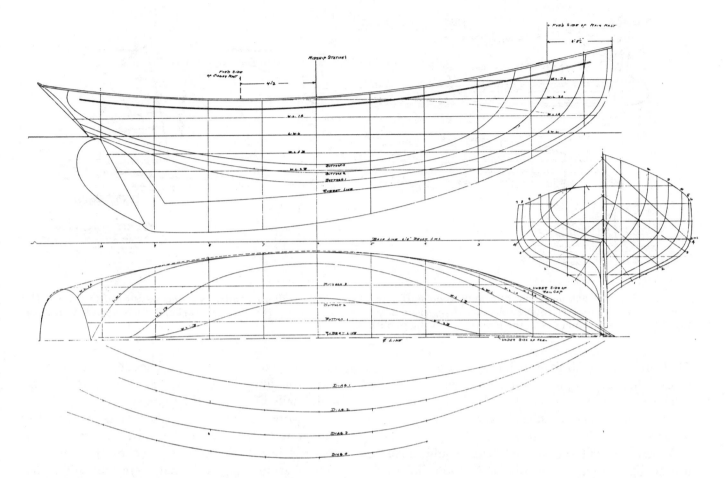

Above: The ketch's lines show her to be stiff and able, and, with her forefoot cut away, handy and maneuverable. (*Rudder* Magazine, © 1911, Fawcett Publications, Inc.)

Below: Her deck and arrangement plan shows a cabin that appears cramped, but with so much stowage space aft, it could be devoted entirely to living. (*Rudder* Magazine, © 1911, Fawcett Publications, Inc.)

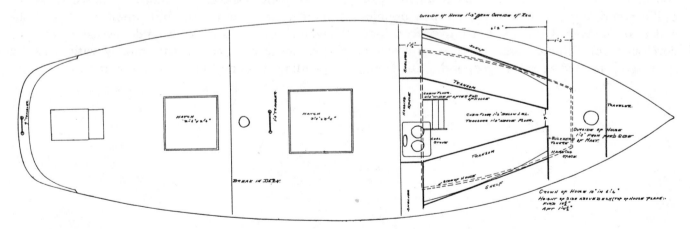

way into the cabin to compete with people for space. Headroom in the cuddy is 5 feet 6 inches. McKean lived aboard her eight months of the year.

The rig of the ketch looks eminently practical if you don't mind reefing the mizzen, and there's no reason anyone should mind such good sailorizing work. She can balance well under mainsail alone and sail like a reefed catboat. Or she can go well in heavy going under jib and reefed mizzen.

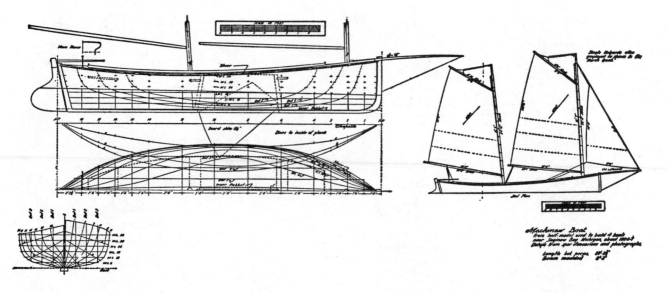

The Lake Huron Mackinaw boat, or Collingwood skiff, a local type of open double-ender, was one ancestor of the ketch. The other was the Gloucester fishing schooner. (*American Small Sailing Craft* by Howard I. Chapelle, W.W. Norton & Company, Inc., © 1951. Reproduced with the permission of the publisher.)

The self-tending jib is most handy; the only thing to do when tacking is to put the wheel over.

The ketch naturally needs the usual main vang led to the mizzen masthead, and she needs her mizzen gaff peaked up more.

A main topsail set on a tall club would make a useful light sail. So would a balloon jib that could be poled out when running off. Such a sail is particularly handy on a single-head-rigged boat, because it can be jibed across so easily.

The ancestor of this boat, as far as her rig is concerned, is the Lake Huron Mackinaw boat, or Collingwood skiff, a local type of open double-ender from twenty-six to thirty-five feet long developed for fishing. Some of these craft were sprit-rigged instead of gaff-rigged, and, until 1882,

according to Howard I. Chapelle, had no bow-sprits or jibs. They were characterized by two major sails of almost the same size.

By pure coincidence, rather than through any connection that can be shown, the rig of this ketch is nearly identical to that of the fifty-five-foot pearling "luggers" that were still sailing out of Broome, Northwest Australia, in 1930. These were handsome and able vessels that tended divers on long cruises to the pearling grounds well offshore.

Looking back on the design of this little Alden ketch, one can't help but think what fun she would be to knock around the coast in, and perhaps even make a little money with, whether pearling, fetching-and-carrying, or fishing.

Chapter 8

The *Fundulus*

Center Harbor is a small, deep, Maine cove created by a protecting island just off the shore of Eggemoggin Reach; in the summertime, it shelters an assortment of wonderful boats, their number all out of proportion to its size. Once, easing through the fleet, looking it over, I started, as I realized I was looking at a boat built to Bill Hand's design of the Fundulus. It was a thrill to see a full-size, three-dimensional vessel representing plans I had pored over for so many hours. That's what happens when you spend a lot of time with boat plans: The plans become more real in your mind than the boat, so that the boat seems to represent the drawings, rather than the other way round.

Here was the Alisande, built by Joel and Steve White and their crew at the Brooklin Boat Yard in Center Harbor in 1981 for Kim Faulkner. She was not only real, but also handsome, with her gleaming, black topsides. Her owner is well pleased with her.

Harold Bryan, a boatbuilder in St. George, New Brunswick, wanted to build a vessel for his family of four to take voyaging. He chose the design of the Fundulus, did a fine job of building her, and launched her in 1988 as the Patience B. The Bryans cruised in her for the next three years, sailing to Tasmania and back. Because they had rigged and fitted her out simply, they spent their time sailing and enjoying their travels, instead of working their way through lists of repair tasks. Harry did admit he had to replace one of the mizzen lazyjacks because it had almost chafed through.

The Patience B was given a bigger, airier cabin than the Fundulus, for she was to be a family home. The cabinhouse was extended aft. She has a sleeping cabin forward, with a double berth; a lovely main cabin, with off-center table and U-shaped settee to starboard, and another settee opposite, with pilot berth outboard; next aft, a big chart table to port, and an L-shaped galley to starboard; then a pair of quarter berths all the way aft, with the engine in a box between them.

Last summer, I sailed the Patience B, using her as a school ship for seamanship students. We found her very easy to handle in all conditions, including a gusty northwester that blew more than strong at times. She was faster than I expected her to be under working sail in light weather. Harry Bryan says she is a wonderful boat in heavy weather. We had a fine sail in the hard northwester. We were traveling among Maine islands on many different points of sailing, and we tried her under a lot of different sail combinations. As it breezed up to its strongest in the afternoon, we settled her down with double reefs in jib, mainsail, and mizzen. She loved it. On the wind, in the hardest gusts, she would just put her rail down. We asked her to fetch into a little gap between a ledge to windward and Crow Island to leeward, and she answered by jamming her bowsprit a bit closer to the wind, putting her shoulder down, and thundering through.

And now, as this book goes to press, Harry Bryan tells me he's just learned that he and I are cousins!

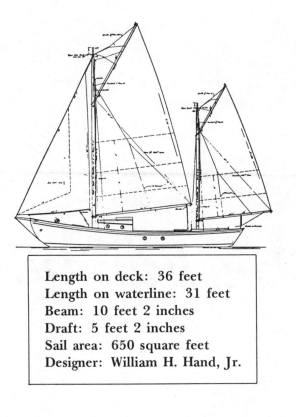

Length on deck: 36 feet
Length on waterline: 31 feet
Beam: 10 feet 2 inches
Draft: 5 feet 2 inches
Sail area: 650 square feet
Designer: William H. Hand, Jr.

It blew a moderate gale out of the southeast all night on the coast of Maine not long ago, and looking out over Penobscot Bay at first light you could just barely make out through the gray scud the whiteness of the tops of most of the waves as they rolled over and foamed on their march up the Bay.

It wasn't blowing all that hard, but as the first gale of the winter, it was impressive.

Whenever I see rough water like that, I always begin wondering how various boats I know, either through sailing them or studying their plans, would behave out there. The Beaufort scale says, under "Action of Fishing Smack" for Force 7, "Remains in harbor, or if at sea, lies to," but it is always tempting to imagine putting out in a modest-sized craft under such conditions to see what she will do. The temptation of indulging in such vicarious voyages is particularly hard to resist, in that they involve neither danger nor discomfort.

Looking out on what the southeaster was doing to the Bay that early morning, one vessel that came to mind as a candidate for beating out through those seas to Matinicus Island was the thirty-six-foot ketch *Fundulus*, designed by William H. Hand, Jr., more than sixty years ago.

With a single-reef down all around, she would have worked to windward in that seaway in reasonable comfort and speed and with great style.

This ketch was built by the Greenport Yacht Basin and Construction Company at Greenport, Long Island, New York, in 1913. She is 36 feet long on deck, with a waterline length of 31 feet, a beam of 10 feet 2 inches, and a draft of 5 feet 2 inches. Her sail area is 650 square feet.

The *Fundulus*, later named *C. D. B.* [?], and, still later, *Cynosure*, is quite reminiscent of the John G. Alden ketch described in the preceding chapter. The *Fundulus* is a bit more sophisticated. Incidentally, she was thought to be one of Bill Hand's very best designs by another John G., John G. Hanna.

The *Fundulus* would make a fine long-distance cruiser for two people, in my opinion. She is a bit under-rigged for my taste, but she was designed for safety and comfort rather than for speed. None of her owners ever claimed she was a fast boat. One said she would do seven knots, but no more, under ideal conditions, and that going to windward in a fresh breeze and rough sea, she would make a good 2¾ knots to windward. He said she was "not close-winded," but only made a half

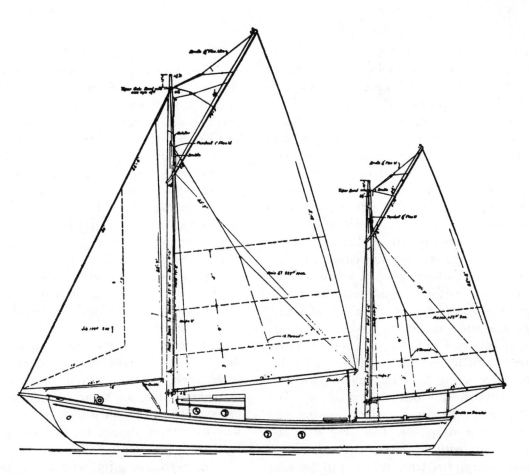

Above: The *Fundulus* is a handsome, able ketch that would make an admirable long-distance cruising boat for two. (*The Rudder Treasury* edited by Tom Davin)

Below: Her ends are well balanced and buoyant; she has a reputation for dryness in rough water. (*The Rudder Treasury* edited by Tom Davin)

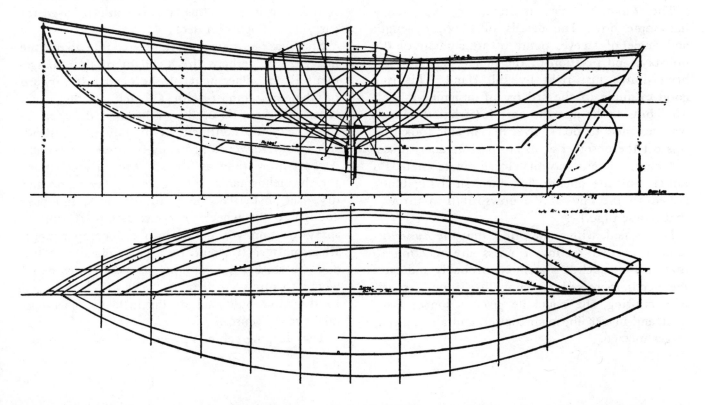

point of leeway at the most. I would guess that she would be sailed about six points off the wind when full and by and would thus make good a course of perhaps 6½ points off the wind. All of this indicates a reasonable, but not outstanding, performance, as far as speed is concerned. (As the *Cynosure,* she came in fifth out of eight boats in the 1930 St. Petersburg-Havana Race.)

Where the *Fundulus* comes into her own is in the comfort department, especially in a rough sea. Comfort in rough water in a small vessel is a relative thing, of course, but it implies at least a rather strong feeling of security and confidence in the boat on the part of her people, a reasonably easy motion, and reasonable dryness on deck. These things the *Fundulus* can certainly provide.

In a head sea, such as the one I was subjecting her to during that early winter sail, her buoyant bow and fine stern let her lift her head easily. It would take quite a big breaking sea to smother her bow. Nor would she bury her nose or take undue water over the stern when running or broad-reaching in a steep sea. The deep drag to her keel, combined with her moderately cut-away forefoot, would keep her from wanting to broach when hard-pressed off the wind.

The ketch's midship section shows plenty of sail-carrying power to make up for only a modest bearing aft; her stern is almost like that of a dory.

The *Fundulus* has, I think, an exceedingly handsome bow. The details of bowsprit length and angle of steeve, point of attachment of the bobstay, and position of the hawse pipe have all been drawn just right by Bill Hand. This is a good example of the artistry of designing a boat. That bow looks just the part for what the ketch was designed to do. It gives her an able look that tips off the observer as to her performance at sea. (Of course I must say that to eliminate chafe, I'd rather run the anchor line through a big block lashed to the end of the bowsprit than through that hawse pipe.)

It was said, with some pride, that the *Fundulus* seldom needed reefing. I guess my reaction to that is that such a statement probably indicates she needs more sail. Certainly for summer coastwise cruising, she could be given a longer bowsprit and bigger jib, main topsail, and a somewhat bigger mizzen.

There is no quarrel with the handiness of her rig. To tack, roll the wheel over. To shorten down for a squall, or make a run in a real breeze, take the mainsail off her. To work her around the harbor, or make a run in a strong breeze, sail her like a catboat with mainsail alone.

The main topping lift probably would be handier rigged in the usual style to the mainmast rather than to the head of the mizzenmast. What should be rigged to the head of the mizzenmast, of course, is my favorite piece of rigging, a vang. She probably should have a boomkin so you could reach the clew of the mizzen without nearly throwing yourself overboard.

The seven-eighths-length club on the jib is a good rig. It lets the sail set better than with a full-length club, yet it can be self-tending. It would need lazy jacks to keep the sail off the deck when rounding up to a dock or anchor, or when picking up the home mooring with its inevitable coating of slime after being away on a cruise. The storm jib should be set farther up the headstay than shown in the sail plan. A good light sail for the ketch would be a big, high-footed, overlapping jib, with a pole to wing it out when running.

Bill Hand gave the *Fundulus* an unusual and most practical arrangement. Her open deck amidships, at the widest part of the vessel, gives a sense of spaciousness and a working area seldom found in a boat of this size. It could be used for carrying a dinghy on deck.

She has a snug steering cockpit abaft the mizzen, but perhaps the highlight of the arrangement is the placement of the head just forward of the mizzenmast with a hatch to the deck. When the head is used as a head, it does, to be sure, have the confinement of only sitting headroom. But it would probably be used as a second cockpit more than as a head. What a great place for the helmsman's watchmate to stay warm and dry, yet instantly handy to the deck and near enough to the wheel for conversation. If a bit of spray or rain got below into the compartment, what matter? It would be a great place to stand and watch her go—as long as you remembered where to put your feet. A "cockpit" seat hinged to the after bulkhead of the little compartment might make sense.

The sleeping cabin is private, not too sunny for

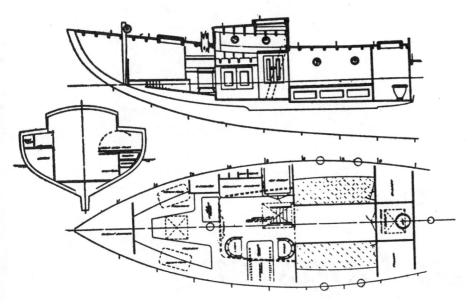

The ketch's arrangement is unusual, but practical, with real chairs in the saloon, a private, quiet, sleeping cabin complete with portholes, and a head compartment that could double as an admirable auxiliary cockpit. (*The Rudder Treasury* edited by Tom Davin)

the off-watch during the day, and it has all the headroom needed for sitting up in bed and reading or drinking the morning mug-up. It should be a quiet place.

There is full headroom under the short trunk cabin, which houses a galley and saloon combined. The chairs are a real luxury afloat. A chair is a lot more comfortable to sit in than is a bunk to sit on. These ought to be fastened down, of course, but they ought to be turnable, so you could swing them around to different positions and lock them in place. Facing the table, as shown, is fine for eating or playing cribbage in harbor, but you'd want to be able to face the chairs to starboard when eating a meal below at sea with the boat heeled over on the starboard tack, and you'd want to be able to face to port when in the same situation on the port tack. It's no fun trying to hold yourself in a chair that's trying its best to tip you out of it, especially if you are trying to eat at the same time.

The ketch has opening ports in both the hull and trunk cabin. I wonder how much real ventilating is done by these opening ports facing athwartships. You used to see them open in the topsides of big yachts at anchor with rounded metal scoops projecting out from their after semicircles trying to catch a little air and send it in. This boat has three hatches to let air in aft and out forward, and I doubt if the opening portholes add much to the circulation. I'd prefer to have them fixed in place and plenty strong. Opening or fixed, the ones in the sleeping cabin would be a joy. It's great to be able to wake up and look

out at the water from a porthole by your bunk. The only time I've ever been able to do it (except in my patented "high" bunk in the skipjack I had) was in an eighty-eight-foot schooner. Those bunk ports are a nice touch in this design.

The *Fundulus* was used by several owners cruising between Nova Scotia and Cuba and into the Gulf of Mexico. She may still be going, for all I know. The people who did this cruising were unstinting in their praise of the ketch. They particularly commented on her good behavior in rough going. One owner wrote: "With the exception of rare occasions when curling seas have slopped over her rails, she has shipped green water on but one occasion, a memorable night when we thrashed to windward against a snortin' no'ther in the Gulf of Mexico under full sail, at a time when able fishing smacks ran under the beach and anchored. Our decks would have been virtually dry that night had we furled the mainsail."

The same owner also commented on her ability to run inlets on the New Jersey shore in breaking seas. Here is his description of running Barnegat Inlet one time: "Owing to the course of the narrow channel through the bar, it was impossible to hold her dead stern-to when a huge comber roared down upon us. Down the forward slope of that hill of water she raced at a pace which backed her sails against a fresh breeze! Yet she showed no tendency to broach or disobey her helm and crossed the bar with only a little spray on her after deck."

Chapter 9

The *Coaster*

The version of Murray Peterson's Coaster that I keep turning to for a dreamship is the big three-master, the Don Quixote del Mar. I'm captivated by her rig, which, to me, combines the romance of the full-rigged gaff schooner, complete to square yard, with the romance of Captain Slocum's yawl Spray. I can see the Don, rolling along, moderate breeze abaft the beam, all ten sails full of wind, and all those lofty spars tracing their slow arcs across the sky. As it breezes on, we shorten her down to "just" her six lowers — imagine having a vessel with six lowers! I can see her short-tacking in the strong williwaws of a channel between steep mountains, clawing to windward under her four inboard lowers, and nothing to do to put her about but roll the wheel up. Or, I see her hove-to in a gale offshore, her head tucked under the wing of her reefed foresail. I've sailed her a lot of dream miles, and, no matter what the weather, she always has a perfect sail combination.

When John G. Hanna, the Sage of Dunedin, Florida, and the writer of the column, "The Watch Below," in the old Rudder magazine, saw the plans of the original Coaster, he wrote that the vessel appealed to him greatly. His only criticism was that the galley was too small to suit him. He cautioned would-be modifiers of the design not to join the two cabinhouses into one, saying, "The bracing of the hull amid-ship by uncut deck beams is worth far more than headroom." The separate cabinhouses also give the vessel handsome looks and deck space. I hope the original Coaster is still sailing.

Still another version of the Coaster is the Defiance, a centerboarder. She is 44 feet, 7 inches long on deck; 37 feet on the waterline; beam, 13 feet, 6 inches; and draft, 4 feet, 6 inches. Her rig is most similar to that of the Coaster II; her sail area is 1,140 square feet. She has a two-person fo'c's'le forward, full-width galley with a head in its corner next aft; main cabin with pilot berths outboard of the transoms; a wonderful single stateroom abaft the mainmast to port, with bureau, desk, and stove; head opposite, with bathtub; and, right aft, a big oilskin locker and a generous chart table. There's a separate engine room with entrance through a hatch in the after port corner of the after house. Some fine schooner, I call her.

Murray Peterson's schooners, designed after the American coasting schooners, were probably not known to Hervey Benham, a recorder of the story of the sailing cargo vessels of the east coast of England, but his words about one of his favorites apply so perfectly to my concept of the Coaster and her cousins that I cannot resist quoting them: "She was a coaster in miniature, and the authentic sea-going lines applied to so diminutive a hull made her a particular delight to the eye."

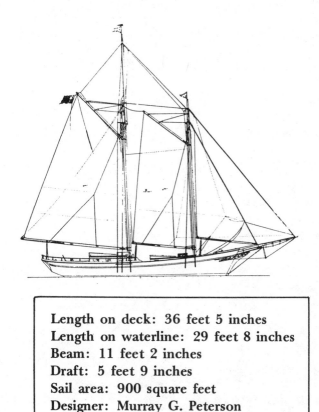

Length on deck: 36 feet 5 inches
Length on waterline: 29 feet 8 inches
Beam: 11 feet 2 inches
Draft: 5 feet 9 inches
Sail area: 900 square feet
Designer: Murray G. Peterson

Upon looking around the anchorage off Burr's Dock, New London, Connecticut, after we had dropped the hook there many years ago, I was delighted to see the little schooner *Coaster* tied up at the wharf. I had often admired Murray Peterson's plans of her, and here was a chance to see the vessel herself.

Inspection from alongside in the dinghy and then from the dock showed her to be just what the plans indicated: every inch an able and handsome vessel. Finer lined than her big cargo-carrying ancestors, she was nonetheless beamy enough to have plenty of stability and full-ended enough to rise to a steep sea without making much fuss over it.

But would she sail fast? Her nicely hollowed entrance said so, but then it came out to form an almost bulbous shoulder, well forward; her straight run said so, but it was more steep than flat.

The fellow on deck who was delivering her someplace for the owner answered my question. "She's nothing spectacular in light going," he admitted, "but give her a breeze o' wind and she sails like a fool, just like a fool."

Judging by the bone in her teeth in Edwin Levick's fine photo of her sailing full-and-by under plain sail in a gentle breeze, she's no slouch.

The *Coaster* is 36 feet 5 inches long on deck, with a waterline length of 29 feet 8 inches, a beam of 11 feet 2 inches, and a draft of 5 feet 9 inches. Her sail area is 900 square feet, with 796 square feet in the four lowers.

What a wholesome design this is for a cruising boat. First off, she's pretty. Some say the Peterson schooners (for there were later variations on the theme of this design) are too pretty. I guess they mean that if she's supposed to resemble a coasting schooner, then she ought to look more like one.

The *Coaster* certainly resembles the workaday schooners of the past, but she has her own style and grace—and why not, since her good looks don't compromise her ability. Capable of a good turn of speed, especially when she gets her favorite weather, she is also eminently seaworthy and seakindly. She'd be easy on her crew, an important attribute in a cruising boat, though one not always achieved in today's designs.

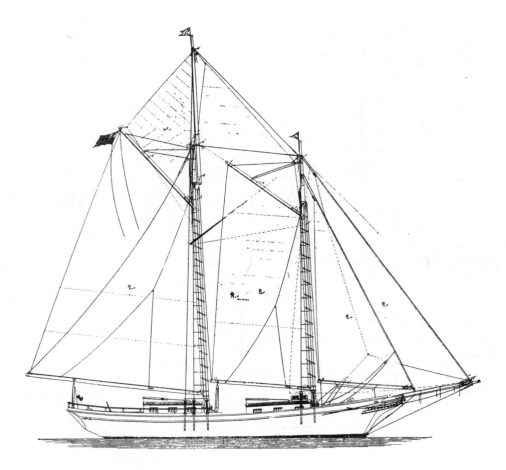

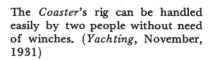

The *Coaster*'s rig can be handled easily by two people without need of winches. (*Yachting*, November, 1931)

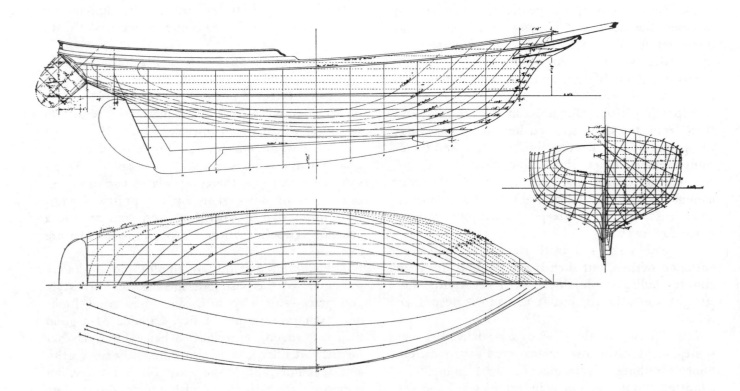

Her lines show her to have a deep body, considerable drag to the keel, and a long run. (*Yachting*, November, 1931)

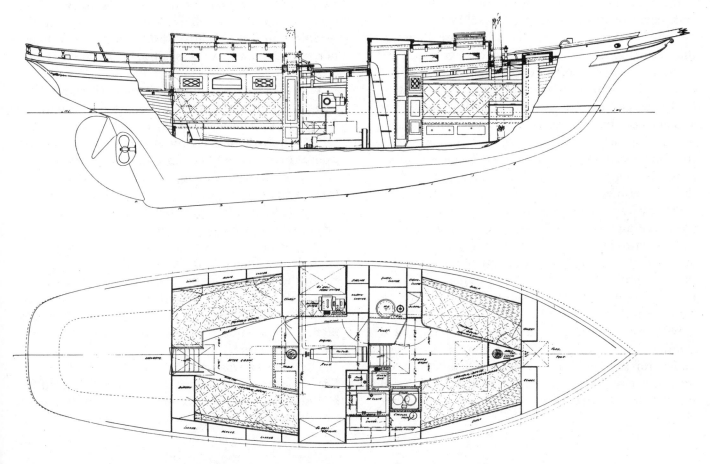

Above: The *Coaster* has comfortable accommodations for four. (*Yachting*, November, 1931)

Below: The original *Coaster* slipping along nicely. (Edwin Levick Collection, Mariners Museum, Newport News, Virginia)

Easy on her crew, with all those sails, spars, and pieces of running rigging? Absolutely.

Four working sails to set with rope halyards that are easy on the hands and enough purchase so that winches aren't needed. Light sails that are fun to play with and that set far enough aloft to really catch the best of a small breeze, but enough sail area without them so there is no need for a big overlapping headsail with its heavily straining single-part sheet. A stiff enough boat (note the fairly hard turn of the bilge just below the waterline) so that reefing wouldn't be necessary until there was real weight in the wind. (And reefing that overhanging gaff mainsail in a breeze with the boat jumping isn't all that hard, provided you keep the boom under control with sheet, topping lift, and gallows frame, and keep the clew earing rove off so you don't have to climb out on the boom.)

With jumbo, foresail, and a reefed main, she'd stand up to plenty. And she'd run off in a gale under foresail and jumbo. If her people needed rest, she could be brought up with just a reefed foresail to lie with her head tucked under her wing.

It's the very complexity and versatility of her rig, the many ways she can be sailed to suit the weather and the wants of her crew, that make her, in the end, an easy boat to handle when cruising.

The *Coaster* has good accommodations for four people. The two pairs of bunks are well separated for privacy. The after cabin makes a comfortable saloon immediately handy to the cockpit, and its house protects the cockpit. The weight of the engine, a 25-h.p. Falcon, is in the middle of the boat, and in this position, the motor can be low enough so its shaft can be nearly level, yet the wheel will be well submerged.

The galley doesn't interfere with saloon-to-cockpit traffic, yet it is immediately accessible from the deck. Looking back on this boat forty years after she was designed, perhaps the most notable feature of her layout is that she has plenty of room for four people, rather than not enough for more.

The *Coaster* was built by Goudy and Stevens at East Boothbay, Maine, and was initially sailed by her designer. She is still going strong on the West Coast, having been cruised to Alaska via the

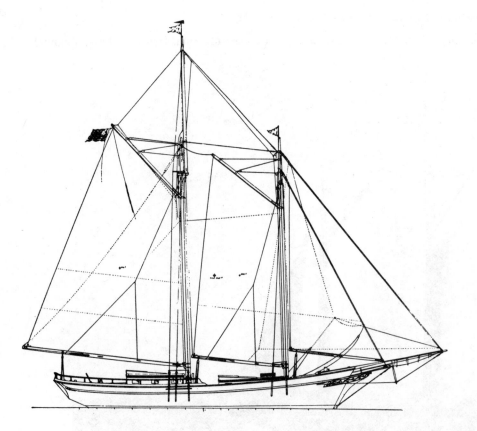

The *Coaster II* is big enough for a dolphin striker. (*Yachting*, December, 1933)

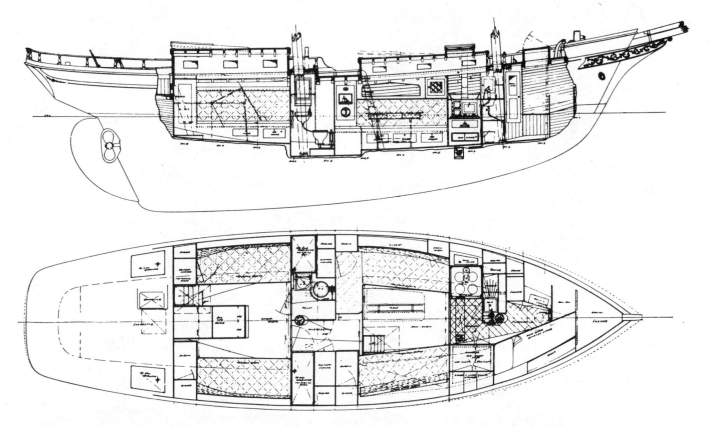

Above: In the *Coaster II*, the engine is aft and there is a single-berth fo'c's'le forward. (*Yachting,* December, 1933)

Below: Owned by H. E. Hock of Little Neck, NY, *Herandis* thrashes her way to weather.

The *Coaster III* is 41'2" long on deck, 33'8" long on the waterline, with a beam of 12' and a draft of 6'3". (*Yachting*, June, 1937)

Panama Canal and Hawaii by Dodge and Layle Morgan a few years ago.

At least two sisterships have been built: the *North Star*, by the Camden (Maine) Shipbuilding Company in 1962, and the *Serenity*, by Malcolm Brewer at Camden, Maine, in 1964.

In 1933, Peterson designed a larger version, the *Coaster II*. Her dimensions are: length on deck, 42 feet 7 inches; length on the waterline, 35 feet 2 inches; beam, 12 feet 3 inches; draft, 6 feet 6 inches; and sail area (four lowers) 1,005 square feet. Two years later came the *Coaster III*, a similar model 41 feet 2 inches long on deck. The *Silver Heels*, built by the Camden Shipbuilding Company in 1963, was a near sister to the *Coaster III*. Peterson also designed an interesting

offshoot, a ketch-rigged version of the original *Coaster*.

A larger successor to these craft was the *Don Quixote del Mar*, a modified fifty-seven-footer that Peterson designed in 1937 for Frederick R. Rogers for ocean cruising. As can be seen in her plans, she is shoaler and a little fuller than the *Coasters*, her additional dimensions being: length on the waterline, 47 feet; beam, 15 feet; and draft, 6 feet 10 inches.

The *Don*'s rig is intriguing, the traditional schooner sail plan having been broken up into smaller units for ease of handling. The main boom has been cut off and a leg-o'-mutton mizzen added. The jib has been given a full club so it can be self-tending; this rig is reminiscent of that on some of the biggest of the coasting schooners. The jib topsail sets low and well forward, to keep it clear of the square foretopsail that has been added. The triangular foresail, set from the yard, won't be blanketed as much by the mainsail as it would if it were square, doesn't require sheets and tacks on the clews, and, in any case, preserves the most efficient part of a squaresail. This sail is reminiscent of the laborsaving mizzen of some of the later four-masted barks.

Her layout below looks just as practical as her

rig, with spacious charthouse aft and galley amidships where the motion is least. She even has a piano in the main saloon! Who wouldn't sell his farm and go to sea?

All in all, it is instructive to look back on these designs of Murray Peterson. They represent a distinctive type of cruising boat, a type that never seems to go out of style, a type that borrows good looks and seagoing ability from traditional American working vessels and makes the most of them.

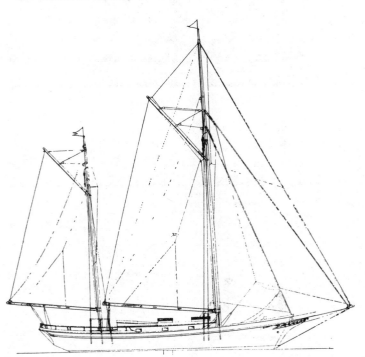

The ketch-rigged version of the *Coaster* sets 737 square feet of sail in her four lowers. (*Yachting*, May, 1935)

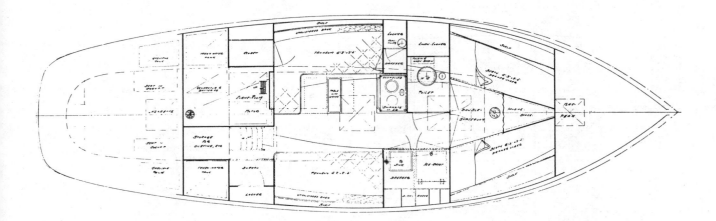

The ketch is laid out for four people. Her hull dimensions are identical to those of the original *Coaster.* (*Yachting*, May, 1935)

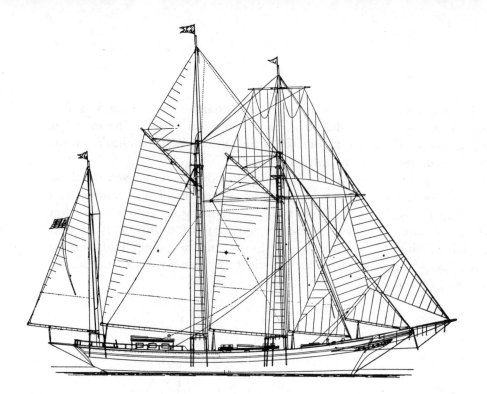

Left: The interesting sail plan of the *Don Quixote del Mar.* (*Yachting,* June, 1937)

Below: The *Don*'s lines show her to be a husky, moderate-draft version of the *Coaster* type. (*Yachting,* June, 1937)

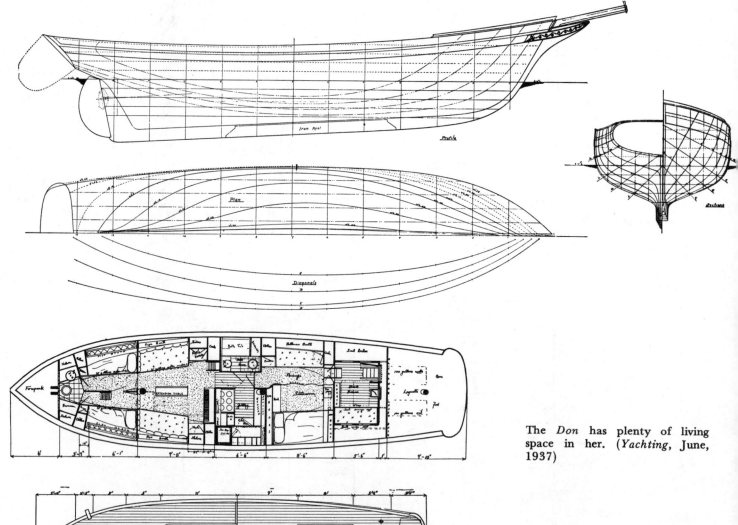

The *Don* has plenty of living space in her. (*Yachting,* June, 1937)

The *Don*'s deck plan shows the break in her quarterdeck amidships and deck stowage positions for two small boats. (*Yachting,* June, 1937)

Chapter 10

The Cogge Ketches

I wish the Urry brothers had designed 100 boats instead of a handful; their designs show great imagination and wonderful artistry. Their 50-foot Cogge ketch remains my favorite of all favorite dreamships. I love to go cruising in her in my mind's eye; she is a great boat to sail and an exciting boat just to be in. A lot of sailors have written me of their dreams of building her; if wishes could launch boats, a fleet of Cogge ketches would grace the Seven Seas.

One correspondent threatened to build the 50-footer of ferrocement. Another predicted that his Cogge ketch would be one of "no less than six" that would be built. A man in North Carolina had all the necessary lumber paid for and stacked, ready for a start. The Northwest School of Wooden Boat-building at Port Townsend, Washington, finished the hull of the 50-footer, put an engine in her, decked her over, built her house, and even gave her a monkey rail she didn't need, but then the owner ran out of money. To my knowledge, the only Cogge ketch that has been completed is William Kinsella's model.

The 50-foot Cogge ketch has spawned at least two more imitations; both are far better designs than that of Mr. Nedwideck in this chapter, but neither is quite a Cogge ketch. Both designers credited the Urrys for their inspiration. William Garden, of Victoria, British Columbia, lengthened his design a foot on the waterline and gave her seven inches more beam. He figured her displacement at 67,500 pounds. She has nearly 400 square feet less sail area than the Cogge, in a handsome ketch rig, with double headsails, a gaff mainsail with thimble-headed topsail set above it on a pole mast, and a Marconi mizzen. She has a bigger galley than the Cogge, a large stateroom with double berth in place of the half-deck cabin, and three berths and two heads forward. Not built.

Al Mason, of Virginia Beach, Virginia, shortened the waterline of his version of the 50-footer by 6 inches, gave her 6 inches more beam, and decreased her draft by 1 foot, 2 inches. He figured her displacement at 64,380 pounds. He cut down her sail area by 550 square feet, drawing a Marconi ketch rig with double headsails. He retained the basic layout of the original design. A boat was built to this Mason design; I saw her offered for sale recently in a boating magazine.

F. Wavell Urry argued for bringing back the stern cabin to yachts — such comforts were common in Samuel Pepys' day — in an article in Sea magazine in 1940 and illustrated it with designs for a 68-foot, deep, narrow Marconi cutter, and a 96-foot seagoing motor yacht, both with stern cabins beautifully incorporated into their then-modern hulls. He even wrote me that he was thinking of installing a great cabin in a modified stern on his Jenetta, an Alfred Mylne 12-meter!

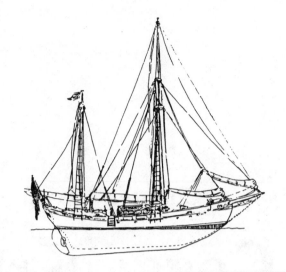

Length on deck: 50 feet 4 inches
Length on waterline: 42 feet 6 inches
Beam: 13 feet 11 inches
Draft: 7 feet 6 inches
Sail area: 1,480 square feet (four lowers)
Designers: Douglas P. Urry and F. Wavell Urry

After I had arrived at the ripe old age of fourteen, I was allowed to explore the closet of my father's study on the third day of a northeaster, the day when the continued restrictions of his children's youthful energies made it mandatory that my father secure peace at any price. He knew that my being allowed into that particular place would have the desired effect on me, but, being an orderly man, he was a bit wary, I think, of my going through his neat stacks of old boating magazines.

He had the issues from 1926 right up to the then-current 1945 numbers. It was tremendously exciting to pull out a stack I had not yet explored and look through them for the first time, knowing not what fantastic schooner or ketch might lie in wait on the next page. For I was a naval architect in those days and was intensely interested in discovering "good" boat designs, separating them from the many "lousy" boats whose plans were published.

A "good" boat had to be well proportioned in hull and rig; she could be rugged or dainty, but she had to please the eye. Any ugliness was sufficient reason for the epithet "lousy boat," with perhaps a "too high-sided" or "not enough sail" thrown in.

The "good" boats were pored over, studied, and absorbed; dimensions and sail areas were ingested beyond mere memorization. The vessel under examination would be imagined sailing in a variety of conditions, and the rig would be shortened down mentally, or light sails would be set to suit the full extremes of wind. Sometimes the route and weather conditions of some actual cruise would be applied in imagination to a newly discovered "good" boat, to both test and enjoy her abilities. Maybe a rolling run from Block Island to Cuttyhunk in a busting sou'wester would be remembered, and the new discovery would have to make the same run on the same day to see how she behaved.

Of course there was always a little editing that had to be done on even the best boats. I never tampered, however, with the hull. If the counter was too heavy for the bow, it was no use pretending she was finer aft than she really was. It was no good wishing that a flat sheer line cocked up nicely. If you had to make basic changes like that, you just had a "lousy" boat—and that was that.

There was one piece of editing I used to do, though, that came very close to hull-tampering. Every now and then I'd come across a boat I

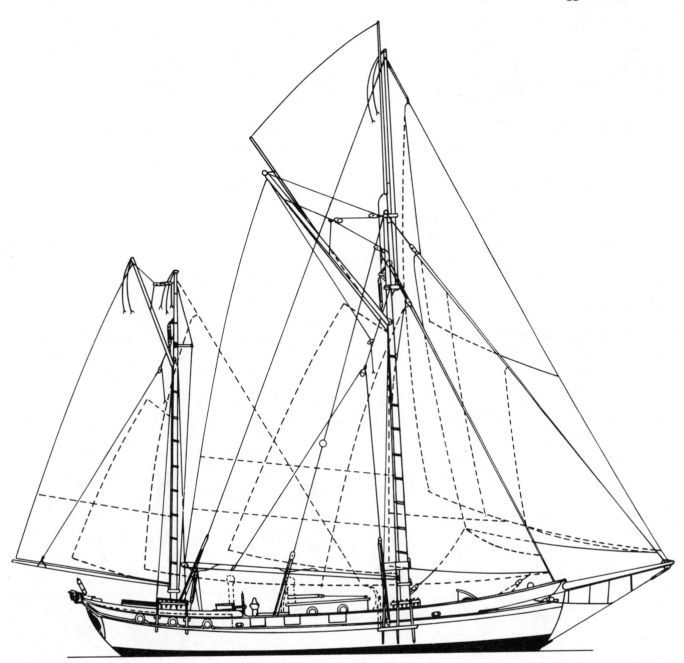

The Urry brothers' 50-foot version of the Cogge ketch, third of the type they designed, but the first one I discovered. (F. Wavell Urry)

really liked, except that it was obvious she didn't have enough lateral plane to do really well to windward. In a case like that, I'd just shut my eyes and stick in a centerboard right down through the keel without changing another thing.

Most of the changes required were either to the rig or to the interior arrangement, and these were limited to minor modifications. A traditional three-headsail rig might have to become a more modern double-head rig if the jib topsail shown were ridiculously small. More often, topmasts, or at least club topsails, were added to bald-headed, gaff-rigged boats. Or, down below, a huge head taking up most of the best part of the boat would have to be relegated to the fo'c's'le to make room for a really decent chart table.

A standard design change at the easily pure age of fourteen was the instant removal of all

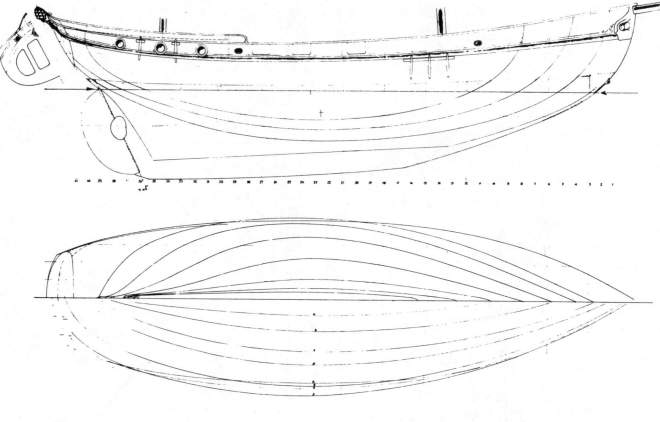

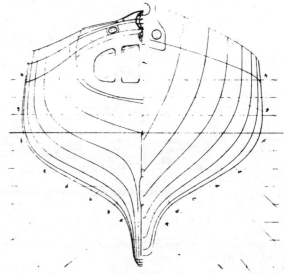

More than twenty years passed before I got a standard
lines drawing of the Cogge ketch. (F. Wavell Urry)

engines, and then the more deliberate determina-
tion of the use for the space gained. It was
always particularly pleasant to close up the
propeller aperture.

There was one issue of *Yachting* that I used to
keep returning to. It was November 1927. In it
was the most wonderful boat I'd ever found. She
was labeled, "A 50-footer of the Cogge type,"

and then it said in smaller print, "Something
between the intriguing *Nonsuch* and the *Coggette.*"

The first time I saw this design, it was quickly
obvious that here was a good boat. The Cogge
ketch, as I termed her, was designed by Douglas P. and F. Wavell Urry. She was 50 feet 4
inches long on deck and 42 feet 6 inches on the

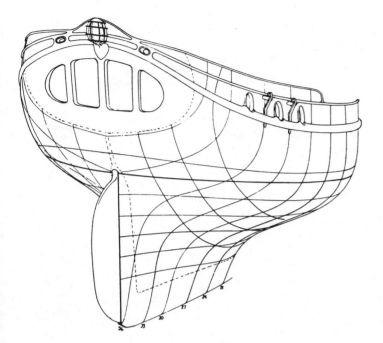

Left: This is the perspective lines drawing that appeared in the November, 1927, issue of *Yachting.* (*Yachting*, November, 1927)

Below: The 50-foot Cogge's arrangement plans. (*Yachting*, November, 1927)

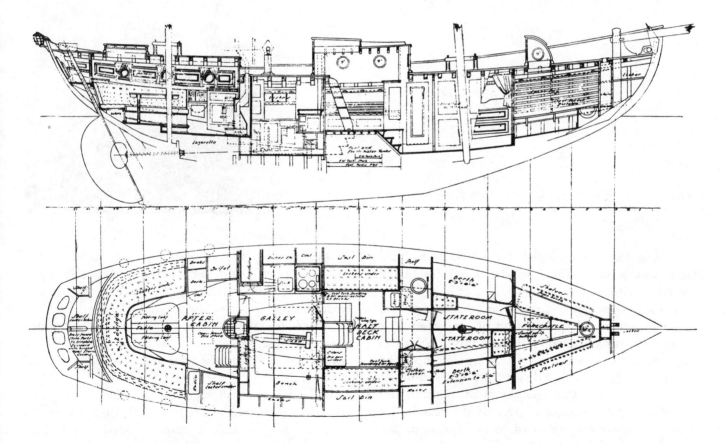

water, with a beam of 13 feet 11 inches and a draft of 7 feet 6 inches. She carried 1,480 square feet of sail in her four lowers.

Her hull was well balanced, with high ends, a bold sheer, and nicely curved, short overhangs. She looked able. And, most exciting of all, she had a raised poop and a great cabin with a fireplace and stern windows! She carried a boat on

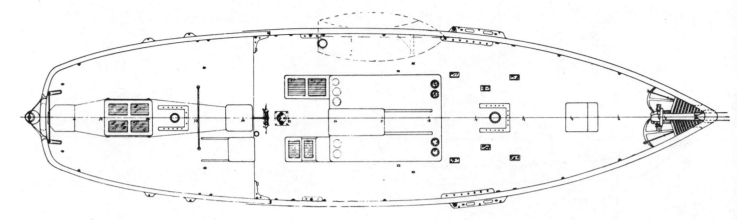

Above: The 50-footer's deck plan. (*Yachting*, November, 1927)

Right: A model of the 50-footer built by William Kinsella of Greenwich, Connecticut. (William Kinsella)

deck and had a substantial deckhouse amidships. Here was a great find, a boat that clearly deserved much scrutiny.

It took some time to take in this design and come to some real appreciation of the vessel. The lines, unfortunately, were shown only in perspective, from the quarter. The drawing did show the shape of the stern, with its windows and its quarter ports, and that was the most unusual, and therefore hard-to-visualize, part of the vessel. The exact shape of the bow had to be imagined. She was shown with white sides and a nicely sheered boot top. I always thought of her, though, with darkly oiled planking, a coppered bottom, and the rubbing strake and rails picked out in royal blue, with the whole set off by some gilt scroll-

work around the hawse forward, around the quarter ports, and, of course, above the stern windows and just below the lantern, where her name would be richly carved. What with her channels to take the main shrouds, the net under the well-steeved bowsprit, and the booby hatch over the fo'c's'le, she certainly looked the true little ship.

The sail plan showed both main and mizzen trysails, each with a short gaff that could be hoisted on the throat halyard alone—a sensible-looking arrangement. The mizzen gaff was not too long, a typical failing in gaff-rigged ketches. There was a balloon forestaysail, an extremely handy and useful cruising sail. There were two jibs smaller than the working jib, and the smaller of these looked modest enough to stand some real breeze. The huge, light jib topsail looked efficient, either on or off a light air. She was clearly designed for offshore cruising, but she didn't look slow.

On deck, she had handsome gratings by the bowsprit, and the deck plan showed two anchors stowed neatly by the post. There were fife rails at the masts and pin rails around the decks. I always did approve of belaying pins in a boat. You could work her rigging without climbing on houses, tripping over deck fittings, or trying to pull on a level with your toes. Her wheel looked made to stand up to, yet the box was high enough so you could sit down on it and still see forward. And there was the stern lantern.

Below was the wondrous great cabin with, as the article said, "the stern windows looking out on the foaming wake, the cheerful fireplace and the broad lounge or transom seat surrounding the table on three sides." I noticed a flush hatch in the great cabin sole, leading below to the lazarette. I assumed this hatch would be hidden by a carpet so the lazarette could be used for piratical purposes. The galley was well aft, where the motion would be least, and handy to the great cabin. The deckhouse would serve admirably for chart work, the head was out of the way, and there was a good-sized fo'c's'le. I gave the latter over to sails, rigging, spares, tools, paint, and naval stores for the topsides.

It was apparent that any editing done on the Cogge ketch ought to be done with great care and deliberation. Here was a rare, fine vessel; perfunctory changes were neither wanted nor deserved.

First, of course, the engine was removed. That made room for the best stateroom in the ship, opening into the galley passageway. The fuel tanks were purified and filled with fresh water. With the shaft and wheel removed, the aperture was sealed and faired. Ahhh.

On deck, the dinghy stowage turned out to be less than entirely satisfactory. It was a tight squeeze between the boat and the house, and when driving into a big, steep sea, carrying sail to push her through, that boat was a worry on the starboard tack for fear a freak sea would pick her out of her lashings. So she came right in on deck in way of the mizzen on the port side. Somehow,

The Urrys' sketch of the original Cogge, the *Nonsuch*, 56 feet on the waterline. (*Yachting*, June, 1925)

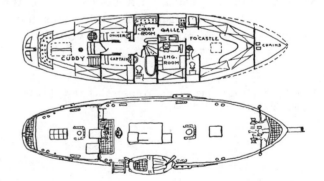

The Urrys' sketches of her deck layout and arrangement below. (*Yachting*, June, 1925)

in the process, she became a slightly longer double-ender, and there appeared lashed in the port mizzen rigging a spar that doubled as boat derrick and boat boom.

Aloft, the two running backstays on each side were brought to a single tackle making down at the break of the poop, so there would be only one backstay tail to set up when tacking. To simplify the tacking drill further, the staysail was

A pen-and-ink of the *Nonsuch* full-and-by, drawn by F. Wavell Urry. (*Yachting*, June, 1925)

THE CUDDY, LOOKING AFT

Wavell Urry put his dream of the great cabin of the *Nonsuch* on paper. (*Yachting*, June, 1925)

cut down a little, given a club and a traveler, and thus made self-tending. This change was carried out with reluctance, since it made the rig less perfect in the name of mere handiness.

The club topsail was stowed away in the fo'c's'le, the clubs being lashed in the starboard waterways on the poop; this sail was saved for showing off in a prolonged calm. In its place, a working thimble-header with hoops on the topmast was bent on, fisherman style. This meant rattling down the main shrouds so you could go

Wavell Urry's drawing of the *Nonsuch* at rest. (*Yachting*, June, 1925)

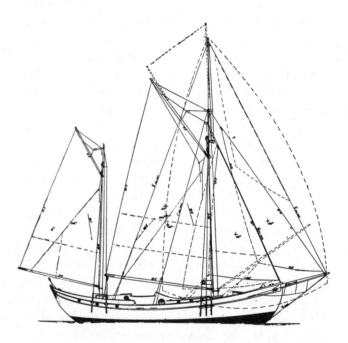

The sail plan of the 42-foot *Coggette*. (*Yachting*, February, 1926)

aloft to furl or loose the sail, a not unwelcome requirement.

Another show-off sail was added, a huge ballooner that filled the whole fore triangle and then some. And, for the trades, a squaresail and raffee were put aboard. The yard was mounted on a gooseneck just above the forestay, and the

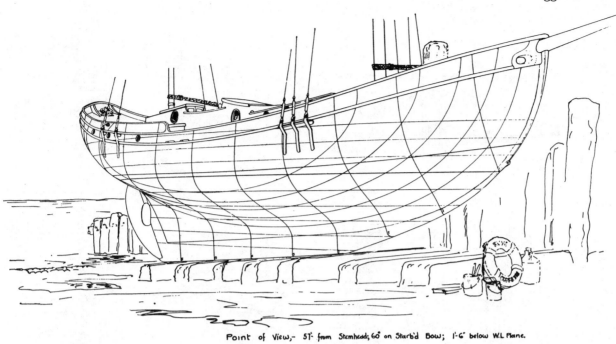

Point of View,— 5ᵀ⁻ from Stemhead; 60° on Starb'd Bow; 1'-6" below W.L. Plane.

The *Coggette*'s lines in perspective from the bow . . . (*Yachting*, February, 1926)

. . . and from the stern. (*Yachting*, February, 1926)

squaresail was rather high cut in the center of the foot so it would clear the forestay. The sail never chafes when full, but it does have to be brailed up in a very light air or calm.

Lastly, a favorite piece of rigging was rove off, a single-part vang leading from the end of the main gaff through a block at the mizzen truck and down to the deck. This keeps the gaff from sagging off and controls the shape of the mainsail. It has one drawback: when the sail is being set or lowered, the vang is slack unless specially tended, and, if the vessel is pitching into a head

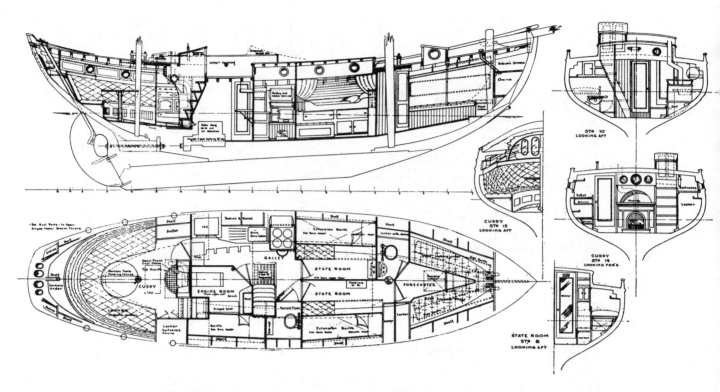

The *Coggette*'s interior arrangement plan. (*Yachting*, February, 1926)

sea, it may wrap itself around the mizzen mast-head. This possibility was an excuse for putting ratlines on the mizzen.

I had taken the Cogge on only a few trial sails

Wavell Urry's sketch of the *Coggette*'s cockpit and quarterdeck arrangement. (*Yachting*, February, 1926)

and was one day inspecting her plans yet again, when, for the first time, I read the text with the plans carefully. I suddenly realized what was meant by, "Something between the intriguing *Nonsuch* and the *Coggette*." These were apparently two similar vessels by the same designers, one bigger and one smaller than my Cogge. I kept admiring the fifty-footer and wondering what her sisters were like.

We lived close enough to the Mystic Marine Museum, as we called what has become the Mystic Seaport, so that I used to visit it often. Once, in 1948, I went there to see Carl Cutler, the wise and patient curator, to ask his advice about a school research paper I was supposed to write.

In the course of the conversation, I mentioned my interest in the Cogge's sister ships, and that remarkable man turned up a magazine that pre-dated my father's collection, and there was the smaller Cogge ketch, the *Coggette*, a forty-two-foot version of the design. I've never been more tempted to steal. A hurried survey of the *Coggette*, however, was all I could accomplish on that occasion. I carried away only a confused mental image of a rather pinched version of the boat with which I was so familiar.

It was 1964 when I finally obtained a copy of the *Coggette* article from the Mystic Seaport Library. I also discovered that the "intriguing *Nonsuch*" had been described in a 1925 article, and the Seaport was kind enough to send a copy of that article too. The *Nonsuch* turned out to be the original of the type. She was fifty-six feet long on the waterline.

Now, having multiplied my dozen-plus years by three, I could at last study and compare all three Cogge ketches. No longer a naval architect by profession, I had, nevertheless, retained a lively interest in that art, and my early prejudices about engines and other features of yacht design had, with advancing age, deepened into fetishes.

Over the years, I had yanked hundreds of engines out of published boat designs, to their great improvement. Yet I had found fewer and fewer boats worth the editorial process. Thus it was with relish that I returned to the Cogge and her two sisters. Since my opinions had strength-

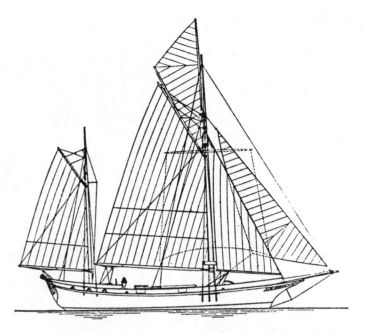

A 55-foot ketch designed by Chester A. Nedwideck in 1932. Though she was presented in *The Rudder* as "extraordinary" and "novel," we can guess at her inspiration. (*Rudder* Magazine, © December, 1932, Fawcett Publications, Inc.)

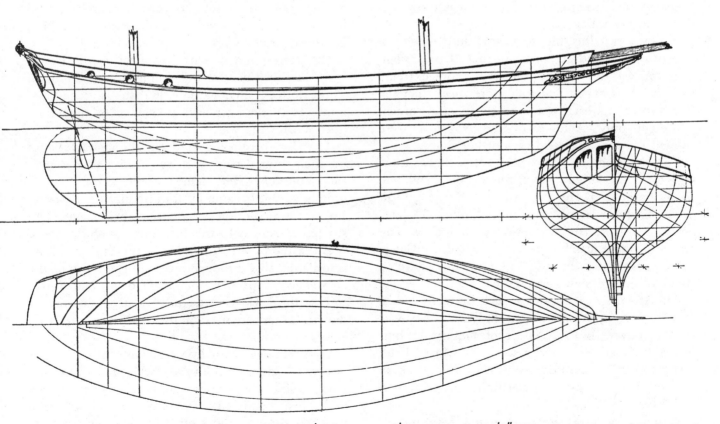

The Nedwideck ketch has a waterline length of 44', a beam of 15', and a draft of 8'6". Her sail area in the four lowers is 1,471 square feet. (*Rudder* Magazine, © December, 1932, Fawcett Publications, Inc.)

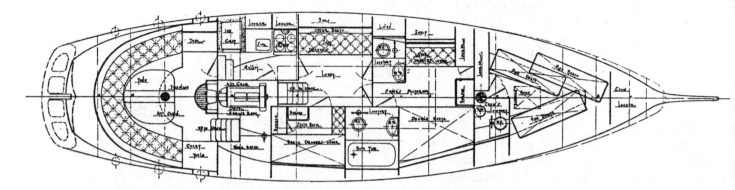

The accommodation plan of the Nedwideck ketch. The perfect proportions of the Cogge ketches are missing in this design, and it is presented only as an interesting sidelight. (*Rudder* Magazine, © December, 1932, Fawcett Publications, Inc.)

ened, rather than merely changed, I found, of course, that my early editing of the fifty-footer stood up beautifully. Inspection of the new Cogge ketches in my possession showed, furthermore, that the same minor modifications as had been applied to the fifty-footer would be desirable in her relatives.

Looking at the big *Nonsuch* and the little *Coggette*, I found it apparent that these design-ancestors of the fifty-footer were more extreme than she was. They had lots more sheer than the fifty-footer—almost, but not quite, too much. Although only sketches of the *Nonsuch* were shown, these gave a good idea of her shape.

For the *Coggette*, two perspective lines drawings were presented, one from the bow and one from the quarter. Her dimensions were: length on deck, 42 feet; length on the waterline, 34 feet; beam, 12 feet; and draft, 6 feet 8 inches. The two additional articles greatly enriched my Cogge ketch resources, but I still did not have a standard lines drawing for any of them.

An attempt to track down such drawings led in 1967 to the information that F. Wavell Urry was in Vancouver, B.C. A letter of inquiry to him brought a nice reply and a set of drawings of the fifty-footer, including standard lines. These showed her hull to be beautifully proportioned and faired.

Perhaps the most interesting new information yielded by the additional articles was a clue to the origin of the Cogge type. Douglas P. Urry, serving in the North Sea in 1916, was reading an old book of voyages while off watch. A phrase, "the Cogge *Thomas*," caught his eye. His imagination began to play with this simple reference to an old, obscure vessel. Douglas Urry surmised she might have been a seventeenth-century northern European trading ketch.

He corresponded with his brother, F. Wavell Urry, about this fleeting vision of an old boat. Those letters, their yarning, and the sketches sent home to Vancouver gave substance to their conjurings after the war.

The Urry brothers sorted out the characteristics of their own Cogge and by 1925 had designed the *Nonsuch*. Her name, aptly chosen for a unique vessel, became all too literally appropriate, for her construction was beyond their means, and she has remained to this day a dream ship.

An attempt to scale down the design to an affordable size produced the *Coggette*, but the Depression kept her, too, from being laid down.

The third Cogge design, the fifty-footer, was drawn for an admirer of the type. But she, too, was never built.

So the Cogge remains a dream, elusive to her designers and her admirers, who may, like me, have sailed many miles in her. Her handsome hull, her regal rig, even her foaming wake watched through the stern windows, seem almost real. Perhaps they may one day become so.

Chapter 11

The *Gloucesterman*

The republication of the design of the schooner Gloucesterman had the happy effect of changing Fenwick Williams' feeling for the vessel from bitter to sweet. Soon after his plans of her were first published, in Yachting magazine in 1932, somebody built her in Hong Kong, using for plans an enlargement of the magazine pages. Williams described the result as "perfectly God-awful." Then a Californian bought her plans from Williams and built her—with considerably increased freeboard.

When Williams gave me permission to bring the Gloucesterman back to the public eye, he was understandably dubious. But a doctor in Germany, Detlef Zschoche, saw the design and got excited about her. He bought large-scale plans from Williams and had a good builder follow them.

The oak keel of the Johan Ehlers was laid by the third and fourth generations of a shipbuilding family, Heinrich Hatecke and Son, at their yard in Freiburg on the Elbe River on June 9, 1982. They laminated her stem, stern post, and frames of white oak and cambala. One sensible modification was to move the engine aft and move the outside ballast forward a little to compensate. The engine is an M.A.N. six-cylinder diesel, delivering 110 h.p. at 2,800 r.p.m.

Dr. Zschoche invited me to attend his schooner's launching at 15.30 Uhr, 11. Juni 1983, at the yard's Basin 1. I wish I could have gone. Soon after she was launched, the Johan Ehlers entered a race in the Skagerrak against some 200 competitors. She came home first and won the race on corrected time. Dr. Zschoche loves his schooner. It's good to know that at last a vessel has been built properly to Fenwick Williams' design of the Gloucesterman.

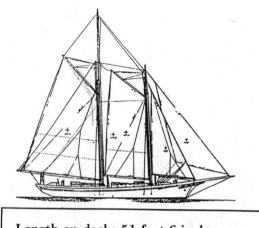

Length on deck: 51 feet 6 inches
Length on waterline: 42 feet 6 inches
Beam: 14 feet
Draft: 8 feet
Sail area: 1,718 square feet
Displacement: 30½ tons
Designer: Fenwick C. Williams

One of the most noteworthy of American vessels in terms of her influence on later designs was the fishing schooner *Fredonia*. She was fast and able, and her general type was copied widely; she spawned a general class of Gloucester fishing schooners that became known as "*Fredonia* models." Her influence can also be seen distinctly on other smaller craft, such as the Friendship sloop.

Actually, naming this class of schooner after the *Fredonia* is a bit like naming the New World America instead of Columbia. The *Fredonia* was a near sistership to another schooner built from the same design, and the other vessel was built before the *Fredonia*. It's something of a mystery why the class of vessels started by this design didn't become known as *Nellie Dixon* models. Perhaps it was because the *Fredonia*, when first launched, was used as a yacht for a short time by J. Malcolm Forbes, and thus gained a wider reputation than her slightly older sister.

The man who created this important design was the great yacht designer Edward Burgess.

The *Fredonia* was launched in 1889 at Essex, Massachusetts, from the yard of Moses Adams. She had a relatively short life, for she foundered in a gale on the Grand Banks on December 18, 1896.

The chief difference between the *Fredonia* and the *Nellie Dixon* is that the *Fredonia* was shortened on deck by some 2 feet 6 inches from the original design. The *Fredonia*'s dimensions were: length on deck 112 feet 5 inches; length on the waterline 98 feet; beam 23 feet 5 inches; and draft 14 feet 5 inches.

The *Fredonia* inspired not only fine fishing schooners, but also fine yachts. One of the best is the schooner *Gloucesterman*, designed some half a century ago by Fenwick C. Williams of Marblehead, Massachusetts. Howard I. Chapelle's description of the *Fredonia*, given in his book *The American Fishing Schooners: 1825-1935*, fits the *Gloucesterman* quite well.

> The design for these two schooners [the *Fredonia* and the *Nellie Dixon*] showed a moderate, graceful sheer; a slightly rockered keel . . . the forefoot had much rounding. . . .
>
> The sternpost had much rake, above which was a short counter and a rather small, heart-shaped transom. The run was long and somewhat convex without straight buttocks, but with very little rounding. The entrance was long and very sharp with a slight hollow in the forefoot. The midsection was formed with a much hollowed garboard, a sharp rise of floor carried straight well outboard, a high and rather hard turn of the bilge, and strong tumblehome

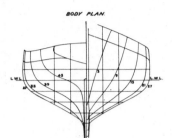

BODY PLAN.

The lines of the Nellie Dixon *and the* Fredonia *from a copy probably made from the plan drawn by Edward Burgess, the designer of these important fishing schooners.* (The National Watercraft Collection, Second Edition, *by Howard I. Chapelle, The Smithsonian Institution and International Marine Publishing Co.)*

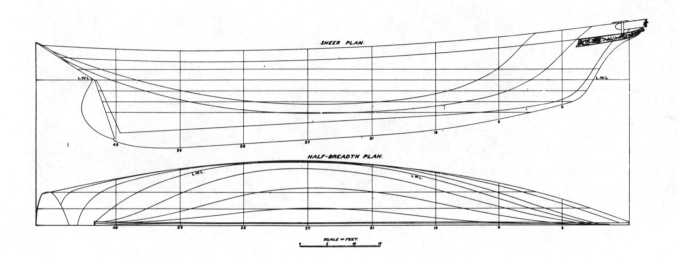

in the topside. In these vessels Burgess seems to have been somewhat influenced by the then scientific "wave-line theory," insofar as the entrance was designed very sharp and long, with the run a bit full and short.

The *Gloucesterman*'s entrance is not nearly as long and fine as that of the *Fredonia,* of course, for the *Gloucesterman* is a much smaller vessel. Her maximum fullness is also farther forward than that of the *Fredonia.* And her transom is oval, rather than heart-shaped.

The *Gloucesterman* is 51 feet 6 inches long on deck, with a waterline length of 42 feet 6 inches, a beam of 14 feet, and a draft of 8 feet. She displaces 30½ tons, with 7½ tons of outside ballast in an iron keel.

The schooner's sail plan is simply a big triangle filled in with six sails. The shape of the triangle, with its rather low-lying leading edge, would be more efficient off the wind than on, which, of course, makes good sense in a cruising vessel that

doesn't particularly care that it takes her 20 minutes instead of 15 to beat a mile dead to windward but wants to be sure of being able to sail at hull speed with ease and safety once the wind frees.

But who can long look at a gaff-rigged schooner sporting a main topmast as a geometrical figure or an aerodynamic exercise? She's a true, living vessel with elegance and huge potential for romance.

Fenwick Williams has made the most of the possibilities. Everything about the hull and rig of the *Gloucesterman* is proportioned just right. Look at the relationship between the profile of her stem, her sheerline forward carried out by the well-steeved bowsprit, and the angle of the foot of her jib. This all looks exactly right, and it looks right because it works well in a head sea. The tack of her jib is 8 feet 3 inches above the water, precisely the same height as the clew of her mainsail.

The schooner's sail area is 1,718 square feet, made up of a mainsail of 598 square feet; foresail,

The drydock manifests the size and beauty of the great **Fredonia**. *(The Smithsonian Institution)*

359 square feet; staysail, 171 square feet; jib, 189 square feet; main topsail, 155 square feet; and fisherman, 246 square feet.

She has deep reefs in both mainsail and foresail. With the first reef tied into the mainsail, that sail is reduced to 450 square feet, an area that can normally be handled by one person. Her reefed foresail is a snug 250 square feet.

Her main gaff would not sag off unduly, for it is peaked up reasonably high and the long foot of the mainsail would help keep the twist out of the sail. The foresail, being tall and narrow with a low-peaked gaff naturally has a vang with which to control the shape of the sail.

The *Gloucesterman*'s engine is right in the middle of her galley, an arrangement with both advantages and disadvantages.

The good news is that there is plenty of room to work around the machine, and you can hardly forget to keep it clean. Hers would not be a neglected power plant. Also, the engine box would serve as an admirable galley table.

The bad news is that clean and polish though you might, the bread might always taste just a tiny bit of diesel oil. Also, if you were making a passage under power in a prolonged calm, you'd probably have to shut her down during meal preparation or the cook would mutiny. Maybe that item should come under the heading of good news also (not the mutiny of the cook, but the occasional, forced shutting down of the engine).

There is a 100-gallon fuel tank in the galley (is this wise?) and a 150-gallon fuel tank back aft in the lazarette. The lazarette also contains a 150-gallon water tank and racks for six 5-gallon water carboys, so you have something substantial to take ashore and hold under that lovely waterfall.

The after companion ladder can be removed to get to the door of the lazarette. A good arrangement here might be to replace that ladder with two vertical ladders, one on either side of the companionway, with the rungs oriented fore and aft. With the boat upright, you can use either ladder or, better yet, use alternate rungs of both ladders.

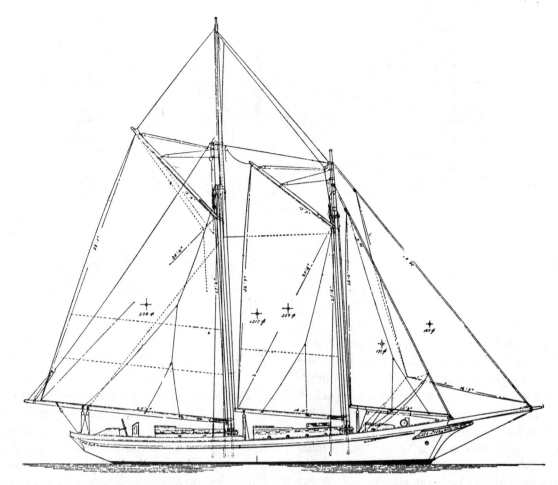

Above: *The* Gloucesterman *is a beautifully proportioned schooner of the* Fredonia *model.* (Yachting, *August, 1932*)

Below: *Though she is less than half the length of the* Fredonia, *the* Gloucesterman *shows unmistakable characteristics inherited from the big fisherman.* (Yachting, *August, 1932*)

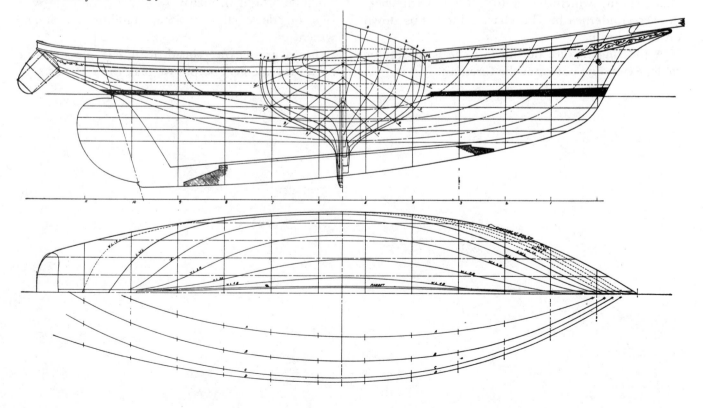

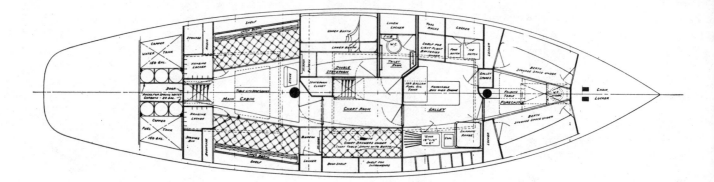

The schooner's layout is versatile; two people could live in her in luxury, nine could squeeze in, and five would find her ideal for cruising. (Yachting, August, 1932)

When she's heeled over, these ladders come into their own, for the ship's crew appreciates the nicely slanted leeward ladder, while the ship's monkey gets ecstatic about the overhanging windward one. The first designer to use this double ladder idea, as far as I know, was Ralph Wiley.

The schooner's saloon is a most comfortable place, with its heating stove alongside the mast and its two big hanging lockers on either side of the companionway.

The forward companionway comes down into a chart room, which has a high bunk with chart drawers underneath. The chart table drops down onto this berth.

A pleasing feature of the fo'c's'le is its folding table, extending out from the foremast.

The *Gloucesterman* has nine bunks, but she would be far more comfortable with five people on board for a cruise of any length. You could have four watch-standers and a navigator-cook. In easy weather, the watch-standers could stand one in four, with the oncoming watch being on call during the preceding watch to take in and reset the fisherman when tacking, or whatever. In hard weather, you'd probably want to double up with two on deck all the time, standing watch and watch.

But I am getting ahead of myself. I guess we'd better lay the keel before we plan the watches.

Chapter 12

The *Poseidon*

Frank Fredette is a designer who deserves to be better known. He designed more than 200 craft, many of them commercial fishermen, many of them handsome and able ketches and schooners that, like the Poseidon, make good vessels in which to live, cruise, and make money. His naval architecture sprang from much seagoing and boatbuilding experience, rather than from mere book-learning.

Fredette was born in Victoria, British Columbia, in 1894 and never left the area, except to go voyaging. From the age of four, he was a child of the waterfront, scrounging stuff to make boats. His first craft was the lid from a discarded steamer trunk, with a shingle for paddle. While still in grammar school, he built a 16-foot rowboat for a customer.

At the age of fourteen, Fredette shipped for the Bering Sea in the sealing schooner Eva Marie. His job on the hunt was to pull an oar in an 18-foot spritsail skiff. The voyage was the start of a seagoing career that included square rig, commercial fishing, and merchant marine service in World War I. Between voyages, he worked as a boatbuilder. He could fashion every part of a plank-on-frame wooden vessel, and he could caulk her seams.

Fredette turned to designing in the early forties. Because he had left school early, he was weak in math, so his wife, a school teacher, did the calculations for his designs. His vessels reflect the best traditions—and the rugged sailing conditions—of the Pacific northwest.

Length on deck: 42 feet
Length on waterline: 32 feet 8 inches
Beam: 12 feet
Draft: 5 feet 9 inches
Sail area: 754 square feet
Displacement: 11 tons
Designer: Francis E. Fredette

One of the many interesting pieces of mail that has come to us as publishers of the *Mariner's Catalog* series is some correspondence from a college in the northwestern United States that was setting up an experimental program with faculty and students to study the whys and wherefores of commercial fishing under sail. This program didn't come under the history department; these folks wanted to go out and do it today.

One of the things they did, with the help of a naval architect, was to come up with a contemporary design for a small sailing fishing vessel. They sent us study plans of the boat, and we had to laugh. The influence, albeit indirect, of the International Offshore Rule for racing yachts was all too evident.

Here is a design for a 42-foot ketch that might better meet the requirements of that college study project. She was designed to be a combination work and pleasure boat, the idea being that the owner would troll for salmon in summer and sail her south and live on board in winter. Not a bad life, eh what?

The ketch is named the *Poseidon*, after the Greek god of water, earthquakes, and horses. (I thought that an odd combination of responsibilities to assign to a Greek god, too, until I

realized that all Poseidon had to master to do his job well was dealing with the unpredictable, perhaps not too tall an order for a Greek god.)

The ketch was designed in 1957 by Francis E. Fredette of Victoria, British Columbia. She was built in Victoria by her owner, Fergus Walker, and was launched in 1959.

She is indeed an able-looking boat. She would not be fast under sail, but would certainly be seakindly and easily handled. She is the kind of boat that might often need a bit of help from her engine to do her work.

The *Poseidon* is 42 feet long on deck, with a waterline length of 32 feet 8 inches, a beam of 12 feet, and a draft of 5 feet 9 inches. She displaces 11 tons. Her sail area is 754 square feet, with 380 square feet in the mainsail, 160 in the mizzen, and 214 in the working jib.

Her power plant is a British diesel, a Parsons Pike of 35 brake horsepower, with 2:1 reduction gear. She cruises under power at 6½ knots.

The ketch's backbone and planking are of fir, and her frames are bent oak.

Her bow is well shaped to deal with a head sea; she has about five feet of freeboard forward. She has fine, high shoulders, a strong sheer, a fairly

*Francis E. Fredette. (Bernadette Mertens,
National Fisherman)*

deep forefoot, and moderate drag to the keel, giving her moderate draft. Her rudder is big and is well aft. Her propeller is well submerged.

Her bilges are firm, but not hard, and she has considerable hollow to her garboards. Her stern sections are flat enough above the waterline to allow her to pick up good bearing aft as she heels. As a matter of fact, she is one of those boats with a bit of flare all around her waterline, so she picks up a little bearing everywhere. That shape also makes a boat look light on her feet.

The *Poseidon*'s ketch rig is well proportioned. She would balance well under mainsail alone or under jib and jigger. There are practical, deep reefs in her mainsail and mizzen, and a small jib is shown.

Whenever I see a pair of headstays meeting at the stemhead, I want to separate them so each can be used for setting a headsail. I think this boat cries out for a bowsprit so that the upper headstay may be taken out to the end of it and then be used to

*Mr. Fredette in his sealing boat replica.
(Bernadette Mertens, William Garden)*

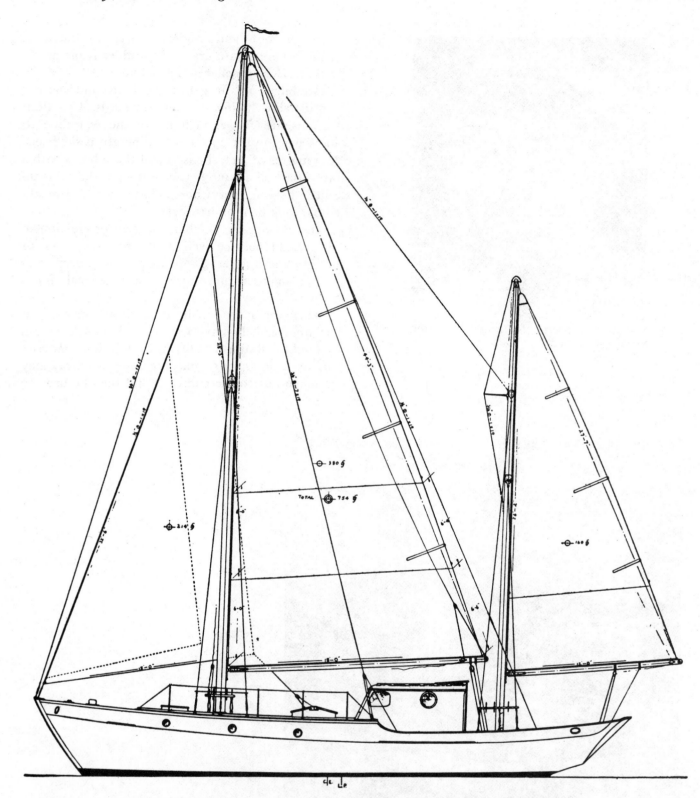

The Poseidon *has a rugged look to her.* (The Rudder, *September, 1959*)

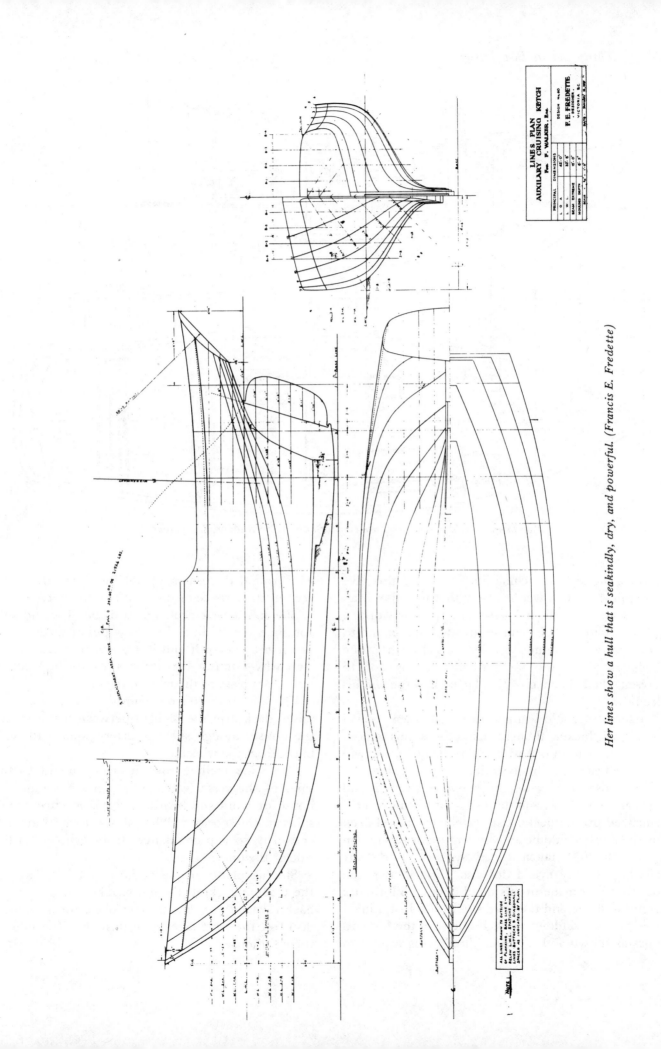

Her lines show a hull that is seakindly, dry, and powerful. (Francis E. Fredette)

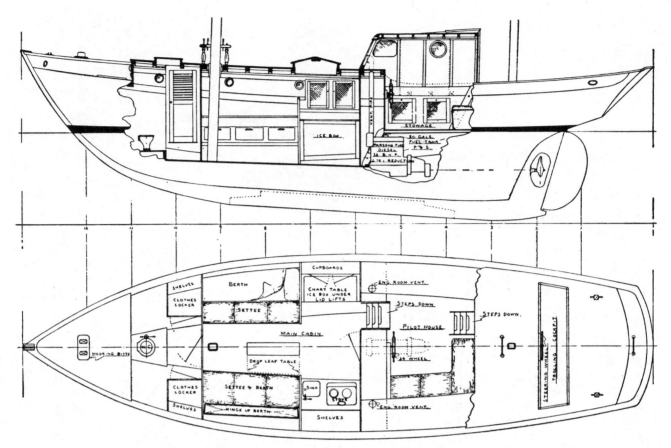

Two people could live in her quite comfortably. (The Rudder, *September, 1959*)

carry a big, light, reaching jib. She might also have a big jib for the lower headstay that would overlap the mainsail considerably to add area for working to windward in light and moderate weather and to pole out as a running sail. Such a sail ought to be high-cut along the foot, though, so as not to present the helmsman with a large blind spot on his lee bow.

I suppose you'd want to carry a mizzen staysail in the sail locker, though such a sail seems seldom to be really useful. And you'd probably want twin running headsails for any serious ocean work.

Her raised deck gives the *Poseidon* strength and dryness on deck and looks good, being nicely balanced by the deckhouse. Either the raised deck or the house could be an ugly feature of this design by itself, but taken together, they work out all right to my eye. I do wish, though, that the designer had made up his mind about a pilothouse window shape and then had stuck with it. I think a row of four windows on each side with the forward ones as shown and the after three being rectangles

with rounded corners would have improved the general appearance of the boat considerably.

She has a well deck forward, but I would still continue the lifelines to a bow pulpit at the stem or on the bowsprit end if a bowsprit were added. And why not run the lifelines aft to the stern as well, or at least to the mizzen rigging?

There is room to stow a nine-foot dinghy on the raised deck over the skylight between the mast and the house, though she'd interfere some with visibility from the wheelhouse.

The wide trolling cockpit gets you out to the sides of the vessel where you can see around the house or work overboard. She has a wheel amidships in this cockpit. What about a wheel at each end of it, so you could steer from right out at the side of the boat?

She has plenty of places for people aft. There is the trolling cockpit, the nicely raked transom for a backrest, and even the perfect place for a chair on deck on the port side up against the after end of the pilothouse.

I think it would make sense from a safety standpoint to consider the *Poseidon*'s wheelhouse to be dispensable. Raise the floor slightly, and make the enclosure into a self-draining, watertight cockpit that just happens to have a house built around it for shelter. Then if that house should be washed away by a freak sea, you'd still have a watertight cockpit. The wheelhouse is a most worthwhile addition to the vessel, however, for it would be a tremendous comfort in bad weather.

The engine was installed farther aft than it is shown in the inboard profile plan, being shoved all the way back under the wheelhouse floor. I prefer the design shown, for an area of full headroom in the engine room is not a luxury to be discarded lightly in return for mere cabin space. There are two 80-gallon fuel tanks in the engine room wings.

She has both a wide and a narrow settee in the saloon and both a built-in and a hinged berth above them. This arrangement gives a lot of versatility for sitting down, lying around, or sleeping. She has a head and a couple of big clothes lockers in the forepeak, just where they should be.

A second craft was built to this design, the *Roebuck Bay*. She was built in Australia of hardwood and is now owned in Victoria by a man who has done extensive ocean cruising in her and likes her very much.

The *Poseidon* was not so fortunate. On a cruise in the Caribbean, she was run down at sea by a freighter and lost. But for anyone who wants a handy little vessel for fishing, cruising, or as a home afloat, whether he is studying in or out of college, this design is well worth considering.

Chapter 13

The *Glengour*

When my uncle Dan Larkin sold his 43-foot, Alden center-board schooner, the Blue Sea, and got a mere powerboat to replace her, he met my shock with the statement: "I'm too old to take another drubbing in an open cockpit." I acknowledged his concession to the comfort of a wheelhouse, but I didn't really understand it. Now, having reached the age at which he made the transition, I do. I notice that when I'm feeling my years, the vessel I turn to for a dream cruise usually has a wheelhouse.

One way I like to take a dream cruise is simply to substitute a dream ship for a real boat in which I've taken a real cruise. An advantage of the method is that it facilitates comparison of the two vessels. Last summer, I seemed to be sailing everybody's boat but mine; it was October before I made even a short, singlehanded cruise in the Goblin. The Goblin, you will remember from the introduction to Chapter 3, was the boat of Fred Taylor, another uncle, and she now has his nephew's hand on her tiller. She is a 23-foot, gaff-rigged, keel-and-centerboard sloop. October is pushing the season a bit in Maine. You expect cold, clear weather. It was cold enough on my trip, but halfway along, the clear weather was replaced by thick fog. After I found the way home to my mooring and got dry and warm at the little stove below, I found myself retracing my courses of the last three days in the relative comfort of W. G. McBryde's Glengour.

The first day, I had patiently worked light and variable airs to travel a few miles from Rockland to my favorite harbor on the whole coast, a little hole protected by Dix Island and her many neighbors, just off the Muscle Ridge Channel. To enjoy the beautiful, though all-too-early, sunset, I'd huddled in the bottom of the cockpit protecting myself from the chilly, after-anchoring breeze with judicious sips of rum. In the Glengour, I steamed right down there at nearly 8 knots, and sunset found me lolling in the toasty-warm wheelhouse, enjoying all the loveliness through clear glass.

So went the comparisons on the rest of the cruise. Instead of beating out blind through the Fox Island Thorofare, bundled-up but damp and shivering, blurred chart dripping, mind racing with disastrous possibilities, paper towel supply dwindling with each drying of my glasses, I just powered straight along in my shirt sleeves, calmly checking off the buoys as they appeared. Oh yes, I get it now, all right.

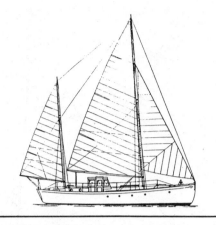

Length on deck: 39 feet 3 inches
Length on waterline: 35 feet
Beam: 10 feet
Draft: 4 feet 11 inches
Sail area: 671 square feet
Displacement: 12.3 tons
Designer: W. G. McBryde

Going through a secondhand bookstore with a good marine section is like going to a party in your hometown. You see lots of old friends and may make one or two interesting new acquaintances. Such was the case the day I discovered a slim, blue volume of at least middle age with "Forty Designs of Motor and Sailing Yachts by W. G. McBryde, M. I. N. A." stamped across its front cover in handsome gold lettering.

Flipping through this book was more like going to a party in a strange town. Among the vessels for which plans, dimensions, and brief commentary were given, there were many interesting new acquaintances, and there chanced to be one old friend.

The old friend was the *Glengour,* a motorsailer, plans and a photo of which I had long admired in Uffa Fox's book *Racing, Cruising and Design.*

Mr. McBryde, in his book, called the *Glengour* a "50-50 cruiser," as opposed to others of his designs that he called "motorsailers." The former term implied to him that the boat would perform quite well under sail alone. The *Glengour* had that reputation, and I agree that there is no reason why she shouldn't sail quite well. In any event, she would certainly be a most comfortable cruising boat for four people.

The *Glengour* was built, I believe in the mid-Thirties, by James Adam and Sons. She is 39 feet 3 inches long on deck, with a waterline length of 35 feet, a beam of 10 feet, and a draft of 4 feet 11 inches. Her sail area is 671 square feet, and her displacement is 12.3 tons. She is powered with two 15-h.p. engines, which give her a speed of 7¾ knots.

The *Glengour*'s hull is long and narrow, with very easy waterlines and buttocks. She would be an easily driven vessel. She has plenty of freeboard for dryness on deck in rough water.

Her short ends are nicely shaped and well balanced. Her hull looks especially handsome in the photo of her at anchor. Her sheered boot top adds greatly to her appearance, in my opinion.

The rig is well proportioned. She would balance nicely under jib and jigger in a strong breeze. Her mainsail has 377 square feet, the mizzen 138, and the jib 156.

She does need preventer backstays pulling aft against the forestay to keep the mast and forestay reasonably straight. I'd also be sorely tempted to pull my usual trick of giving her a bowsprit. That way you could move the "topmast" stay out onto the end of it for a big ballooner. And a bowsprit is an anchorman's best friend.

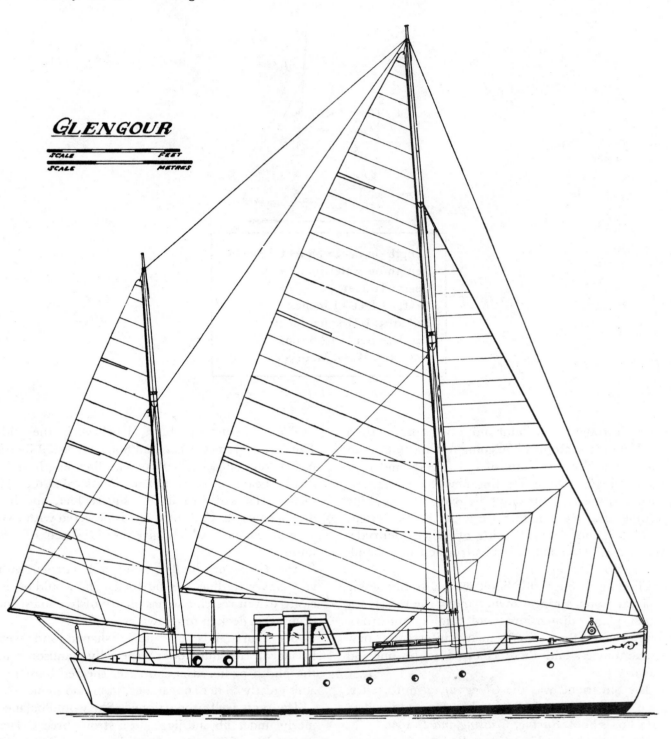

GLENGOUR

SCALE ——————— FEET
SCALE ——————— METRES

The **Glengour** *is a Scottish fifty-fifty cruising boat.* (Racing, Cruising and Design *by Uffa Fox*)

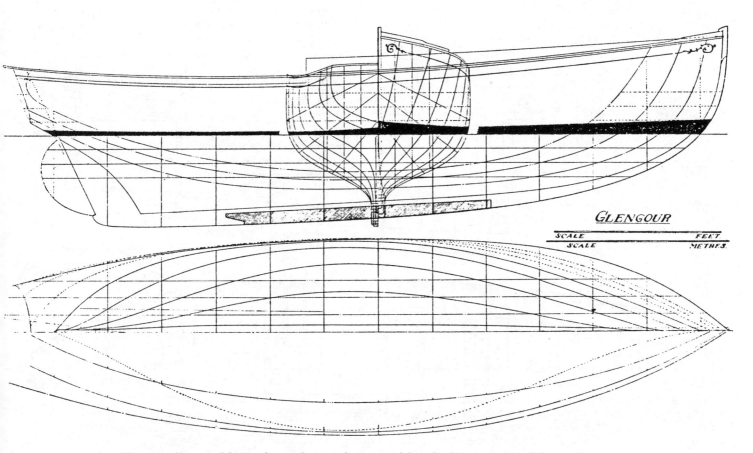

*Her waterlines and buttocks are long and easy, and her sections are powerful enough so
she would stand up well to her sail.* (Racing, Cruising *and* Design *by Uffa Fox*)

In this day and age of extremely reliable marine engines, the increased reliability gained from having two engines instead of one is less important than it was when the *Glengour* was designed and built. Still, having a spare engine, so to speak, could be a mighty comforting thing if you had serious mechanical troubles a long way from an engine repair shop. And what could be more satisfactory when you have to turn her in a short space than to put a twist on—with one engine running ahead and the other astern—adjusting the throttles carefully so she stays in one place, and then just standing around nonchalantly while she turns herself?

The *Glengour*'s deckhouse adds to her looks, to my eye. It gives her a certain air of distinction. And there is something very different about a boat with a real wheelhouse. Standing and leaning in there looking out at the watery world through a glass window, you get the definite feeling that you

are involved with something that can be called a ship. Maybe that's the way to solve the old conundrum about what is a ship and what is a boat: a ship has a wheelhouse; a boat doesn't.

The ketch has a raised flush deck from the deckhouse forward to give her plenty of working space topside and plenty of living space below. There is a small cockpit just abaft the mizzen mast, where you can steer her with a tiller.

On-deck dinghy stowage would be something of a problem. She is fitted with davits on the starboard side, but with a dinghy either hung from them outboard in pleasant weather or swung in on deck in rough weather, the view from the wheel would be somewhat obstructed. A ten-foot boat on deck would reach from the middle of the forward hatch to the after end of the skylight.

The forward companionway from the wheelhouse comes down into the engine room, which has full headroom in its forward end. With the

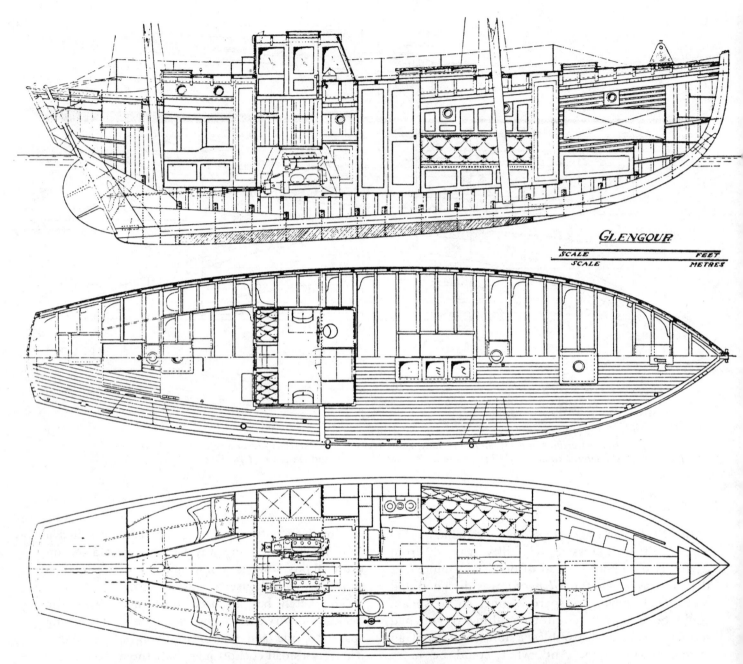

She is laid out with plenty of space for four people and two engines. The wheelhouse would be a joy. (Racing, Cruising and Design by Uffa Fox)

wheelhouse and engine room between the deck and the forward living quarters, little cold and wet should find their way below forward in bad weather. If this boat were to make serious passages offshore, the inside of the deckhouse should, of course, be strong, watertight, and self-draining, and the doors leading below forward and aft should be strong and watertight. When running under power,

you'd want to keep the forward companionway shut to keep the engine noise out of the wheelhouse.

All in all, the *Glengour* does seem to be a true 50-50 cruising boat. Of her performance under sail, her designer wrote, "She is able to go to windward, and remarkably fast for a vessel of this type." Uffa Fox wrote, "Though she is a full-powered motor-

The Glengour *anchored in a peaceful Scottish loch. (*Racing, Cruising and Design *by Uffa Fox)*

boat she is also very able under sail, and strangely enough is as fast as a 23-ton Bristol pilot cutter to windward in a good breeze." That is not to say that the *Glengour* is a fast boat under either sail or power, but she would certainly not be disap-

pointing under either method of propulsion. She is the kind of boat in which it would be tempting to cheat a little, and sail merrily along with the lee engine just ticking over to give her a little extra push.

Chapter 14

The *Calypso*

Roy Blaney finished building the revised Calypso *and christened her the* Jenny Ives. *But instead of taking her on a voyage, as he had dreamed, he sold her. The new owner put her out for charter, and I got to use her for a school ship.*

In the flesh, she is a fine, handsome vessel, turning heads wherever she goes. She's a wonderful boat to sail. All her faults are below deck.

The revised cabin plan turns out not to have enough floor space. All the furniture is built out so far from the sides of the boat toward the centerline that a couple of people, trying to move about in the cabin, seems like a big crowd. Blaney didn't build her interior quite to plan. He squeezed the head aft and made it into what one student called "the torture chamber." That change gave him room to move the stove into a U-shaped galley to port and fill its old space with a nice chart table. But it's all just too cramped, especially in the main cabin, where feet have to kick each other for space under the table. Bunks, seats, and counters all need pruning to make room for the crew to use them.

I took several crews of seamanship students out, each for five successive day-trips. We had some fine sails in the Jenny Ives *on the coast of Maine. On a couple of occasions, we made the most of a good breeze by extending our island-circling track out to as much as thirty-five miles without being late for supper. More often, we were trying to outwit breezes that were light and variable, tides that were inexorable, and fog that blew in or scaled up on its own irregular, unpublished timetable.*

I was surprised at how fast the Jenny Ives *will sail. Once, broad-reaching under the four lowers in a fresh breeze and smooth water, we caught a strong gust and pushed the log to 8.5 knots. We'd fall in with modern, light-displacement sloops sporting huge genoa jibs, and their skippers' faces would express shock at how long it took their go-fast boats to pass the quaint gaff-rigger. We had an interesting brush with an Atkin* Ingrid, *a double-ended Marconi ketch of about the same size, close-reaching in a gentle breeze that gradually dropped out. She crept up and by us, and then, as the breeze eased, we turned the tables. With her topsail set, the* Jenny Ives *is remarkably agile in a light air.*

She heaves-to steadily with the forestaysail aback. She balances well under staysail, mainsail, and mizzen, and you can reef or take in the mainsail without changing her balance significantly. Her rig is as versatile in practice as it looks on paper.

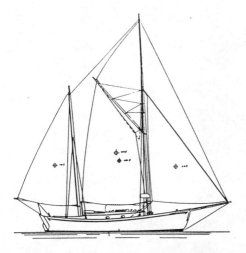

Length on deck: 35 feet 9 inches
Length on waterline: 31 feet 3 inches
Beam: 11 feet
Draft: 5 feet 1 inch
Sail area: 827 square feet
Displacement: 10 tons
Designer: Thomas C. Gillmer

Thomas C. Gillmer, a naval architect in Annapolis, Maryland, designs boats under ideal conditions. His house is, appropriately enough, on Shipwright Street, and the balcony of his design office, isolated from the living quarters by a narrow circular staircase, almost overhangs Spa Creek.

Looking at Tom's place from out on the Creek, you'd swear you were in some exotic place like the Italian Riviera. Looking out at the Creek from the balcony just a few steps from Tom's drawing board, you can see hundreds of boats tied up in marinas, on moorings, and passing in review. The inspiration provided by this setting has to be general, however, rather than specific, for there are mighty few boats in sight on Spa Creek nearly as handsome as the ketch *Calypso,* turned out by Professor Gillmer thirty years ago and modified slightly in 1974.

Calypso, as readers of Greek mythology will recall, was the sea nymph who delayed Odysseus on her island for seven years. Her ketch namesake looks fully capable of singing an effective siren song to anyone who would cruise in comfort in an able, good-looking vessel.

The *Calypso* is 35 feet 9 inches long on deck, with a waterline length of 31 feet 3 inches, a beam of 11 feet, and a draft of 5 feet 1 inch. Her displacement is about ten tons, and her sail area is 827 square feet.

She has considerable sheer, accentuated at the stern by the high crown of her transom, and this sheerline contributes much to her good looks. Her short ends are businesslike; in redrawing the boat in 1974, Professor Gillmer straightened the stem slightly, but left just enough curve in it to keep it soft.

The *Calypso*'s design is one of moderation. She has moderately hard bilges, moderate deadrise, and moderate draft and depth of forefoot.

She has a hollow entrance, but there is considerable flare above it. This combination makes for a bow that drives into a head sea fairly easily, yet without taking a lot of water on deck.

The ketch has good lateral stability; she should steer well and shouldn't try to round up too much when heeled. The keel has considerable depth below the rabbet line to give an effective lateral plane. Her rather low wetted surface would con-

Tom Gillmer, who designed the Calypso *and her little sister, the* Blue Moon, *in the next chapter.*

tribute to general smartness under sail. All in all, she has a rather easily driven hull, and she should never be cranky.

In the modified design of the *Calypso*, Professor Gillmer has increased her ballast-to-displacement ratio considerably (from about 31 percent to about 43 percent), for 6,250 pounds of iron outside ballast has been replaced by 8,600 pounds of lead.

It is interesting to compare the *Calypso*'s rig of 1945 with the modified rig given her in 1974. With the old rig, the masts were a bit farther forward, and she had a single headsail, a bigger mizzen, and a separate, fidded (offset athwartships, rather than forward) topmast with a bigger topsail. The modification of the rig gave the *Calypso* double headsails and a pole mainmast a little shorter than the older version's lower mast and topmast. In the new rig, the mainsail has 299 square feet; the mizzen, 147; the forestaysail, 121; the jib, 173; and the topsail, 85. All her sails are loose-footed.

The *Calypso*'s new rig is, of course, most versatile. She would balance well under main and staysail, jib and jigger, or staysail and reefed jigger, to name but three combinations.

The roller-furling jib makes great good sense with this rig. It is a most handy sail and can be used reaching or when sailing full-and-by on a passage when weatherliness is not critical. (The problem with roller-furling headsails is you can't

set the luff up really hard so the sail loses a lot of its drive when the boat is jammed right up on the wind.) The roller-furling jib could be sent down out of the way when setting jib topsails on this ketch.

She could profit by having perhaps as many as four different headsails to set on the topmast stay. Three of these would be fairly narrow, only overlapping the forestay slightly, and would be designed primarily for windward work. They might have areas respectively of, say, 100 square feet, 175 square feet, and then a really tall one reaching all the way to the masthead with an area perhaps as large as 250 square feet. The fourth sail to set on this stay would be a big ballooner for reaching and running (poled out for the latter) in light going. With all this use of the topmast stay, one might be tempted to return to the staying arrangement of the old rig, with a slightly taller mainmast so that a spring stay could be used between the mastheads in conjunction with upper mizzen shrouds led well aft. One might even find it advantageous to rig running preventer backstays to the mainmast head for use when one of the jib topsails was really pulling.

It would be good if the sail bins also contained both storm and balloon forestaysails. A nice big mizzen staysail is shown, and it would be a rare joy to watch it pull her along if you were ever lucky enough to be on just the right point of sailing to use it.

Would anyone care to play with a club topsail on this boat in light airs? Such a sail might make a fine high note for the *Calypso*'s siren song.

Note the sensibly rigged peak halyards in both sail plans, supporting the gaff throughout its length and, in the case of the new plan, with a long enough bridle so it won't be unduly strained by the pull of its block. For appearance' sake, I find I want to lift the main boom up parallel to the others. Hopefully, readers will already have been mentally trimming the head of that mainsail with a vang led to the mizzen masthead long before I have gotten around to mentioning what a fine rig that makes.

The *Calypso* originally had a Gray 4-40 engine specified, and Professor Gillmer figured it would drive her at a fast 7½ knots.

The new design has a high-crowned flush deck raised to the level of the rail, instead of a trunk cabin. I think that is an improvement, for it makes

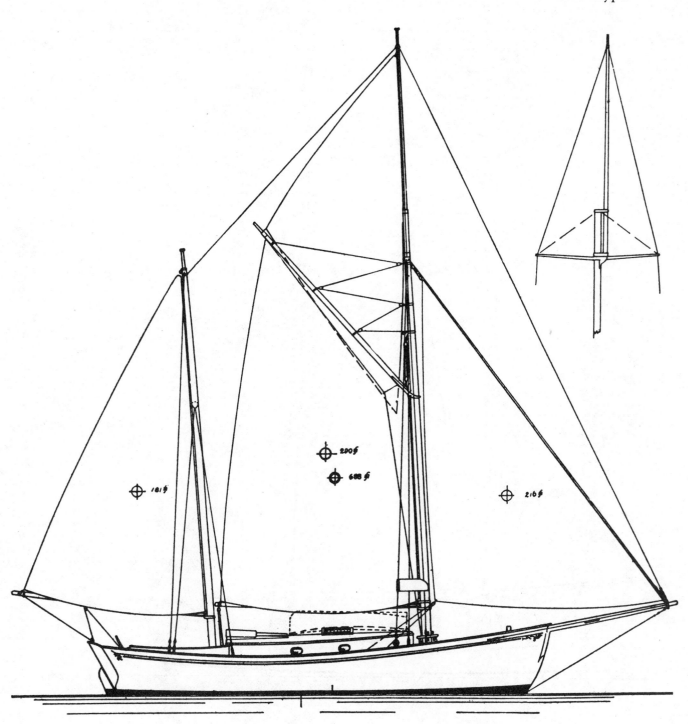

The Calypso *was designed in 1945 and was given a facelifting in 1974. Her original rig had a single headsail, small mainsail, and big main topsail set on a separate topmast fidded athwartships.* Calypso's *new rig has a pole mainmast with a taller mainsail and smaller topsail set above it and a double head rig. (*Yachting, *September, 1945, and Thomas C. Gillmer)*

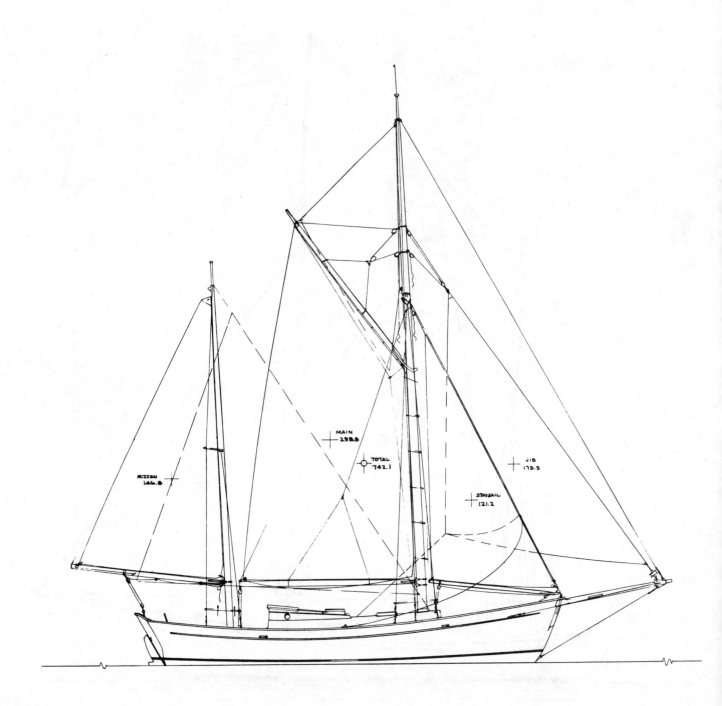

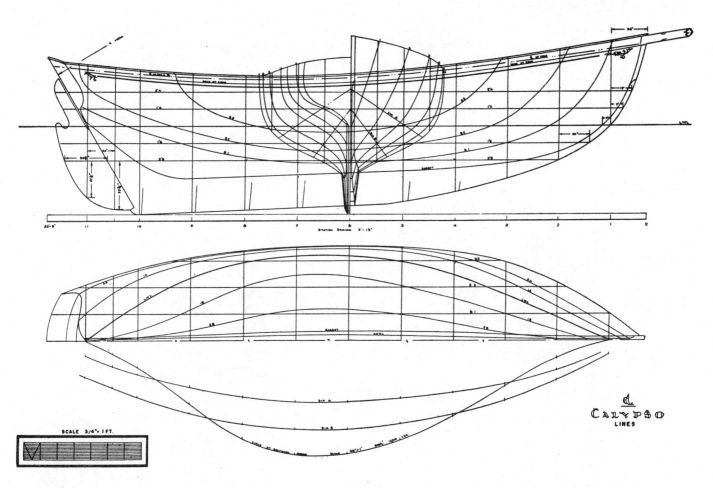

The only change made in her lines was straightening out the upper part of the stem a bit—I am not sure why. (Yachting, September, 1945, and Thomas C. Gillmer)

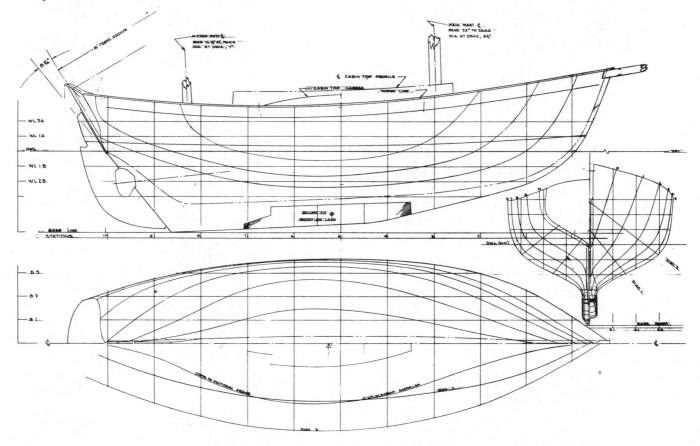

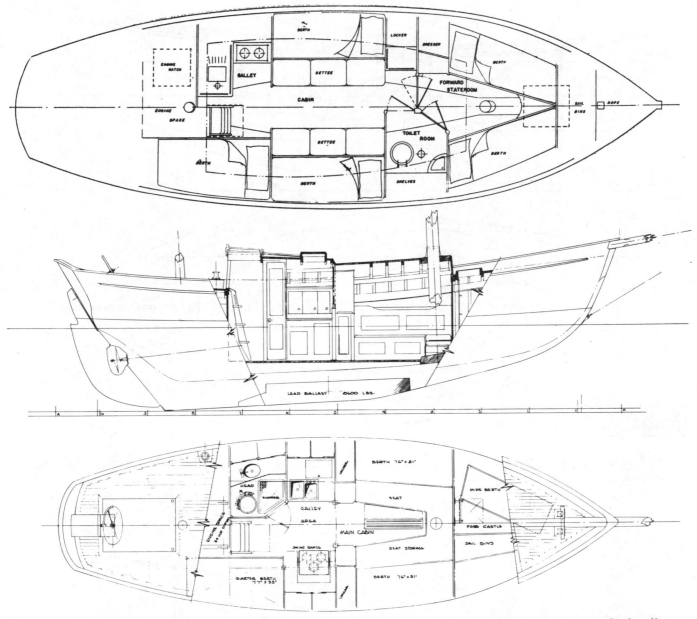

The arrangement plan was changed quite a bit, moving the head aft, the galley and saloon forward some, dead-ending the saloon, and giving her a small fo'c's'le with a single pipe berth instead of a forward stateroom. (Yachting, September, 1945, and Thomas C. Gillmer)

a strong, watertight arrangement and increases the working space on deck. Of course this construction would make it more desirable to have lifelines running between the shrouds.

I would prefer a cockpit coaming on this boat rather than having the cockpit open all the way to the rail. Without a coaming, dollops of water come right into the cockpit when she is being driven a bit, while, with a coaming, the cockpit stays a lot drier.

The original design for the *Calypso* had a standard accommodation plan, with a quarter berth aft to starboard opposite the galley, and a saloon amidships separated from a forward stateroom by a head to starboard and lockers to port. The new accommodation plan shows quite a different arrangement with one less berth but the great advantage of a dead-end saloon. There's nothing like sitting down at the cabin table with the sure knowledge that no one is going to ask you to get right up again so they can "get through." The old arrangement was designed for cruising in the tropics, while the new plan is for cruising in northern waters. In any case, the new layout looks ideal to me for three people for a long cruise. And the separate fo'c's'le makes a simply glorious place for the boatswain to keep his gear and do his work.

A Maine boatbuilder, Roy Blaney of Boothbay Harbor, is building this design for his own use. Now that's really living.

Chapter 15

The *Java* and the Concordia Yawls

I have learned that Llewellyn Howland, the man behind the Concordia yawl, had a remarkable quality that I knew nothing of as his young friend. A new edition of his book, Sou'west and By West of Cape Cod, *was published in 1987, bringing back into print fourteen of his wonderful stories of sailing, learning, and tasting life on and around Buzzards Bay. Howland is recounting his experiences as a young man; a vital figure in these experiences is "the Skipper, a cousin of a degree and of an older generation . . . with no family of his own and with both means and leisure at his disposal." The Skipper takes young Howland under his wing; takes him sailing; teaches him to catch fish; takes him exploring; introduces him to fascinating men — and a notable woman — of the sea; and feeds him plain, native fare from salt water and saltwater farm, made delectable by perfect preparation.*

John Rousmaniere wrote an introduction to the new book in which he laid out some Howland family history. Llewellyn Howland's father, William, owned and managed two textile mills in New Bedford in the 1890s. He was an enlightened manager in an era when management was equated with harsh treatment of workers. His mills failed, and he died at the age of forty-four, when his son was a freshman in

college. Soon after Llewellyn's retirement from his own business career, his wife died. Llewellyn Howland's life had had its share of heartaches. Writing stories of an idealized past was a way for the widower to succor his emotions. Part of the process was to invent for himself a fairy godfather — the Skipper.

At first, when I read in Rousmaniere's Introduction that the Skipper and the stories were fictitious, I couldn't believe it. I knew of no heartaches in Llewellyn Howland's life. I only knew a man "of an older generation" who took me sailing in the Java, fed me plain, delectable fare, gave unstintingly of his wisdom, and allowed me the privilege of calling him Skipper.

Now I know that Llewellyn Howland was a magician: He could transform things. He could take the terrible loss of his father and make a fairy godfather, and then share him with the world. He could take an imaginary Skipper and make a real one — himself.

When Llewellyn Howland lost his beloved boat, the Escape, in the 1938 hurricane, he said, "That's the end of boating for me." But then he conjured up the Concordia yawl, one of the best boats of all. He could change defeat into victory, a very hard trick.

Length on deck: 39 feet 10 inches
Length on waterline: 28 feet 6 inches
Beam: 10 feet
Draft: 5 feet 8 inches
Sail area: 618 square feet
Displacement: 9 tons
Designer: C. Raymond Hunt

Some of us schoolboys groaned when we heard that the speaker for a meeting of our boating club was going to be some old geezer who had graduated from the school who knows how many decades back in history. We were pretty confident that we knew just about all that was worth knowing about boats, so we sauntered along to the gathering place fully prepared to be both patronized and bored. We were neither.

Llewellyn Howland hurried in from Padanaram, Massachusetts, face aglow and eyes atwinkle, and absolutely bowled us over with the wit, charm, and enthusiasm with which he yarned to us about boats and cruising. For a couple of us, the occasion marked the beginning of a precious friendship between old and young, shellback and greenhorn, a friendship that lasted ten years until that grand old man died. During those ten years, we were lucky enough to be the mirthful audience for his well-told tales by the fireside in the big terracotta house in Padanaram that is no more, to make a Buzzards Bay cruise with him in his lovely yawl, the *Java,* and to earn the right, in his eyes at least, to call him "Skipper."

In the summer of 1893, Llewellyn Howland, aged 16, needed to convalesce from typhoid fever. He had the same kind of a friendship with an old man, wise in the ways of the sea, whom he called "Skipper." It was to that Skipper's cottage, overlooking Buzzards Bay, that Llewellyn Howland went to rest.

The resting began and ended the first night he was there. On that night, his "Skipper" showed him a large, beautifully made model of the *St. Esprit du Conquet.* The model was of an 86-foot armed lugger, probably of the Chasse-Marée type—deep, powerful vessels with three lugsails stacked up high on fore and mainmasts and two more set on a small mizzen mast, balanced off with a long, low jib set on a running bowsprit. The fully rigged model was one of a pair ordered built by the Minister of Marine in Paris from lines and specifications furnished by "Monsieur le Capitaine Pierre Reynard." Capitaine Reynard had built the *St. Esprit* in his own yard at Le Conquet, a fishing village near Brest, in 1799 and had used her for running contraband in what was then for a Frenchman a very dangerous English Channel.

Llewellyn Howland.
(Skipper,
April, 1957)

Waldo   Howland
(Skipper,
April, 1957)

The model of that lugger was totally romantic and beautiful to Llewellyn Howland, and he studied her every detail of form and fabric.

The next morning the Skipper put Llewellyn Howland to work. The task they shared was the intensive testing of a dozen three-foot sailing models, all with identical rig but different hull designs, six being moderate craft and six being extreme. The models were tested not only for speed, but also for how they sailed and behaved in rough water. When the objective analysis was completed, the model with the highest marks was one of the moderate ones, and it was not lost upon the experimenters that her lines were the fairest, most harmonious, and prettiest of the lot. Llewellyn Howland continued to study the model of the *St. Esprit* with her own fair, harmonious, and pretty lines, and he understood well why she had served her captain so successfully.

Skipper Howland was not one to lock away the knowledge and wisdom he acquired. He shared it via many friendships and via the excellent writing he did later in life. His story of the model of the *St. Esprit* is part of an article he wrote for the *Atlantic Monthly,* "A Boat is Born," reprinted, with a number of his other stories, in the book *The Middle Road,* published by the Concordia Company, South Dartmouth, Massachusetts, in 1961, four years after his passing. He wrote a grand series of articles for the *Rudder* in the mid-Forties,

gathered together in the book *Sou'west and By West of Cape Cod,* published by Harvard University Press in 1947. He published himself in 1953 a little book called *Triptych,* containing three of his writings out of his own experience in life, writings that mean much to those who knew him.

Llewellyn Howland ended the article, "A Boat is Born," with an acknowledgment of the debt he owed Capitaine Reynard and his *St. Esprit du Conquet* for the creation of his own excellent cruising yawl, the *Java,* in 1939.

The hurricane of September 21, 1938, left Skipper Howland boatless. He immediately began making plans with his son Waldo and Waldo's partner at the Concordia Company boatyard at Padanaram, C. Raymond Hunt, for the designing and building of the best small cruising vessel they could create. She was to be designed specifically for Buzzards Bay, where the sou'wester comes breezing on with great regularity and the seas are high and steep.

Llewellyn Howland wrote, "I freely called on the time and skill of many willing hands to help me carry out my plan for the creation of a 40-foot boat which, in essence, should sail on her bottom, not on her side, and, at that, approach the speed limit of her length under the widest range of weather conditions likely to be met with off or along shore on our Atlantic seaboard. All other details were subordinate to these cardinal qualifi-

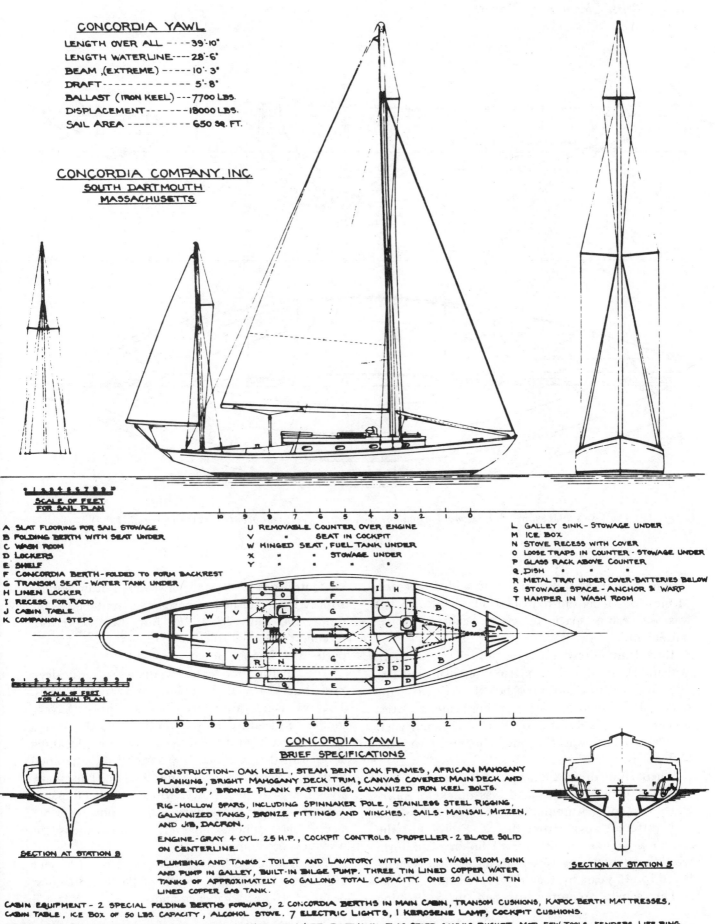

CONCORDIA YAWL

LENGTH OVER ALL	39'-10"
LENGTH WATERLINE	28'-6"
BEAM (EXTREME)	10'-3"
DRAFT	5'-8"
BALLAST (IRON KEEL)	7700 LBS.
DISPLACEMENT	18000 LBS.
SAIL AREA	650 SQ. FT.

CONCORDIA COMPANY, INC.
SOUTH DARTMOUTH
MASSACHUSETTS

SCALE OF FEET
FOR SAIL PLAN

A SLAT FLOORING FOR SAIL STOWAGE
B FOLDING BERTH WITH SEAT UNDER
C WASH ROOM
D LOCKERS
E SHELF
F CONCORDIA BERTH-FOLDED TO FORM BACKREST
G TRANSOM SEAT - WATER TANK UNDER
H LINEN LOCKER
I RECESS FOR RADIO
J CABIN TABLE
K COMPANION STEPS

U REMOVABLE COUNTER OVER ENGINE
V   "   SEAT IN COCKPIT
W HINGED SEAT, FUEL TANK UNDER
X   "   "   "   STOWAGE UNDER
Y   "   "   "   "

L GALLEY SINK - STOWAGE UNDER
M ICE BOX
N STOVE RECESS WITH COVER
O LOOSE TRAPS IN COUNTER - STOWAGE UNDER
P GLASS RACK ABOVE COUNTER
Q DISH
R METAL TRAY UNDER COVER-BATTERIES BELOW
S STOWAGE SPACE - ANCHOR & WARP
T HAMPER IN WASH ROOM

SCALE OF FEET
FOR CABIN PLAN

SECTION AT STATION 8

SECTION AT STATION 5

CONCORDIA YAWL
BRIEF SPECIFICATIONS

CONSTRUCTION- OAK KEEL, STEAM BENT OAK FRAMES, AFRICAN MAHOGANY PLANKING, BRIGHT MAHOGANY DECK TRIM, CANVAS COVERED MAIN DECK AND HOUSE TOP, BRONZE PLANK FASTENINGS, GALVANIZED IRON KEEL BOLTS.

RIG- HOLLOW SPARS, INCLUDING SPINNAKER POLE, STAINLESS STEEL RIGGING, GALVANIZED TANGS, BRONZE FITTINGS AND WINCHES. SAILS- MAINSAIL, MIZZEN, AND JIB, DACRON.

ENGINE- GRAY 4 CYL. 25 H.P., COCKPIT CONTROLS. PROPELLER - 2 BLADE SOLID ON CENTERLINE.

PLUMBING AND TANKS - TOILET AND LAVATORY WITH PUMP IN WASH ROOM, SINK AND PUMP IN GALLEY, BUILT-IN BILGE PUMP. THREE TIN LINED COPPER WATER TANKS OF APPROXIMATELY 60 GALLONS TOTAL CAPACITY. ONE 20 GALLON TIN LINED COPPER GAS TANK.

CABIN EQUIPMENT - 2 SPECIAL FOLDING BERTHS FORWARD, 2 CONCORDIA BERTHS IN MAIN CABIN, TRANSOM CUSHIONS, KAPOC BERTH MATTRESSES, CABIN TABLE, ICE BOX OF 50 LBS. CAPACITY, ALCOHOL STOVE. 7 ELECTRIC LIGHTS, 1 KEROSENE LAMP, COCKPIT CUSHIONS.

OTHER EQUIPMENT - RUNNING AND RIDING LIGHTS, ANCHOR AND WARP, BOAT HOOK, FLAG STAFF, CANVAS BUCKET, MOP, FEW TOOLS, FENDERS, LIFE RING, DOCK LINES, COMPASS AND BINNACLE, LIFE LINES, PULPIT.

FINISH - SPARS BRIGHT, DECK TRIM AND HOUSE SIDES BRIGHT, DECK PAINTED BUFF, TOPSIDES WHITE, BOTTOM GREEN, COCKPIT FLOOR TEAK, BARE.
INTERIOR: PINE BULKHEADS, HARDWOOD TRIM, ALL BRIGHT. UNDERSIDE OF HOUSE TOP WHITE, FLOOR PAINTED, TOILET ROOM WHITE EXCEPT FOR FLOOR.

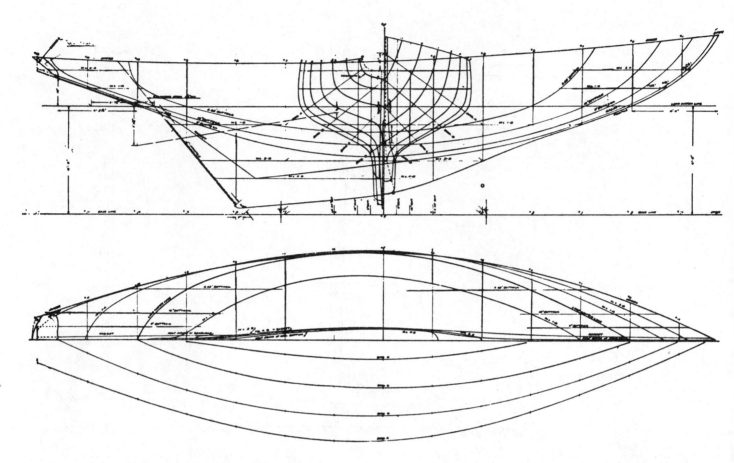

The Java's *lines show a fair, harmonious hull of great power, yet great beauty. (*Yachting, *April, 1952)*

cations." And, as Waldo Howland added recently, "Rules for racing did not determine anything, nor was big cabin space or great headroom a requirement."

Ray Hunt drew the lines of the new boat. William Harris did the construction plan and layout. Waldo Howland says he "fussed with the details like Concordia berths, cabin heaters, stoves, hatches, cockpit design, etc. But father knew what he wanted and was the one who conceived the basic ideas."

When Hunt drew the new boat's lines, he made them—as Llewellyn Howland was quick to appreciate—fair and harmonious to the eye. She was a very different vessel from the *St. Esprit,* but she shared a general inspiration of boldness of form with that fascinating vessel, an inspiration remembered for 45 years by Llewellyn Howland.

The general requirements and their resulting

characteristics of the new yawl were not unfamiliar to Ray Hunt, for he had designed a similar boat, the *Cinderella,* built in 1936. But there were differences that led the new design close to the perfection Skipper Howland sought.

The yawl has moderate overhangs, a fairly deep keel, but rather shallow bow and buttock lines. The waterlines are quite convex, but with very moderate deadrise in the midsection, the boat's lines are still quite fine. The remarkable thing about this design is her very hard bilges, combined with tumblehome, at the midsection. This shape gives the yawl great power to carry sail and makes her stiff and dry. This extraordinary power for her size is not gained, however, at the expense of heaviness or clumsiness.

The new design had a length on deck of 39 feet 10 inches, a waterline length of 28 feet 6 inches, beam of 10 feet 3 inches and a draft of 5 feet 8

The Java *outside Padanaram harbor making the most of the afternoon sou'wester. (Norman Fortier)*

inches. The displacement was 18,000 pounds, with 7,700 pounds of outside ballast in an iron keel. The sail area of her yawl rig with a working jib was 618 square feet.

The boat was built at Casey's yard in Fairhaven, Massachusetts, and was launched in 1939. She was christened the *Java,* after a lucky vessel among those owned by Llewellyn Howland's New Bedford ancestors. The *Java* was beautifully built and was always perfectly maintained. Every inch of her had the patina of a piece of polished furniture.

The *Java* was a most successful boat, attracted attention, and begat a long line of sisterships and near sisters that became known as the Concordia

The Cinderella, *designed by Ray Hunt two years before he drew the plans for the* Java. *(*Yachting, *June, 1936)*

The Polaris, *a sloop-rigged Concordia stretched out to 41 feet long on deck. (Roberts Parsons)*

H. A. Taylor, Jr.'s Sumatra *driving to windward.* *(Norman Fortier)*

Above: *Looking aft in the main cabin. (Norman Fortier).*
Below: *The stern on the yawls is quite narrow. Here are the cockpit back rests ready for use. (Norman Fortier)*

yawls.* The fifth Concordia yawl (the *Suva*, in which I was lucky enough to sail many times) was the first of the class to be built in Hamburg, Germany, by Abeking and Rasmussen. More than 100 Concordias have been built, many of them by Abeking and Rasmussen. Some of the boats were built to a design that was lengthened to about 41 feet. Some have been rigged as sloops, and some, especially the newer boats, have been given masthead rigs.

The Concordia yawls have proven to be fine boats for cruising, daysailing and racing, and ocean racing. Some have made notable ocean cruises and some have won major races, such as the Marblehead-Halifax Race, the race between Newport and Annapolis, and the Bermuda Race. These honors gladdened Llewellyn Howland's heart, but they were mere by-products of the happiness he felt

*For a quite complete history and catalog of most of these boats, see *The Concordia Yawls: 1938–1978*, edited and published by Elizabeth Meyer. For a luxurious sequel, see her *Concordia Yawls: The First Fifty Years*.

Above: *Looking forward in the main cabin. (Norman Fortier).* Below: *Up forward in the Suva. (Norman Fortier)*

each time he sailed out into Buzzards Bay in his beloved *Java*.

The rig makes sense for the fresh and strong breezes of Buzzards Bay, but for other sailing areas where a higher percentage of light weather may be encountered, additional sail area might be desirable. For most folks nowadays this means setting a Genoa jib, but that's the hard way, in my opinion. A Concordia yawl based on the Chesapeake Bay, for example, might do very well with a bigger mizzen and a bowsprit, setting an extra jib. These sails are easier to handle than the big overlapping jibs; they would be stowed in a hard breeze, and the yawl would then become a jib-and-mainsail boat. A larger mizzen would also balance better when sailing under stem-head jib and mizzen than does the small mizzen, though the small mizzen does work in this regard. Notice that the mainmast is set quite far forward in this boat, a sensible arrangement to keep the rig simple by giving it a single headsail. My proposed double-head rig for light weather may seem unduly complicated to some folks, but I maintain it is a more sensible cruising rig than a big, deck-sweeping Genoa jib with its heavily straining, single-part sheet and its creation of a big blind sector forward.

There are some very nice details worked out on the Concordia yawls. The boats with the older seven-eighths rig have running backstays, and these terminate in a slide running on a heavy track along the deck. Lines lead forward and aft from this slide (the forward one leading through a block and then aft) so that the slide may be pulled forward or aft along the track from the cockpit. With this rig you can set up the backstay a lot harder and with less effort than with a purchase.

The yawls have a wide, flush covering board along the outboard edge of the deck with a toerail set inboard of it three or four inches. This arrangement looks very handsome, emphasizing, as it does, the tumblehome of the topsides amidships.

The two-part forward hatch is hinged on each side and has athwartships strongbacks that rest on deck when the hatch is open in such a way that the two halves of the hatch cover are level and become fine little seats. At the after end of the cockpit seats, there are hinged backrests that fold down out of the way when they are not wanted. Note the setback of the seat risers in both cockpit and cabin to give more room for feet.

The arrangement below is the standard one for a four-person boat. It's really hard to improve on in a boat of this size.

The Concordia berths are most ingenious contraptions, making nicely curved wooden slat backrests when you are sitting on the transoms and folding down to make comfortable canvas berths for sleeping. When the berth is folded back, it can also be used to store bedding out of the way.

Llewellyn Howland's wonderful boat—born out of the destruction of the hurricane of 1938; inspired by a model of a French lugger of 1799; created by the Skipper himself, his son Waldo, Ray Hunt, William Harris, and those who built her; and sailed for many years by Skipper Howland and his friends—has well deserved the emulation of her many sister Concordia yawls. Long may these fine vessels continue to spread Llewellyn Howland's wisdom.

Chapter 16

The *Marco Polo*

The second boat I'm going to have built when I win the lottery is a Marco Polo. I want to see for myself just what her roll is like. Evidently, she is quite wonderful at coping with a big seaway, but her crew, hanging on below in a motion that Captain Beebe describes as "quite violent," pays the price.

And it turns out that Captain Beebe, in his description of his passage in the Marco Polo Talaria, didn't want to ruffle Francis Herreshoff, and so pulled his punches. Here is part of what he wrote to a prospective Marco Polo builder after Herreshoff's death:

My feelings about the Marco Polo model are somewhat mixed. It is certain that her performance at sea under sail in any kind of weather will be remarkable. I have never seen anything like it, the way she behaved crossing the Gulf Stream with a full nor'easter blowing against it. As far as the boat is concerned, she could go anywhere. But the crew is another matter. In deference to Francis, I played this down in the article, but the motion below decks was so bad it was hardly possible to do anything, cooking, sleeping, going to the head. All of the crew were seasick. I expected to be, as I lose my sealegs easily and had not been afloat for about seven months. But the other three, all experienced yachtsmen, claimed they had never been sick like that before. It was the way she rolled. She seemed to have no stability but the keel weight. No matter what amount of sail we carried, she would roll equally each side of the vertical. In effect, she was rolling like a motorboat in a rough sea, than which nothing is worse. Our course by necessity was a reach across wind all the way and it never let up. It was a "pendulum roll."

And here is some of what Beebe wrote to Herreshoff:

The whole question of motion cannot be divorced from the layout below. This was particularly borne out by the incident described on the fourth night when I was steering. As I said, the wind increased in a short time to something better than 25 knots. We were carrying jib, fore, and main, and I was holding her up to a fairly close reach. As the wind increased, she really started sailing, so the phosphorescence alongside from her bow wave (it was very dark) seemed to flash by at tremendous speed. I would say she was doing better than ten knots. It was glorious sailing as far as I was concerned. But, as she leapt over the waves with the greatest abandon, down below it was perfect hell.

The best-looking Marco Polo I've seen (because she was built unusually close to the design) is called the Roll and Go, *apparently a perfect name. I have no doubt the* Marco Polo *can do plenty of both; I can hardly wait to get that winning ticket.*

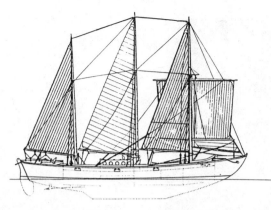

Length on deck: 55 feet
Length on waterline: 48 feet 9 inches
Beam: 10 feet
Draft: 5 feet 6 inches
Sail area: 812 square feet
Displacement: 19 tons
Designer: L. Francis Herreshoff

One of L. Francis Herreshoff's early designs, drawn in 1922, was that of a lifeboat-like, three-masted, auxiliary-powered ocean cruiser 100 feet long. Her outboard profile and sail plan make a most interesting study.

Nine years later, in 1931, Mr. Herreshoff expanded the idea for the design up to a length of 130 feet. The 130-footer, in particular, might make a good passenger cruising vessel for today, if ocean cruises could be made to pay.

Both these designs turned out to be dream ships only, for neither was built.

But then during the latter part of World War II, Francis Herreshoff brought this idea for the design of a safe, fast, simple auxiliary ocean cruiser down to a length of 55 feet. He figured that during the War a lot of Americans were being introduced to ocean voyaging and that after the War some of them might want to return to the out-of-the-way corners of the world they had seen, but on their own terms. What better way than in their own able vessel, one that could make long, fast passages under sail and power? He even designed the craft with a set of hoisting eyes for the world cruiser whose time was more limited than his wallet.

Mr. Herreshoff named his 55-foot world cruiser the *Marco Polo,* saying of the great explorer, "Comfort and show were not the main objects of

his life, but to get onward and visit strange places was more to be desired."

The *Marco Polo* is 48 feet 9 inches long on the waterline, has a beam of only 10 feet, and a draft of only 5 feet 6 inches.

She displaces about 19 tons depending on her loading. The load waterline is drawn in on her lines as if the vessel were light, with her tanks and lockers empty. Loading for a long cruise could bring her down in the water as much as ten inches, according to her designer, and one of the objectives of the design was that the vessel not change her stability characteristics much with changes in loading. This was achieved in part by making her topsides somewhat "slab-sided," and I hasten to add that that is Mr. Herreshoff's expression, not mine.

The *Marco Polo*'s sail area is 812 square feet, divided as follows: jib, 142 square feet; foresail, 201 square feet; mainsail, 261 square feet; and mizzen, 208 square feet.

Her lines show a hull that is extremely buoyant and dry. The turtlebacks in the ends of her provide extra reserve buoyancy, as well as an unusual amount of interior space in the bow and stern. The after turtleback gives the cockpit a bit of extra protection from a following sea.

She has very long, easy buttock lines and, in

L. Francis Herreshoff. (Muriel Vaughn)

fact, the very fine lines throughout of a long, narrow hull. The *Marco Polo* is very easily driven, which satisfies one of the primary requirements for the design—that she be easily and thus economically driven under power.

Yet this design is an unusual combination in that, though she is long and easy, she is also very powerful, with her nearly 15,000 pounds of lead outside ballast and her high, straight sections above the waterline. She could be driven very hard under sail without putting the rail under. And Francis Herreshoff wrote of her, "It is believed this model of vessel can be driven very hard in a following sea as she has a small midship section, an easy run, and a cutaway forefoot—all of great importance in running." Mr. Herreshoff envisioned her being driven under sail and power 24 hours a day at ten knots, though she would probably be far more comfortable at something between eight and nine, which of course would be a remarkable sustained speed for a vessel of her displacement.

Complete construction details of the *Marco Polo* were presented by Mr. Herreshoff in a series of articles in the *Rudder,* reprinted in his book *Sensible Cruising Designs.* Here are just a few highlights: her wood keel is 3¼ inches deep by a varying width from 5 to 14 inches; her floors are 2 inches thick; the frames are molded 2½ inches and sided 2 inches, being sawn in the ends of her and bent throughout the midships stations; deck beams are molded 2¾ inches and sided from 1⅜ inches to 3 inches; shelf, 2½ inches square; clamp, 5 inches

by 1½ inches; planking, 1½ inches; and deck, 1¼ inches.

Her three-masted rig is both intriguing and practical. There is something about a three-master: when she rolls a bit, you really have a lot to watch happening. The three-masted rig keeps the center of effort low on her narrow hull, gives considerable versatility in the way of sail combinations, and allows a big shift in the center of effort fore and aft depending on what you want to do with her. The masts are raked progressively aft, with the foremast having a rake of two degrees; the main, 3½ degrees; and the mizzen, five degrees. Mr. Herreshoff did this purely for aesthetic reasons, as far as I know.

Note the running backstays on the foremast. The one *Marco Polo* I've been aboard, the *Morning Star* of Cohasset, Massachusetts, nicely built of wood-core fiberglass by her owner Arthur Rowe, Jr., had runners fitted on the mizzen also.

For the rig of the *Marco Polo,* Francis Herreshoff used turnbuckles, sail track, wire halyards, one-of-a-kind masthead fittings, and so forth, all of which he engineered and designed for extra strength without great weight. Doubtless all of this gear would work very well indeed, its one drawback being that none of it is reparable without fairly sophisticated skills and equipment. When something does carry away in a far corner of the world, that is when gear like the deadeyes and lanyards that Mr. Herreshoff showed for the fore and mizzen rigging of his 1922 design comes into its own.

The *Marco Polo*'s rig is designed primarily for ease of handling in a fresh breeze and in heavy weather. Yet she does have a couple of light sails, a balloon jib set flying to a portable nose pole, and an overlapping, light-weather foresail. It would be a great temptation for me to fit the vessel with a permanent bowsprit to carry the ballooner and also to help in handling anchors.

In thinking about light sails for the *Marco Polo,* no one should be tempted to add main or mizzen staysails; these, in my opinion, would be more trouble than they would be worth.

Mr. Herreshoff designed this rig so that the largest sail, the mainsail, would be a light and moderate weather sail and would be the first to be taken in when shortening down. The sail is cross-cut and its spars and rigging are of lighter weight

Francis Herreshoff's drawing of life on the beach after the great gale suggests the reward that might accrue to a sailor with a Marco Polo. *(The Rudder, 1945)*

than those for the foresail and mizzen. You will note, too, that while the mainsail is cross-cut, the foresail and mizzen are vertically cut for greater strength, giving up in return a bit of performance when close-hauled, but giving up nothing when off the wind. She would run or reach nicely in a gale under foresail alone.

L. Francis gave considerable attention to the rig for running before the wind. He shows boom guys on all three booms for holding them forward when she's rolling along before it and coasting down the seas. He describes a bifurcated trysail set on a track on the forward side of the foremast with the slides running up the middle of the sail. This sail would be like twin spinnakers all in one piece. Mr. Herreshoff wrote with some hesitancy, "It is believed she will be partly self-steering with this rig in heavy weather." Nor was he much more sanguine about the squaresail shown. The yard goes up the track on the forward side of the foremast, the sail is laced to the yard, and the problem comes when sail and yard must be taken down as the breeze grows too strong for it. There are no brails, and Mr. Herreshoff admitted it would be a rather ticklish, all-hands evolution. Brails and clew lines would probably pay their way.

Though Mr. Herreshoff shows the *Marco Polo* as a single-screw vessel, he also envisioned that she could be built with twin screws or even in a triple-screw configuration. He specified a folding propeller for minimum drag when sailing. I think the *Marco Polo* would be an ideal application for the variable pitch wheel, since she would often be propelled by both sail and power.

Another objective of the *Marco Polo* design was very long range under power; she has two big fuel tanks reaching from sole to deck amidships, each holding 507 gallons.

On deck, there is space for a dinghy between the fore and main masts. L. Francis designed a very nice 11½-foot rowing and sailing pram especially for the *Marco Polo*. So she will fit down over two hatches on deck, she has a removable midships rowing seat, removable mast partners, and leeboards instead of a centerboard. In all but heavy weather, the hatches can be left open under her protection.

The *Marco Polo* has stout, high, lifelines and no bulwarks so that should a sea come aboard, it will be the crew and not the water that is retained on deck.

She is designed to be handled by one person on watch; all halyards lead to the cockpit, and all sails have downhauls.

Mr. Herreshoff suggested four anchors for the *Marco Polo*, of 100 pounds, 90 pounds, 75 pounds, and 40 pounds. He allowed as how the Herreshoff pattern would do. He gave her a stout anchor windlass just abaft the turtleback on the foredeck.

The dotted lines shown above the cockpit in the profile construction drawing show that the helmsman when seated can see over the deckhouse and can also see the compass mounted inside the after bulkhead of the house without shifting his line of vision greatly.

The *Marco Polo* steers like a sports car; one revolution of the steering wheel turns the rudder 45 degrees. This is reminiscent of the Herreshoff steering gear that Francis' father designed and built for boats like the Newport 29's. They took some getting used to, but once you have the feel of such a steering gear, you can control the boat like a dinghy. Of course such a high steering gear ratio will only work if the boat is well balanced and light on her helm.

It might be nice to add a second steering position, perhaps a horizontal wheel atop the after end of the deckhouse, similar to the arrangement

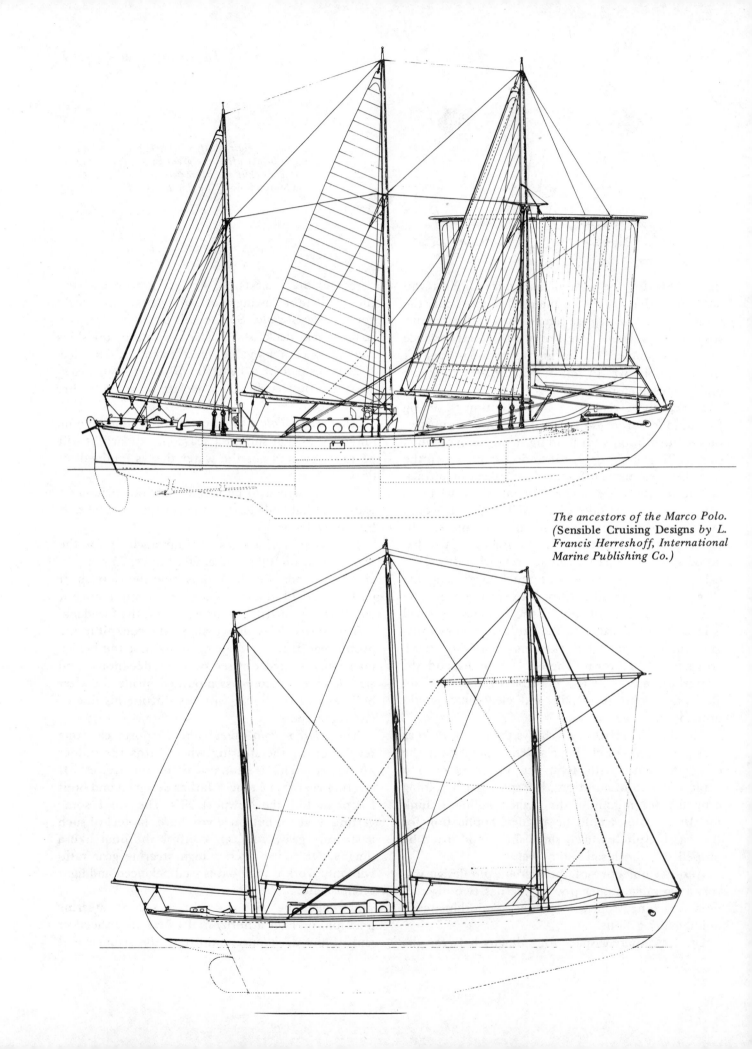

*The ancestors of the Marco Polo.
(Sensible Cruising Designs by L.
Francis Herreshoff, International
Marine Publishing Co.)*

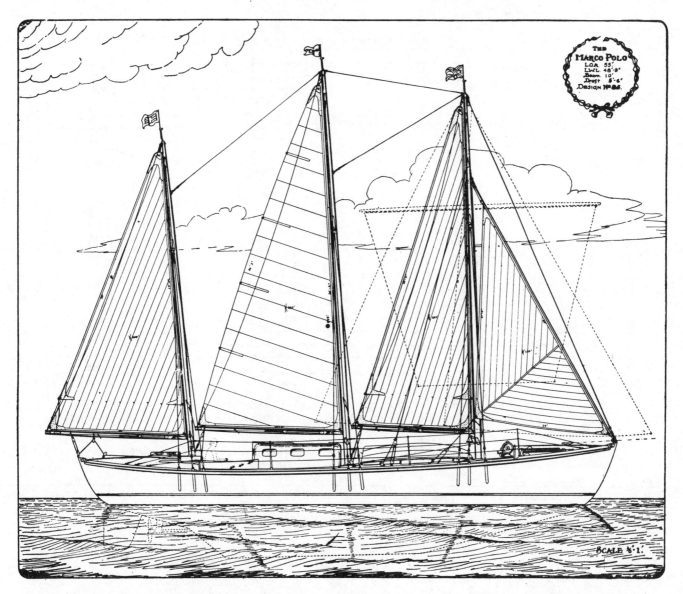

Francis Herreshoff's concept of an ideal world cruiser, designed at the end of World War II. (Sensible Cruising Designs by L. Francis Herreshoff, International Marine Publishing Co.)

L. Francis designed for his big ketch, the *Landfall*. You could even add a dodger that could fold up over the after end of the deckhouse to protect its companionway and this second steering position.

The *Marco Polo*'s balanced rudder is interesting. Mr. Herreshoff claimed it could stand as much abuse as a deadwood. In any case, it is high enough so that it shouldn't hit anything if the vessel should take the ground. The *Marco Polo*'s rudder and wheel do look a bit exposed to me, however.

The three-master's accommodations are divided into three completely separate compartments, each of which must be entered through its own hatch from the deck. Modern sailors seem to love to be able to walk from stem to stern of their vessels without even having to duck, but I would gladly

trade that feature off for the remarkable amount of privacy—perhaps quite important on a long cruise—that L. Francis has achieved with his arrangement for the *Marco Polo*.

In a way, she is arranged like a destroyer. Mr. Herreshoff gave top priority to the spaces for the engine and fuel that would be responsible for driving the vessel thousands of miles and then devoted what was left over in the ends of the boat to the crew. And he clearly wanted his engine room to be a well-frequented and joyful place, not a dark hole to be avoided. He wrote, "A large engine room makes a good workshop and a safe retreat away from the ladies. This engine room could have a workbench on one side and a leather covered transom seat on the other." With such an

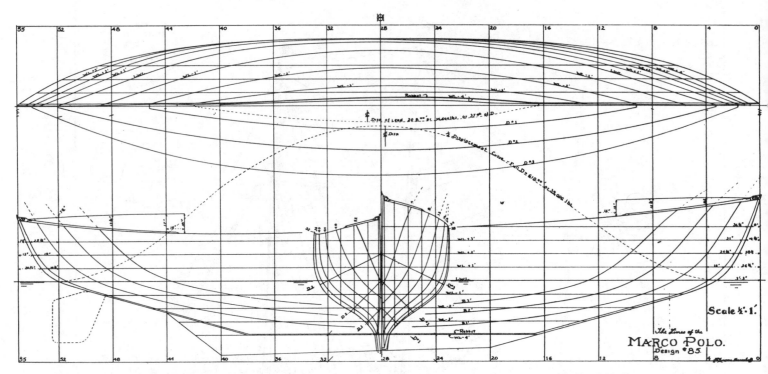

Above: *Her lines show a vessel that combines the speed of a long, narrow hull with the extreme seaworthiness of a lifeboat.* (Sensible Cruising Designs *by L. Francis Herreshoff, International Marine Publishing Co.*)

Below: *The construction drawing shows many features of a vessel that looks as if she just plain wants to go to sea.* (Sensible Cruising Designs *by L. Francis Herreshoff, International Marine Publishing Co.*)

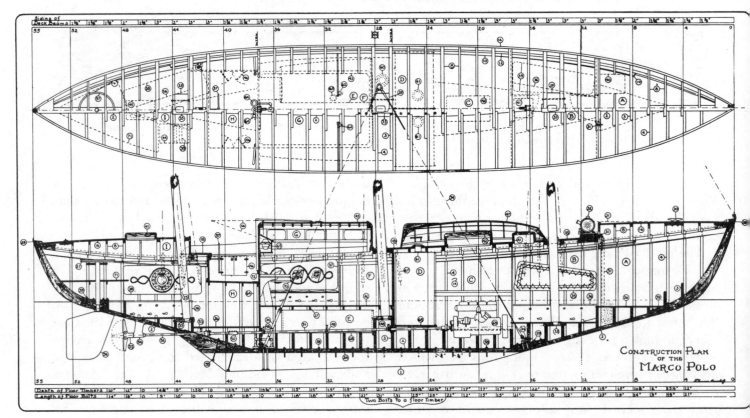

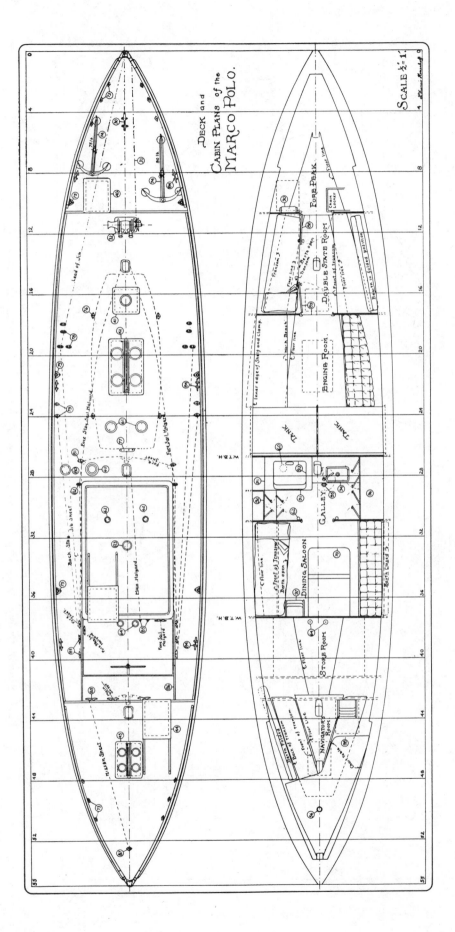

DECK and CABIN PLANS of the MARCO POLO.

SCALE ½"=1'.

The Marco Polo is arranged with a well-protected cockpit, a good place to stow her dinghy out of harm's way, a big engine room, plenty of fuel tank space amidships, and accommodations for up to five people in three well-separated compartments. (Sensible Cruising Designs by L. Francis Herreshoff, International Marine Publishing Co.)

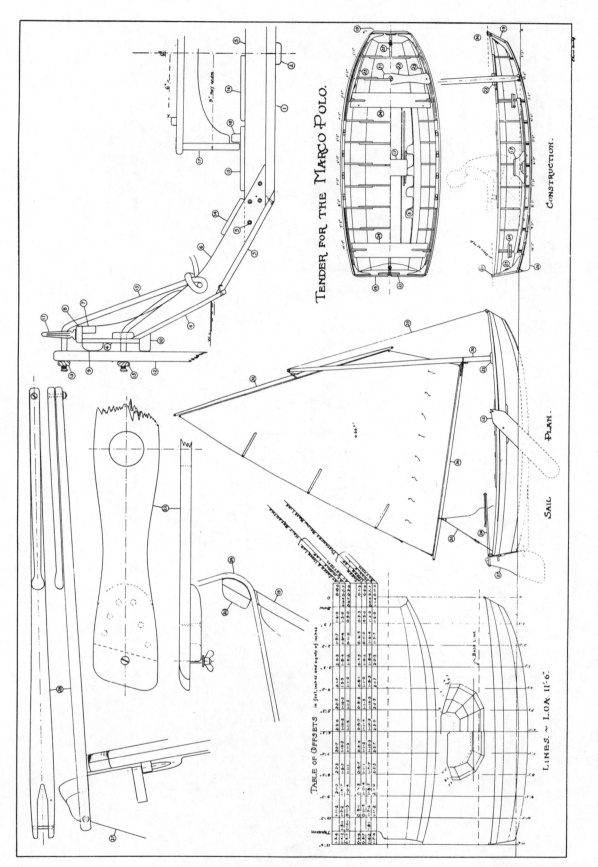

TENDER FOR THE MARCO POLO.

CONSTRUCTION.

PLAN.

SAIL

TABLE OF OFFSETS in feet, inches and eighths of inches

LINES. ~ L.O.A. 11'-6".

The plans of the 11½-foot pram that Mr. Herreshoff designed especially to be the tender for the Marco Polo. (Sensible Cruising Designs by L. Francis Herreshoff, International Marine Publishing Co.)

A Marco Polo, the Talaria, *under sail. Note that her deckhouse has been extended forward of the mainmast.* (Sensible Cruising Designs *by L. Francis Herreshoff, International Marine Publishing Co.)*

arrangement, you could hardly help but take good care of the engine.

L. Francis was well known for his predilection for the cedar bucket. He wrote: "The forepeak has enough space for a pump water closet for those who are fond of this mechanical contrivance." And again, "On a long cruise, nature needs every encouragement and if one can retire to the place of his choosing—bucket in hand—the whole business is simplified. And if by coincidence nature should call all of the crew at the same instant, then if there is a whole nest of buckets all can be accommodated."

L. Francis believed in simplicity in the cabin, and he told his readers why:

> Although I do not like either water closets or ice boxes, I do not want to force my peculiarities on anyone even if I do know that it will save them from much expense and disagreeable drudgery. I should like to impress on the minds of contemplated owners of *Marco Polo*s that extreme simplicity is the only practical way to reduce the cost of a boat of this kind. On many yachts of this size the hull costs thirty percent, the spars, sails and rig thirty percent, and the interior thirty percent. It is very doubtful if saving in cost of the first two mentioned is economical, but, if one sticks to extreme simplicity in the cabin arrangements, he can save several thousand dollars and, strange to say, have the best time in the end for such arrangements are so much easier to take care of. In fact the principal art of cruising is to learn how to take care of yourself easily and quickly so you will have time left over for enjoyment.

The saloon in the deckhouse is a light and airy place. L. Francis suggested sliding glass windows. The table folds out from the after bulkhead of the house.

The galley has much locker space and there is a huge storage area in addition beneath the cockpit. There are two 172-gallon water tanks beneath the galley.

The navigator has his own cabin in the stern with a chart table to envy. Here he can practice his magic without anyone looking over his shoulder, exulting in his pinpoints or wondering about his triangles, as the case may be.

L. Francis designed folding wooden berths for the *Marco Polo*. There are narrower transoms under them, and the bottoms of the berths—for which he showed handsome decorations—become the seat backrests when the berths are folded away.

Mr. Herreshoff suggested that if someone wanted a *Marco Polo* for short-range cruising, one of the water tanks could be converted to fuel, a smaller engine could be installed beneath the cockpit, and you would then have the space taken up by the big engine and the big fuel tanks for more accommodations, such as a head and another stateroom. (This is the way the first *Marco Polo* built, the *Talaria*, was, in fact, arranged.)

The *Marco Polo* would be a wonderful vessel in which to cruise offshore. She could be sailed nicely singlehanded, or comfortably with up to five on board. And true luxury at sea is to have several watch-standers and the need for only one to be on watch at a time. I remember one submarine cruise when we had six qualified officers-of-the-deck on board. Instead of complaining that it couldn't be your turn again already, you looked forward to the rare privilege of being allowed up on the bridge for four hours out of the twenty-four.

Captain Robert P. Beebe, U.S. Navy, made a passage from New York to the Bahamas in the *Talaria,* Josiah Newcombe's *Marco Polo,* in November, 1957, and described the trip in detail in an article for the *Rudder.* With his kind permission, I quote the parts of the article that pertain to *Talaria's* performance:

Saturday. Beginning to get some sea and learn *Talaria's* ways in such going. Decks wet but not much spray. Navigator finds the motion in the after cabin too much for him and moves his gear into the main cabin. Sea legs not all that might be desired. Barnegat light vessel at 1950. 7.8 knots.

By this time we were getting offshore and the seas were building up. Reaching right across them gave the ship a very quick motion and made the helmsman's task difficult. We are learning that she steers easily, but must be steered all the time.... *Talaria's* short and taut rigging gives off a peculiarly high pitched moan that sounds much worse below than it does on deck. We are gradually realizing that the boat is by no means being pressed and is ready to handle much bigger things than this.

Sunday. By dawn we were well offshore, with the seas getting impressively high. Helmsman told to keep her moving at maximum speed. Is a fast reach in a beam sea the worst course for motion? It seemed that way....

With the wind drawing aft, and everyone's spirits reviving after a rugged first night, it was agreed the sooner we got across the Gulf Stream the better. So we hoisted the main and made her jump. She registered twenty miles in two hours on the log once and was not far from it the rest of the day. Glorious sailing, though life below was far from comfortable unless one was in a bunk....

Past Norfolk by sunset. Time to gybe over and commence the run through the Gulf Stream. Seas steadily building up, wind still thirty knots with higher gusts. At 2100 lowered jib and main to snug down for anticipated squalls in the Stream. Wind still well aft. Several violent gybes as the boat ran off course and hit wind shifts in the lee of the seas.

Top batten of the foresail caught under shroud several times and had to be freed by luffing. Rigged a preventer on boom. This did not keep the head of the sail from gybing and catching the batten again. The mizzen caught similarly, but in this case tore before it

could be freed. Herreshoff was right in leaving the battens off. Tremendous struggle to lower and secure the mizzen due to precarious footing on aft turtleback and no way to keep the boom from flogging from side to side when held by sheet and topping lift only. Joe [Newcombe] finally did it while well belayed with a heavy safety line.

Sailing under fore only, quite sufficient considering the heavy Gulf Stream squalls building up. It appears we were in the Stream from about 2200 on the tenth to 0800 the eleventh. Wind from the north northeast varying from gusts of forty knots to quiet periods of about fifteen. Typical Gulf Stream weather, only more so, with the northerly blowing against it. Black squalls bearing down, sea confused from the shifting of the wind, and building up towering crests against the current. Motion below quite violent. On deck it is a different story. *Talaria* can be seen by the light of the moon to be making her way through the seas in tremendous fashion. We are learning to love the hull and the way she rides over the biggest breaking combers with no apparent effort. The ones we think will come aboard, great towering giants with breaking crests, never do so. There has been no solid water on deck throughout the voyage. The lee rail has never been under.

Monday. The log showed an average of nine knots since previous noon. Much rejoicing at our getting across the Gulf Stream and south of Hatteras in less than two days from New York....

Tuesday. Wind moderates and continues to veer toward east. Sea much reduced. Joe suggests that now is the time to try out the squaresail. Navigator all for it, but points out we may be sorry later.

We turned to on the gear. The exact arrangement shown on the plans was not quite finished, notably the blocks at the masthead for the topping lifts. Solved this by hoisting blocks on fore halliard. When lifts, braces and sheets were ready and everything led properly to be on the correct side when hoisted, we raised the yard alone to see how it went. No strain. Hoisting the crane and handling lifts to bring the yard nearly vertical to swing by the shrouds and out is very easy to do. Lowered yard to bend squaresail in stops. It swings up and out with ease. Man sheets and braces and break her out. A perfect break. The sail sets beautifully and off we go before the wind, making about five knots in a twelve to fifteen knot breeze. Beer for all hands. A half spoke is all the steering she needs....

Sailed all night under squaresail at about six knots. It was a comfortable night and the first real sleep for some of us....

Wednesday. At 1115 we lowered squaresail. It came down with the greatest of ease, with the yard held just off the lifelines under perfect control while lashings were passed as far out as could be reached. Then hoist again, top up one end and back through on deck.

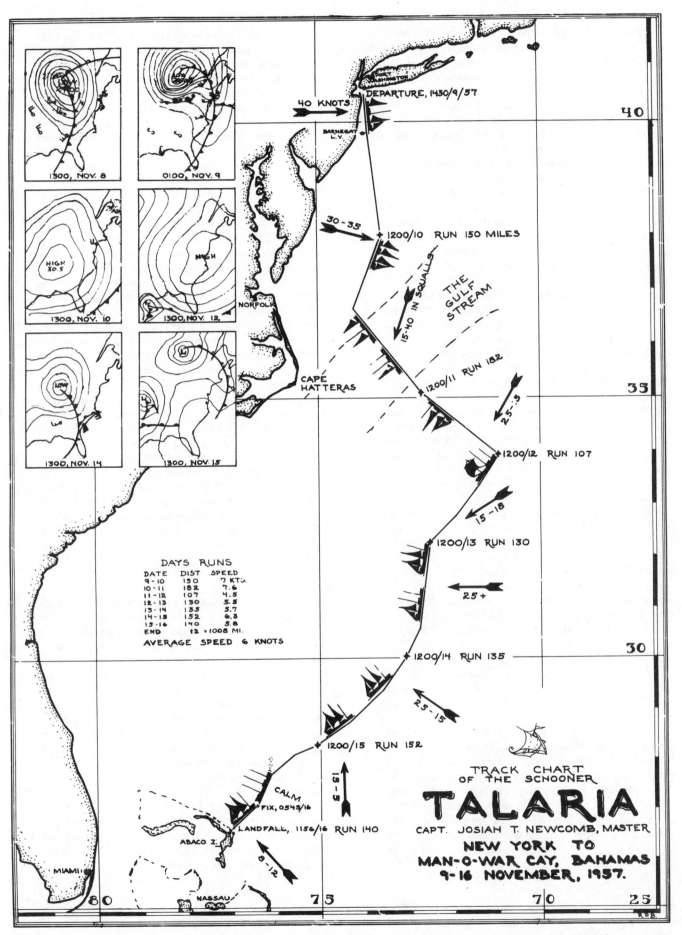

Captain Robert Beebe's chart of the Talaria's passage south. (Captain Robert P. Beebe, U.S. Navy, Retired)

Although twenty-four hours cannot be considered an all-out test of the squaresail rig we were all most pleased with it and the way the gear performed. No signs of strain anywhere. The yard made a perceptible difference in the roll, causing it to be slower and deeper. However this was not objectionable. . . .

After sunset, squalls clear off. Wind continues to increase, reaching about twenty-five knots, more in gusts. Why is this? Navigator at the helm, reluctant to bear off and lose precious southing, holds her to it. The ship is going faster and faster until finally the shocks and rolls become excessive as she leaps over the swells like a live thing. Loud complaints from the watch below holding an after dinner kaffeklatsch in the cabin. Decide we had better get the main off her as this wind seems sure to hold steady and is no squall. All hands require oilskins and safety belts. It takes fifteen minutes to get ready and for eyes to become adjusted to the dark. Then the main comes down with no trouble and is secured. This was our only rugged night sail drill of the whole trip. The 251 square foot sail posed no difficulties compared to the tales one hears of struggles with really big sloop and ketch rigs. Score another point for *Talaria*.

Thursday. At dawn the wind is southeast, twenty-five knots, sea somewhat confused due to veering of the wind. I suddenly realize what it looks like—the sea in Winslow Homer's *Gulf Stream*, a big copy of which hangs in my office. She steers easily with jib and fore at about six knots, which is enough in this sea. We are cruising, not racing.

At 1530 hoist main and increase speed to seven knots or a bit better. . . .

Friday. Joe breaks out the loose footed overlapping foresail which is rigged with ease and sets well. Adds about a knot to our speed. Not now laying Man-o-War, but on such a perfect day who cares? Could sail around like this for a week. Speed about five knots. Would like to try reaching jib also, but gear is not installed to rig it. Some talk of firing up the engine and making like a motor sailer as Herreshoff suggests. Conclude this would not prove anything. Things are nice the way they are.

Saturday. Pass northern tip of Man-o-War Cay at 1345, six days twenty-three hours and fifteen minutes from Sandy Hook, 1008 miles. Average speed six knots. . . .

The hull. The hull is terrific. The action of the boat in a seaway was a joy to behold. At night, by the light of the moon, it was easy to imagine that she was picking her way through the waves with intelligence, never making a wrong move. This may not be a very scientific description, but I have known boats that seemed determined to hit waves just the wrong way whenever possible, banging about and throwing spray all over in an impressive, but essentially futile, display. *Talaria* never did this.

There was no wake at all at any speed to affect the breaking of the seas. She never took solid water on deck. When Joe was securing the mizzen the second night, and we were running off slowly under fore alone, a sea came up astern and barely topped the rail with about a bucket of water that immediately slid off the turtleback. The bow never did get down into a wave or even close. For this trip the turtlebacks were unnecessary. But the sea can get a lot tougher than we had it and I would not venture an opinion as to whether it would be a good thing to leave them off. If they were absent sail handling would be easier of course.

The motion was described in the log several times as violent. However I am sure it was no worse than other types would have displayed in the seas and on the courses we followed. There is no doubt in my mind that *Talaria* can be driven much harder than more conventional vessels of the same weight. It is the crew that will cry for mercy, not the hull. We were quite content with six knots whenever the sea built up. This is a speed well below the potential of the hull though excellent by most standards for heavy weather. She rolls deeply and easily. Our thoughts were inconclusive as to whether more stability with the risk of a sharper snap-back would be worth while. Personally I would say no, for the really vicious rolls that caused havoc below were the result of climbing over big waves that came in on the beam. We spent over half the trip on courses that met the seas in this way. The confusing combination of convex, concave, hyperbolic and parabolic curves such a gray-beard can offer made contemplation of stability as expressed on a nice flat piece of buff drawing paper seem somewhat remote. But I was ready to agree with Herreshoff that the waves seemed quite "helical." It did seem that the idea that a narrow beam will reduce the "pitch-out" at the top of one of these mountains was demonstrated.

Steering. The unusual rudder is a *Marco Polo* feature. There is no doubt that she steers easily. Furthermore it did not seem to make any difference what combination of sails she carried. The amount of helm required stayed about the same. On the other hand, she had to be steered constantly. There was no leaving the wheel to get a cup of coffee or fiddle with the sheets. If you let go of the wheel she was sure to run off in short order to one side or the other. Is this a drawback? We never did agree. My own feeling is that the ease of steering makes a watch a pleasure compared to some boats and the attention required is hardly a chore. After all, that is what you are on watch for.

[But recently Captain Beebe wrote me, "On reflection it seems to me essential that she have an autopilot for occasional use. In this way the single watchstander can take care of all the little things during his watch without calling a relief."]

The Vivienne of Struan *is a school ship operated by the government of Western Australia.* (Sailing, March, 1978)

Sail and battens. The sail battens were heartily cursed. The sails were bought with them to give the best performance in light summer airs. They proved just a nuisance at sea, as has been related, particularly as the sails are rather narrow and the shrouds have an unusually wide angle which almost corresponds to that of the leech to the mast. The solution, of course, is two sets of sails. A rather expensive solution, I am afraid.

The jib was comparatively easy to muzzle and there was good support for the man who did it on the forward turtleback. The fore and main gave no trouble. But something must be done about the mizzen. My own solution would be to install a rather small inconspicuous (on such a large hull) patent stern. The lifelines could then be led farther aft and a permanent gallows installed to rest the boom upon while working the sail. The other booms have securing straps, but the mizzen does not. Consequently the boom swayed from side to side, putting a big strain on the mast and the topping lift at every roll during the five days when there was no sail spread on it. The patent stern would also allow spread for a kicking strap. The fore boom is well held down by the way it is sheeted. On the main we used a strap to one of the cockpit cleats and it improved performance perceptibly. There is no way to rig one on the mizzen at present. As it is sheeted to centerline blocks, the boom rise is excessive on a reach and probably one cause of catching the battens and tearing this sail.

General gear. Except for the torn mizzen, which took a day to repair, every piece of gear functioned perfectly throughout the voyage. There was no chafe. No seizing, no repairs were necessary. She was ready to return or to go on around the world the day we arrived. This certainly shows the hand of a master designer. . . .

The *Marco Polo,* as represented by *Talaria,* can do everything claimed for her. She is a tremendous sea boat, easy to work, quite suited to a one-man watch. She has all the room and more to make a real working oceangoing accommodation. She even exudes an impressive feeling of power while lying at anchor. What more could one ask?

Thanks to L. Francis Herreshoff for designing such a vessel.

Captain Beebe and L. Francis corresponded about the *Talaria*'s performance on the passage south, and I quote a few pertinent comments by L. Francis:

I am much surprised that she has a quick or sharp roll and think the seas at times must have coincided with her period of roll. Also I can't help thinking the seas were unusually steep for their length, and this condition may not often occur. If the crew of *Talaria* were more accustomed to her I think they would have carried more sail which would have had a great dampening effect. Of course if *Talaria*'s center of weight were higher she would have a slower period of roll, and this would have been the case if she had had a heavy motor near the water line, and large fuel tanks whose centers were above the LWL.

The desired amount of stability has always been a moot question on an ocean liner, but if you are close to dangers when struck with a squall, then a vessel that will remain manageable is desirable, and I think an H-55 can carry all sail and be manageable (or steer well) in a strong squall. With less stability, perhaps not, so the answer may be that bilge keels should be used on a vessel with light and low spars, but the added surface of bilge keels will reduce the cruising radius under power. . . .

As to the quick steering or unsteadiness of *Talaria,* I will say that all nautical designs have to be a compromise. If I had designed the H-55s with a deadwood and long run aft then they would have held their course much steadier, but it would then be very difficult to lay them to with the bow well to windward. Few people today realize how delightful it is to lay-to in disagreeable weather, and few of

today's yachtsmen have done it for the simple reason that it cannot be done with most of the modern yachts. But on a vessel like the H-55 if you lay-to say from 1200 to 1600, again from 2300 to 2400, the voyage will be ever so much pleasanter and sometimes seasickness done away with altogether. Sometimes I think the days' runs are nearly as much with these stops for then the crew will carry on and drive her harder when sailing.

However, to me a vessel that cannot easily be made to lay-to is no ocean cruiser, but don't forget that a light headed sail boat is easier to be made to steer herself than a long keeled vessel, and I believe *Talaria* can be made to steer herself much of the time when it is not rough. Also the quick steering vessel can be made to hold her course with proper helmsmanship while the long keeled types are apt to take wild yaws that cannot be quickly corrected. So we can't have both—both a quick and a slow turning craft, but there will be times when you will bless the quick turning vessel for its ability to avoid dangers and tack ship positively under all reasonable circumstances.

You have spoken of *Talaria*'s ability to "pick her way through the waves with intelligence, never making a wrong move." This is mostly because she does not have a deep forefoot and long deadwood aft which would allow the center of lateral resistance to jump from way forward to far aft when crossing the crest of a wave. However, if *Talaria* does require constant attention at the helm this has the advantage of keeping the helmsman awake in the dog watches, and to me a much pleasanter pastime than trying to correct a slow turning, deep yawing, vessel which, as you say, is prone to pick the bad spots.

As for the leech of the mizzen catching under the shrouds, I must say emphatically that the mizzen should not be set when there is a sea and the wind aft of wind-on-the-quarter. The principal reason for this is that the mizzen sail has a very bad effect on the forward sails for it causes the wind under its lee to draw in from one side then the other in a distressing way that causes bad steering, and causes the forward sails to want to jibe. Of course in light weather and no sea the mizzen can be carried running before it.

I think the mizzen boom, as all the booms, was designed with a strong boom bail to take a forward guy or cross tackle, for with high, narrow leg-o'-mutton sails when running freer than wind-abeam, (particularly if there is a sea), the boom must be held down and out, to prevent the sail from pressing so hard against the shrouds and spreaders.

Perhaps the mizzen boom should carry port and starboard boom forward guys always attached which lead to strong cleats just inside the mizzen rigging. But you must always remember to cast these off when tacking ship. You will ask why I didn't show these cleats on the design, and I will say that he who makes no mistakes does nothing. I think if the mizzen

A sketch of the Marco Polo *drawn by her designer. (Muriel Vaughn)*

is never carried when running before it in a sea and wind, and the booms' forward guys are properly tended, then there will be no need of one going out on the after turtle deck, but if desired a stanchion each side, as there is forward, could be erected to carry the life rails further aft.

As for the turtle decks at both ends—these were adopted to give head room in the ends of the vessel, but I suppose some sort of a fiddly deck house could have been built on the after deck instead. To my knowledge there have been three H-55s built in various parts of the world without the turtle decks so apparently others do not approve of them, so I don't know. One way is better when below deck, the other better above deck, but I happen to like the looks of them.

And, from a later letter:

I got the idea of the sharp rolling not so much from your article as from conversing with Mr. Fisk, and I think the trouble is not with the model or the height of the center of weight but rather that the masts, although very strong, are light because they are pretty scientific. On account of there being three masts, the center of weight of the mast is lower than usual.

The way to heave *Marco Polo* to is to simply take in all sail excepting the mizzen, and have the main sheets about close hauled, and the rudder turned in whatever direction it wants to go. Under those conditions she will neither forge ahead nor go backward

but will lay with her head about 45 degrees from the wind, making a dead set to leeward of 90 degrees from her center line. Under these conditions the boat can be in a very rough sea and the motion seem very slight.

Years later, Mr. Herreshoff wrote to an inquirer about the *Marco Polo* design:

There have been very few *Marco Polo*s built, and as far as I know, only four or five rigged as planned. There have been ones with no rigging, some with sloop rigs, and some with staysail schooner rigs. Only God knows why. One with sloop rigging has been up in the Arctic Circle three different years, and one rigged as designed was sailed across the Atlantic by a man crippled below the waist, a woman, and a man who had had no previous sailing experience.

I would conclude that if the *Marco Polo* has any basic fault, it may be a rather lively motion in a seaway. Captain Beebe's account and, apparently, Mr. Fisk's remarks to Mr. Herreshoff, indicate that the *Talaria*'s motion could be a bit quick and uncomfortable. If this be true, it is probably a trade-off for extreme seaworthiness, buoyancy, and dryness on deck.

L. Francis Herreshoff wrote of the *Marco Polo*, "Though some auxiliaries in the past have been called 50-50 boats, we hope and expect the *Marco Polo* will be better than that. She should really sail well in moderate and heavy weather with her modern scientific sails, spars, and rigging. Under power she should go further and faster than many straight-power boats, so perhaps it would be safe to call her a 90-90 boat."

I ain't going to argue with him.

Chapter 17

The *Aria*

It has amazed me that the Aria and her three sisters haven't spawned a big fleet of Buzzards Bay 25-footers, for she is indeed a wonderful boat.

The Concordia Company, of South Dartmouth, Massachusetts, made a nice job of building a Buzzards Bay 25-footer in 1983; she was named after the water nymph Naiad. Best of all, she was given the original gaff rig that Nat Herreshoff designed for her.

My friend Lloyd Bergeson launched a modified Buzzards Bay 25-footer in 1986. I never expected that I would applaud changes to any design of Nathanael Greene Herreshoff, much less to the Buzzards Bay 25-footer, but, in the case of Lloyd's boat, that is just what I did. Lloyd loves Herreshoff boats, and he likes to be able to make offshore passages when the spirit moves him. After losing his New York Yacht Club 30-footer to an ultimate wave in the North Atlantic, he decided his next boat would be a Buzzards Bay 25-footer, modified so she could go offshore. He raised the design's freeboard about six inches; gave her a small, watertight cockpit and the low cabinhouse with continuous, rectangular windows that is a Herreshoff trademark; and designed a moderately tall Marconi rig for her. He calls her Tore Hund, after a Norwegian seafaring ancestor; she is a most successful little vessel.

The Buzzards Bay 25-footer is so low-sided that she is one of the few good boats that can stand having her freeboard increased without spoiling her looks. The result in the Tore Hund is a boat that has both the grace of the original Buzzards Bay 25-footer, with her long, lovely bow, and the more seaworthy look of the somewhat higher-sided and snub-nosed Alerion and Newport 29. I once lay anchored near the Tore Hund in her home harbor on Isle au Haut, Maine, during a southerly gale that produced waves big enough to make her do some dancing. She looked absolutely gorgeous, swinging to the gusts and pitching into it, her beautifully curved bow cleaving each little sea into spray.

The century-old praise of an English fisherman for a small beach yawl applies very much to this Herreshoff model: "You see, sir, she don't stop to look at nothink, but goes right through everythink."

And here is late-breaking, good news about the Aria herself: Her last owner, Paul Bates, has given her to the Herreshoff Museum in Bristol, Rhode Island, where she will be a permanent exhibit. Her gaff rig will go into Maynard Bray's sistership, the Anita.

Length on deck: 32 feet 3 inches
Length on waterline: 25 feet 4 inches
Beam: 8 feet 9 inches
Draft: 3 feet 1 inch
Displacement: 4-1/3 tons
Designer: Nathanael G. Herreshoff

Pop swapped the yawl *Brownie* for a Herreshoff Buzzards Bay 25-footer, the *Aria*, in the fall of 1948. As in the case of all even swaps, each party thought he had the best of the deal. The *Brownie* was described in Chapter 3, and the *Aria* is described right here, so you can judge for yourself.

In any event, Pop never got to capitalize on the arrangement; the following spring he got the new boat overboard but died before he could take her sailing the first time. So the *Aria* became my legacy, and I guess no 17-year-old whipper-snapper ever had better. I kept her ten years and never could get used to her speed. She is some boat.

She was designed by Nathanael Greene Herreshoff and built by the Herreshoff Manufacturing Company in 1914 for one C.R. Holmes at a contract price of $2,000.

She is Herreshoff hull number 738, and her original name was the *Whitecap*. She is one of a class of four D Class half-decked sloops designed for racing on Buzzards Bay and generally known as the Buzzards Bay 25-footers, from the length of the waterline. These boats are the *Mink*, No. 733; *Vitessa*, No. 734; *Bagetelle*, No. 736; and the *Whitecap*. All four were built in 1914.

The boats never became popular as a racing class, and the Herreshoff Company turned out no more of them. They supposedly gained a bad reputation when one of them filled and sank when she was left on her mooring with her mainsail set and sheeted flat and was struck broadside by a squall. They are certainly not tender boats. The only time that the *Aria*'s coaming went under while I had her was when she was struck by a heavy puff just after I had cast off the mooring and, without good steerageway, she was slow to luff.

The *Aria* is 32 feet 3 inches long on deck, with a waterline length of 25 feet 4 inches, a beam of 8 feet 9 inches, and a draft of 3 feet 1 inch. Her sail area is 490 square feet, and her displacement is just under 4½ tons.

The design is a modification of Captain Nat Herreshoff's third *Alerion*, hull No. 718, which he designed and built for his own use in 1912. The *Alerion* is smaller than the *Aria*, with a waterline length of 21 feet 9 inches. She has a bit more freeboard and somewhat shorter ends than the *Aria*, but the basic hull shape is the same. The *Alerion* is preserved in beautiful condition at the Mystic Seaport. A near sistership to the *Alerion* is the *Sadie*, hull No. 732, built in 1914, now also preserved in a museum, that at St. Michaels, Maryland.

Nathanael Greene Herreshoff. (Muriel Vaughn)

A further modification of this basic design resulted in the Newport 29 class of which three boats were built in 1914: the *Dolphin,* No. 727; *Mischief,* No. 728; and *Comet,* No. 737. These boats have the short ends and high freeboard of the *Alerion,* and they are keel boats without centerboards. They are 36 feet long on deck, with a waterline length of 29 feet, a beam of 10 feet 4 inches, and a draft of 5 feet.

Seven of these nine boats built by the Herreshoff Manufacturing Company in or before 1914 are going strong, and the other two may be also for all I know.

Of the three versions of this design of Captain Nat Herreshoff's, the *Alerion,* the Buzzards Bay 25-footers, and the Newport 29s, the Buzzards Bay 25s have the finest lines. The *Aria* was always a sweet and pretty boat to look at and to sail.

Her sections look deceptively easy and gentle, for her bilge is not hard, her draft is quite shoal, and her freeboard is low. Yet she was a powerful boat and could stand driving due to her considerable outside ballast, rather high ballast-to-displacement ratio, great flare in the topsides, and considerable beam. Her broad stern helps her stiffness by giving plenty of bearing aft.

She has about the prettiest bow I have ever seen on a boat. I think the stem profile is the most artistic one Captain Nat ever modelled. The entry is quite hollow, but above the waterline her bow has a lot of flare. The skipper of the only boat that ever beat her in a serious race told me that when the breeze lightened and we began to creep up on him, he was nearly mesmerized by the beauty of that approaching bow with its never-ending, delicately swept back bow wave.

That bow could pound on very rare occasions. When she was well heeled down, one sea in a whole afternoon might be shaped just wrong for her, and she would slap it like a beaver. One time in Gardiner's Bay we ran into a whole succession of such seas and she made such a commotion that I went below to see if she was cracking any frames up forward. The flexibility of her structure under attack was unbelievable. The give was very visible, but she wasn't even weeping.

But that bow loved to cope with 999 out of 1,000 head seas. It would spit 'em off to leeward and in the process seemed to wedge the boat to weather, so that instead of letting the seas knock her off, she seemed able to use them to shoulder her way to windward.

The bow and buttock lines are shallow for low resistance. She has a very long and flat run for such a small boat.

Her profile gives just the right compromise between steadiness on the helm—it was certainly no work at all to make her go straight—and maneuverability. She could do some fancy stepping and spinning for a 32-footer; we used to wriggle in and out of some narrow waters with glee, and, of course, no engine ever came anywhere near this boat.

The tiller is a small, skinny piece of locust that is beautifully shaped; it looks too small for her, but it isn't.

The *Aria* had a 6-meter rig in her when Pop got her. It suited her well, and the rig conversion had been carried out intelligently.

The mast was 47 feet long from keel to truck. The first time I hoisted it out, I simply cast off all the standing rigging, tied it off on the spar, slid the hook on my sheerpole fall a little way above what I thought would be the balance point, and hoisted away. Everything went fine until I began lowering the thing down to the horizontal, and then it about

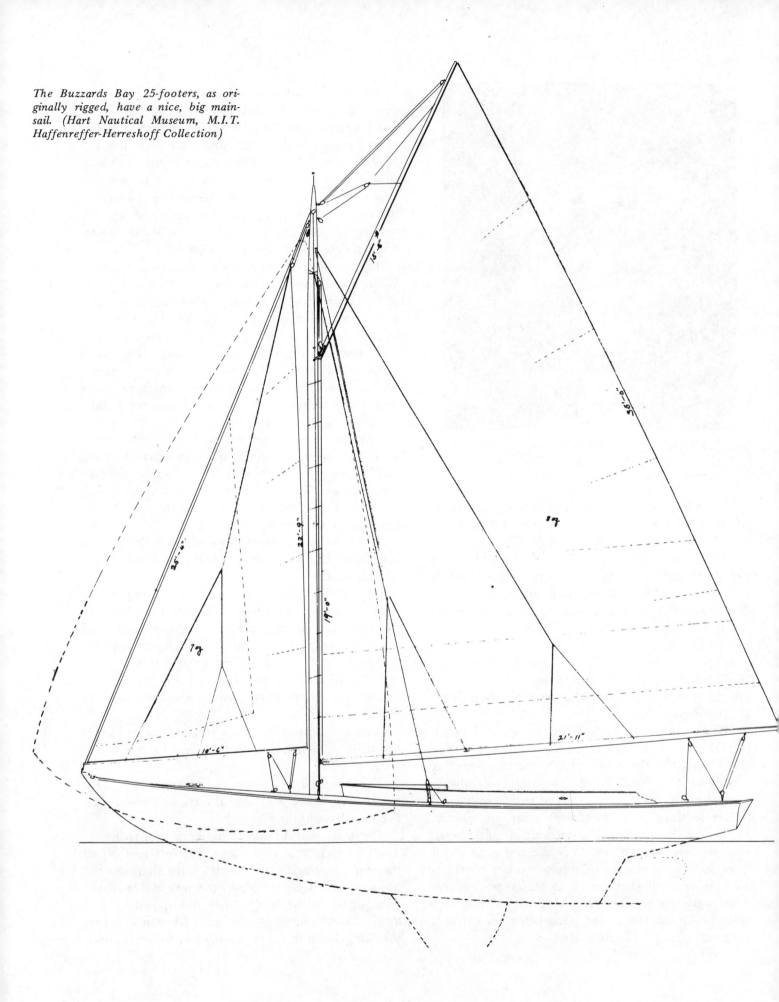

The Buzzards Bay 25-footers, as originally rigged, have a nice, big main-sail. (Hart Nautical Museum, M.I.T. Haffenreffer-Herreshoff Collection)

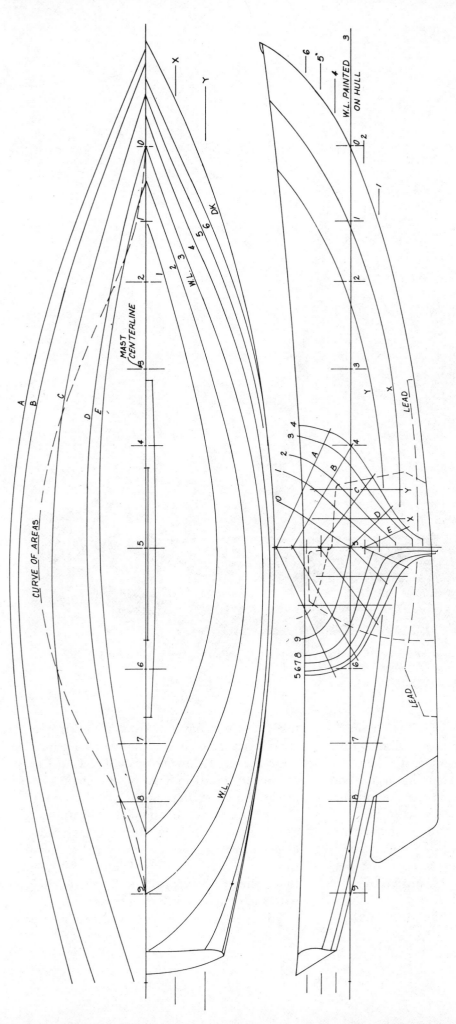

She has a sweet set of lines. The sections are deceptively gentle looking, for she is a powerful boat that will stand a bit of driving. (Edson A. Schock)

The Mischief, *a Newport 29, beating down Narragansett Bay under her original rig. That's the U.S. Naval War College over her bow. (David Cabot)*

bent double under its own weight and that of the rigging. I had no idea that spar was so limber, and figured I had just destroyed the mast. It held.

With a spar that limber, the standing rigging had to be set up pretty tight to keep the rig straight. There were plenty of wires to play with. She had three sets of spreaders, one set of jumper struts, five pairs of shrouds, one pair of jumper stays, double headstays, running backstays, and a permanent backstay. That made 17 pieces of wire with 15 turnbuckles to adjust it all.

Captain Nat hadn't designed the *Aria*'s hull to

take the strain imposed by that tall rig with its taut standing rigging. Whoever put the rig into her had done the right thing by installing a steel strap from the sheer clamp in way of the chain plates down under the mast step and up to the opposite sheer clamp. Doubtless this helped hold things together, but after two seasons of sailing her fairly hard, I began to worry about the way the seams in way of the rigging were working. It just didn't seem fair to that delicate, 35-year-old hull to wrench away at it with such a tall, tightly stayed rig.

So, in 1951, another swap was engineered.

Most of the Aria *with some of her 6-meter rig showing. (Roberts Parsons)*

Sam Jones of Essex, Connecticut, had one of the *Aria*'s sisters, the *Mink,* and he still had her original gaff rig. He wasn't using it, and he figured a spare 6-meter rig would be a lot more valuable to him than a spare 1914 gaff rig. So we swapped rigs. Putting the original gaff rig back into the *Aria* was one of the most useful things I have ever done, so Sam, wherever you are, thanks again for the trade.

The gaff rig has about the same sail area as had the 6-meter rig. The mast is 32 feet long, instead of 47 feet, and is hollow. I could just carry it on my shoulder once it was stripped of all the rigging, so you can see it was a nice, light spar. The mast position is the same with both rigs.

The gaff rig has one extra piece of running rigging, the peak halyard, but has only five pieces of standing rigging, a single shroud on each side, a headstay, and a pair of running backstays. So there are five pieces of wire instead of 17 and three turnbuckles instead of 15.

The sails that came with the gaff rig had been made at Herreshoff's, and the mainsail was the most beautifully setting gaff sail I ever saw. There was a club and traveler for the jib, but I had gotten used to the loose-footed jib of the 6-meter rig and so left the club and traveler off and set the new jib loose-footed. When the 6-meter rig had been put in, a nice pair of Luders winches with folding handles had been mounted, one on each after corner of the cuddy roof, and these were so handy I kept them with the gaff rig.

The boat went just as well to windward with the gaff rig as she had with the 6-meter rig. She was never all that close-winded even with the tall, Marconi rig. Deep, narrow boats with tall rigs, like the Eastern Interclubs, could outpoint her with ease, but she had no trouble beating them badly to the windward mark because she footed so fast. The only time she didn't sail as well with the gaff rig as she had with the Marconi rig was in very light airs, when she missed that tall triangle of sail way up high where there is often a little more breeze.

One of the things Pop did during the winter he was looking forward to sailing the *Aria* was to make her a yuloh. This is a Chinese sculling oar that Pop had come to know on China station in the Navy. It has been described in *The Mariner's Catalog,* Volume III, and it has been written up and drawn by real experts like George Worcester, so I won't go into it here. Suffice it to say that the yuloh worked just fine on the *Aria* on those evenings when we had overstayed our welcome in Fisher's Island Sound and were coming up the Pawcatuck River in a flat calm. You could shove her along at a knot or two depending on whether you were lazy or energetic.

The *Aria*'s dinghy has also come in for its share of mention in the *Mariner's Catalog.* The dinghy's name was the *Ano,* by which you can readily see that it had once been a canoe but had had each end cut off. The *Ano* was at its best when stowed on the *Aria*'s deck, across the stern with the Marconi rig, and moved to the foredeck with the gaff rig so it wouldn't foul the mainsheet. If the *Ano* was

That's me misspending my youth in the Aria.

for a storm anchor. And the 15-pounder always left you worrying a bit; a 25-pounder would have been easy enough to handle and would have given more peace of mind.

The boat has plenty of deck space. There is a lot of room around the mast and her widely flaring bow makes a fine platform for handling headsails. The rather extreme flare to the topsides forward up near the rail makes a fine hand-hold when she's jumping a bit.

The *Aria* has a huge, deep cockpit, easily the most comfortable cockpit I have seen in any size of boat. The seats are about 9½ feet long, the coaming is slanted outboard just right for a backrest and is high enough to give you plenty of support and protection. The seats are high enough off the cockpit floor so that you have a really comfortable seat, and when the boat is heeled you have good foot braces in the centerboard trunk at the forward end of the cockpit and the opposite seat at the after end. In this cockpit, you feel as if you are sitting down in the boat, not perched up on her. Six people have plenty of room when sailing, and, of course, you can have quite a party on board at anchor.

Her coaming and seats are made of four beautiful pieces of mahogany. Behind the seats under the deck are long, open shelves that provide a great deal of handy stowage space.

The *Aria*'s big, deep cockpit is not, of course, watertight or self-bailing; rain or spray drains through narrow spaces between the cockpit floorboards directly into the bilge. She has a big tarp that goes over the boom and gaff, the peak halyard and lazy jacks being slacked away to the mast to accommodate it. The tarp covers the entire cockpit and provides a big sheltered area with considerable headroom for a rainy day. It also saves pumping out after a rain and protects considerable acreage of varnish work from the weather. At anchor, you can roll it forward to open up as much of the cockpit as you want to; we often used to set it close-reefed, forming just a nice windbreak over the cuddy and across the forward end of the cockpit.

One thing Pop put in during that last winter was a chart drawer on sail track and slides under the after deck. Sitting at the tiller, all you had to do was reach back through the opening into the lazarette, pull out the drawer, and there were the charts right handy.

light and docile on deck, she was crank and dangerous afloat. One night in Great Salt Pond, Block Island, a guest disregarded my strong suggestion that he not try to row ashore in the *Ano* against the usual southwest gale. He turned out to be an awfully good man in a small boat, for it took the *Ano* a full 30 minutes to return him on board, tired, wet, and frustrated through not having come anywhere near his destination.

The ground tackle in the *Aria* consisted of a 50-pound yachtsman's anchor that had been the *Brownie*'s best bower and a 15-pound yachtsman's anchor that Pop had calculated would be enough to hold her under most circumstances. They were just wrong. The 50-pounder was more than she ever needed; a 35-pounder would have been plenty

The 6-meter rig did give her a tall beauty. This was standing out of Marion, Massachusetts, on Buzzards Bay. (Edward Cabot)

No hatch is needed in her cuddy roof, for the cockpit is deep enough so that you can easily stoop and walk into the cabin. Nice louvered mahogany doors can be slid out from under the forward ends of the cockpit seats, slipped onto their pintles, and used to shut off the cabin from the cockpit if desired.

One feature of the boat's construction that Pop said he particularly admired was a pair of strengthening members consisting of fairly wide, straight boards set on edge that ran from each side of the keel up and out to the sheer clamp along the forward face of the bulkhead separating the cuddy from the cockpit. These stiffen her up greatly right amidships without adding much weight to her structure.

In the cuddy there is a narrow seat on each side; there is sitting headroom under the cuddy roof. She has a single pipe berth away forward.

Pop had put in a head at the forward end of the cabin, but I had little trouble rationalizing its early removal and replacement by a nicely varnished, brass-bound wooden bucket. I also got rid of a water tank way up in the eyes of her and another all the way aft in the lazarette, for I didn't think she needed that kind of weight way out in the ends of her—or that much civilization either, for that matter.

In the after starboard corner of the cabin are some shelves and lockers and a fold-down, single-burner alcohol stove. The centerboard trunk is half in the cabin and half in the cockpit, and the cabin half has a folding table leaf on each side.

The *Aria* was hauled and maintained on the

Running up into Buzzards Bay. We have just taken in the spinnaker, which she didn't really need. (Edward Cabot)

railway at Ram Point on the Pawcatuck River that Pop had built for the *Brownie.* Scraping, sanding, red-leading, puttying, and painting her hull, you got to know her shape pretty well, and every spring's work brought a renewed appreciation for the beauty and soundness of Captain Nat's model.

We'd get most of the work done during spring vacation from school, which meant getting her overboard usually about the third week in April. We'd leave her on the cradle a day or two so the lower seams in the centerboard trunk could swell up—aided by a little sawdust judiciously sprinkled down the slot.

I never made a long cruise in her, but did a lot of daysailing and cruised regularly to the eastward to Buzzards Bay and Vineyard Sound.

My first summer with her I sailed her single-handed to Buzzards Bay on a ten-day cruise. I made a couple of errors in judgment, both having to do with entering harbors, but the boat was so maneuverable and so well behaved that she got me out of both mistakes unscathed.

Since the *Aria* was obviously a fast boat, we

wanted to try her out against the competition, so we took her in three Off Soundings races. My regular and best racing crew consisted entirely of Cabots, Ed and Nelson, brothers who had been a major force to contend with in the Herreshoff 15-foot-waterline E class boats on Buzzards Bay and were old enough to remember when the 25-footers came out, and, of course, Ed's son and my very best friend, Dave. These able sailors always took a great interest in the boat and helped me a lot, not just with racing her, but also with her upkeep and general management.

In the three starts in Off Soundings, we took two firsts and a second in Class C, the racing class. The race in which we were beaten was, of course, by far the most interesting. The winning boat was the *Flying Scotchman,* a new—and at that time novel—light-displacement, fin-keeler, with very high freeboard, reverse sheer, and skimpy sail area. It blew quite hard on both days of the racing, and most of the sailing was to windward. Under these conditions, the *Flying Scotchman* had things a bit her own way, but we did notice that the one time

Beating up into Smith's Cove on Shelter Island Sound in a hard northwester under just a reefed mainsail. (Edward Cabot)

On the railway at Ram Point on the Pawcatuck River.

Soaking up. The original gaff rig has been put back into her.

it moderated, we came right up on her until it breezed on again. The boats would probably be a fairly even match for each other under a wide variety of sailing conditions.

I guess the *Aria*'s greatest day while I had her was in a race around Fisher's Island when she beat most of a fleet of far larger boats, including the 72-foot yawl *Bolero,* boat for boat. Granted, it was a flukey northwest day and we played in under the outside shore of Fisher's Island to the point of hitting the board on a couple of rocks so we could catch what few puffs were coming off the land while the bigger boats had to stay farther offshore becalmed. Still, it was all fair, and I have a nice big silver pitcher to help me remember the day.

After sailing her for four years, I went into the Navy, and Uncle Sam's operating schedules began to cut down on our sailing time.

For part of my first summer in a destroyer, though, the ship was actually in her home port of Newport, Rhode Island, and my wife and I lived on board the *Aria* in Brenton's Cove. Early in the fall came a hurricane scare, and an embarrassed new ensign had to go to the exec to request permission to leave the ship in the face of impending danger. It was my fitness report versus Captain Nat's boat, and I figured there were 300 other guys who could look after that tin can with her 60,000 horsepower. The

exec was understanding, and I scooted back home, offered the bride a chance to get ashore dry while she could, and then proceeded to lay out one of the longest scopes of anchor rode ever seen in Newport harbor between Goat Island and Trinity Church. I also tied three reefs into the mainsail, one on top of the other, and generally put away and lashed down everything movable, including the tarp. All we got was much rain, so I spent most of the night pumping.

The *Aria* didn't get nearly the use she should have had in the next few busy years, and when we moved to Chesapeake Bay, I sold her.

Meanwhile, the *Bagetelle,* one of the other Buzzards Bay 25s, had been owned first by an uncle and then by Ed Cabot. Ed had rerigged her as a modern yawl. When Ed died, Dave took over his father's boat.

One time I crewed for Dave in the race around Fisher's Island. The *Aria* was then again owned locally, and she was in the race too. Five of us in the *Bagetelle* worked very hard on a day with changing conditions, shifting to different-sized Genoa jibs, setting and resetting the mizzen staysail, and fussing with spinnaker and spinnaker staysail. Two fellows in the *Aria* sailed her around the course with working jib and mainsail, never doing more than trim a sheet now and then. For all

Looking more like her original self. Ahhhh.

our efforts, we in the *Bagetelle* only beat the *Aria* by a couple of minutes, and the gaff-rigger saved her time on us. I never could figure out who to root for that day.

Whenever I look back on my experience sailing the *Aria*, the chief memory that comes up is her surprisingly great speed under all conditions. A couple of years ago I got to worrying that maybe she really hadn't been all that fast and that my remembrance of her fleetness was more nostalgic than accurate. Paul Bates, the *Aria*'s present owner in Noank, Connecticut, kindly gave me the opportunity to put the worry to the test. We took her out on a nice fresh southwest day, laid her off on a broad reach to Stonington Point, ran up into the harbor and back, and then stood back up Fisher's Island Sound just able to lay Noank, rail down, and going like smoke. It wasn't nostalgia. One more time the boat surprised me with how fast she could sail.

L. Francis Herreshoff once told me that the Buzzards Bay 25-footers were his favorite of his father's designs. That's a mighty powerful statement when you think about it. After ten years of surprises, plus a dividend, I have to agree. I just wish Pop could have sailed the *Aria*. He really would have loved her.

Chapter 18

A Forest Ranger's Patrol Boat

For daydreams of a simple, solitary, beachcombing sort of life, I often turn to D. P. McMillan's Forest Ranger's Patrol Boat. She really goes with that mood of let's-deep-six-everything-but-the-bare-essentials.

This winter, I've been imagining living on board the Red Cedar, basing myself in Pulpit Harbor, a pretty, landlocked millpond of a place on the northwest side of North Haven Island, Penobscot Bay, Maine. The harbor boasts a western view of the Camden Hills out its narrow entrance if you anchor in just the right spot and has a couple of long coves well worth a daily row except in the coldest weather. Pulpit Harbor is quiet enough: Its waters are well protected from winter gales, and the bustle of shore facilities is far away.

I can land at the public dock in the easterly cove and walk two miles on a paved road to the village. Actually, that's impossible; somebody always picks me up in their truck before I get well started, especially on the return trip, when I am often laden with supplies. And if my simple needs should sway toward the exotic, there are plenty of days that are calm enough to run the fewer than ten miles across the bay to Rockland, or even Camden, if need be. You can get anything in Camden. Here's a day in early March, for instance, when it's clear-as-

forever, the northeast breeze is decidedly gentle, and the outdoor thermometer I installed to be readable from inside the wheelhouse will probably hit forty. Shucks, I may go to Rockland just to see what's at the flicks!

One vital logistical need when living on board the Red Cedar in winter is a supply of good, clean, hard coal. Luckily, such is obtainable in Belfast, which means a fortnightly, seventeen-mile run, with a good excuse (because it's the shortest way) to march through Gilkey Harbor between Islesboro and Seven Hundred Acre islands. To go with the coal, I need plenty of firewood. This is where the beachcombing comes in. On every good day, I take much satisfaction in filling a pair of big, canvas tote bags with driftwood left me by the tide.

My tender for the Red Cedar was supposed to be a sailing peapod, but I do like to be able to bring her on board, and I found that the peapod is too big and heavy for convenient hoisting out and stowing. I replaced her with a 10-foot sailing skiff that I used to have down on the Chesapeake. This boat is fairly light to handle and fits across the Red Cedar's cockpit, resting on her rails with acceptable overhangs.

It's fun dreaming these dreams, especially here at my Harborwatch writing table, overlooking the scene of the action.

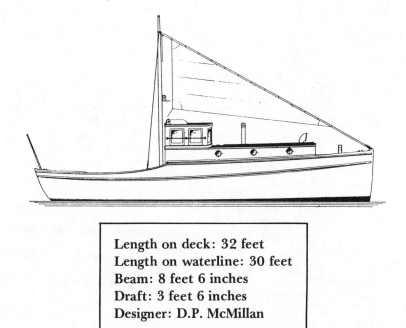

Length on deck: 32 feet
Length on waterline: 30 feet
Beam: 8 feet 6 inches
Draft: 3 feet 6 inches
Designer: D.P. McMillan

I'm like the sailor in Darrell McClure's cartoon in *Yachting* some decades back who was down on his knees praying to God for forgiveness for having taken a cruise in a powerboat and liked it. As a matter of fact, I made two such trips and liked them both.

Once we went aways east in the old roly-poly *Penguin* to pick up and tow back a Herreshoff 15-footer. The other time we stacked four Blue Jays on the working deck of a big Novi, laid their masts across on top of everything, and headed up Long Island Sound in a vain quest for silverware.

Such shenanigans were hardly in the mind of D.P. McMillan of Vancouver, B.C., when he designed a 32-foot double-ended motorboat 60 years ago, for the project had been commissioned by the British Columbia Forest Branch (wonderful name for the outfit!), which wanted a one-man patrol boat for the Forest Rangers. The resulting boats, if given good sailing peapods to tow, would make admirable vessels in which a solitary soul could really soak up the qualities of a coastline. Powerboats seem always to be at their best when associated with smaller sailing craft.

The first boat built was launched in June, 1918, and was called the *Sitka Spruce*. Two sisterships were built the following year, the *Red Cedar* and the *Douglas Fir*. The boats proved successful for their intended purpose.

Mr. McMillan's creation (I'd love to see some more of his designs) makes quite a handsome vessel, in my opinion. The hull is deep enough to have six feet of headroom under the trunk cabin without having to build a skyscraper. Of course some of this height has been gained in the raised deck. This raised deck has just the slightest amount of sheer to keep it from being ugly. The appearance of the boat would have been improved if the top of the house had followed this same very gentle curve instead of being straight. The pilothouse—the focal point of visual interest on the boat—has just the right curved front, just the right crown to its roof, and just the right windows. Bow and stern profiles, sweep of rubbing strake, cabin house portholes, mast and standing rigging, and even such details as the samson post forward and the flagstaff aft, are all drawn with care and perception.

The boat is 32 feet long on deck, with a waterline length of 30 feet, a beam of 8 feet 6 inches, and a draft of 3 feet 6 inches. Note the flare high on the bow to keep her reasonably dry going into a head sea. She has fine waterlines (especially forward), easy sections, and a good run.

A double-ender designed 60 years ago as a forestry patrol boat for use in British Columbia. (The Rudder, September, 1918)

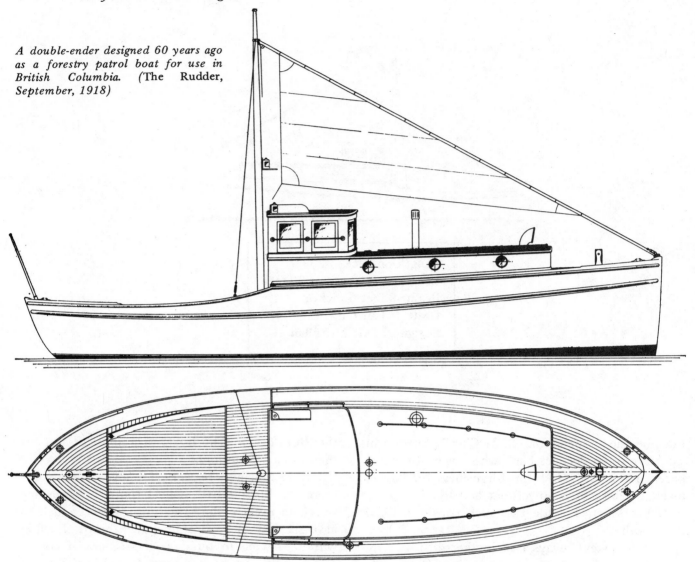

She should be easily driven at low speeds (one of the hot, new low-energy users?) and would be no bruisewater.

It may be that she needs another two or three inches depth of keel. It was written of her that in a small quartering sea, she would "roll considerably." It would also be desirable, in a boat of this type, to be sure to have enough lateral plane to be able to sail across the wind heading for harbor with a damaged or otherwise uncooperative engine.

While examining her hull shape, note that she has a metal strip supporting the bottom of the rudder and protecting it and the wheel. Does this strip have enough vertical dimension?

The boats were fairly heavily built. The keel, of Douglas fir, is five inches square. The false keel is of Australian gum. The stem is fashioned from a 5-inch square piece of white oak. Frames, also of white oak, are 1½ inches by 1½ inches, on 8-inch centers, but on 7-inch centers in way of the engine bed. Floors are white oak, 1½ inches thick. Longitudinals are all of Douglas fir: sheer clamps, 2½ inches by 5 inches; raised deck clamp, 2½ inches by 3 inches; and bilge stringers, 2½ inches by 4 inches. All of these were put in in one length. Planking is 1⅛-inch Douglas fir. Joinerwork is teak and red cedar. She carries a half ton of cement ballast in the bilge.

On deck, that low-angled headstay would be fine to lean on and hang onto when on the foredeck with the boat jumping into a sea. As a matter of fact, its angle may be just right so that you could use it to practice a bit of circus work, presumably with the boat in quiet water. Because of this shal-

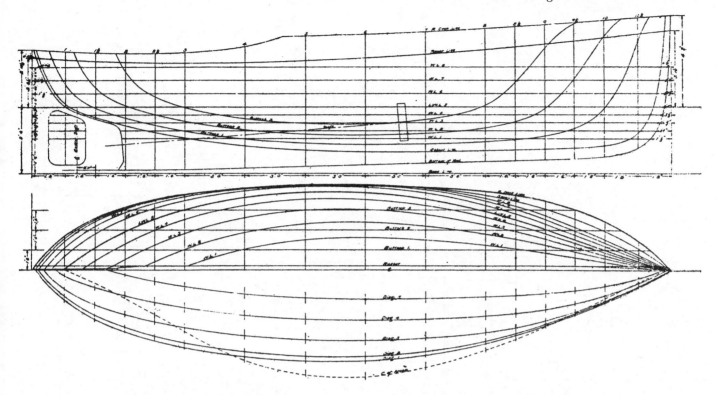

Her lines show a hull that is up to date, for she would be a consummate saver of energy.
(The Rudder, *September, 1918*)

low angle you'd certainly want a downhaul on the riding headsail, because otherwise you'd let go the halyard and nothing would happen.

I'd want to add another sail aft. It would be a trysail setting on a boom on the mast. I'd want the gooseneck quite high, about the level of the grab rail outside the pilothouse windows. The foot of this trysail would be parallel to the foot of the jib. It wouldn't be a big sail, but would help steady her, would really do some pushing with a strong breeze aft, and would help considerably on that sail to shelter with a dead propeller. The boom would double as a derrick for bringing the peapod into the cockpit in a hard chance.

I'd also be tempted to add a second pair of shrouds and give her some wooden "ratlines" and a spreader to stand on, maybe even with some swordfishing hoops. Maybe that's why I liked those powerboat runs. Both boats had A-frame masts with crow's nests. Even at a relatively low height above the vessel, it's a whole 'nother world up there.

You'd want a pair of heavy rope lifelines ready to set up from the shrouds to the stern for that wrong combination of seaway and passengers.

She needs a bowsprit to handle her anchors. The short plank variety—complete with swordfishing pulpit (and that's yet a third world)—would balance the main boom in appearance. These accoutrements wouldn't hurt her looks at all. She would use her anchors constantly, for she's not the kind of boat to lie at a dock longer than is necessary to fuel up, which wouldn't be all that often, given her camel-like efficiency.

The cockpit will take a low deck chair, or even a chaise longue, and it will be down out of the wind. You could also sleep out there, especially if you stuck your feet through the locker door and under the after deck. You could even put a tarp over the boom.

Her bridge deck keeps water from getting below through the pilothouse if she should be pooped; I'd want four big drains in the cockpit floor rather than the two small ones shown.

She cries out to have a big towing bitt amidships at the after end of the bridge deck.

This boat's engine is up in the middle of her to keep its weight amidships and make the engine and shaft fairly level. The thing is certainly accessible; you're living right with it, so it is impossible that it

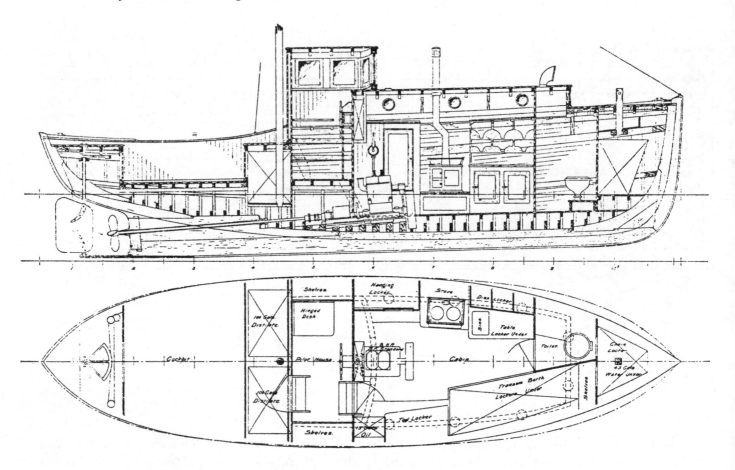

Her slow-turning Union engine, right up in the middle of things, burns "distillate," which Westy Farmer reveals is furnace oil. (The Rudder, *September, 1918*)

will be neglected. The chances are quite good that, out of gratitude, it will run when you want it to.

The *Sitka Spruce* and the *Red Cedar* each had a 10-h.p. Union engine. They cruised at 6.5 knots and could make seven when all buttoned up. The *Douglas Fir* had a 12-h.p. Union; she averaged 7.6 knots for 132 miles on her trial trip and could make eight knots wide open.

The two 100-gallon fuel tanks are under the bridge deck; in Mr. McMillan's drawing, they are labeled to hold "distillate." There is also a little 15-gallon tank high against the bulkhead right above the engine for gasoline. This particular combination of fuels being beyond my tiny motor-boating experience, I asked Weston Farmer what it was all about. Westy explained that the Union engine was a compression-ignition type, like the diesel, that burned furnace oil. He said that on the distillate chain, furnace oil lies somewhere between jet fuel and sludge. They're all distillates of the stuff that comes out of the ground; presumably

Mr. McMillan meant to be a bit vague to the Forest Rangers about the fuel they would be depending on. Westy explained that the gasoline was used to start her up and run her out of the harbor.

She has a 45-gallon water tank in the bow. This ought to be about a three-month supply for one person. It's too bad to have all that weight up there, but I suppose it could be used to give her just the right fore-and-aft trim.

She has a fine layout for the singlehander, though you might want a comfortable seat in place of the tool locker just aft of the berth on the starboard side. At the end of the day's run, you could relax and warm your toes on the very machinery that had given it to you.

The galley looks neat and adequate, and the head is up out of the way.

The pilothouse is not only a great place to run her from in comfort, but also adds greatly to her accommodations. It would be a fine spot, when anchored, in which to supervise harbor activities throughout 360 degrees. Of course it would need a stool placed so you could lean back against the after bulkhead. And I think you'd want a permanent chart table fixed across the whole length of the pilothouse in place of the hinged table shown.

All in all, one of these patrol boats from the Canadian northwest would make a fine little cruiser. Shucks, what are those ragmen after anyway? By the time they get through slatting around waiting for the afternoon sou'wester, we'll be in the cove, anchored, swum, fed, and setting out for an explore round the point to the island in our sprit-rigged peapod just in time to catch that breeze ourselves.

Oh God, what have I said . . . ?

Chapter 19

A Hand Double-Ended Schooner

The late James W. Crawford had some wonderful boats in his day, and he sailed them hard. He circumnavigated in the 60-foot Alden schooner Dirigo II. He made long passages, including crossing the Atlantic singlehanded, in the 61-foot, steel, double-ended cutter Angantyr, designed by MacLear and Harris. In 1974, the Cruising Club of America awarded him its Blue Water Medal.

When Jim Crawford saw the Hand double-ended schooner in Still More Good Boats, he had to have her. Paul Rollins built her for him at York, Maine; she was launched on July 18, 1982. Crawford even christened her with my suggested name, the Simplicity.

The photo added at the end of the chapter shows the Simplicity on her first sail, the day after she was launched. Crawford sent it to me with a note addressed "Dear Godfather." "Some kinda fun!" he wrote.

Crawford wanted his little schooner to be a pure sailing vessel; he installed no motor. If he had to move her around in harbor, he sculled her. Otherwise, he waited for a good breeze and then made the most of it.

Two very experienced sailors, neither known as a champion of the gaff-rigged schooner, were taken out to see what they thought of her. Rod Stephens pronounced her unquestionably reliable, and Dick Newick could suggest no changes. As for me, I just love knowing the Simplicity is out there.

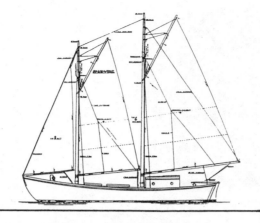

Length on deck: 35 feet 3 inches
Length on waterline: 31 feet
Beam: 10 feet 2 inches
Draft: 4 feet 6 inches
Sail area: 528 square feet
Designer: William H. Hand, Jr.

William H. Hand, Jr., of New Bedford, Massachusetts, was perhaps best known for his designs of fine motorsailers — big, husky ketches like the *Bluebell* and the *Seer*.

But here's a Hand motorsailer that may have been overlooked. This little double-ended schooner was designed and built as an auxiliary fishing boat, I believe about a half century ago.

Her owner was one F.C. Wederkinch, and he used his vessel on the coast of Texas.

(The coast of Texas? One stares at the words in disbelief. Clearly the states of Maine and Oregon have coasts, but Texas? One envisions cowboys warning their herds away from some alien liquid lapping the edge of a ranch. You have to open the atlas to prove to yourself that — yes — Texas really does have a coast. But I digress.)

The schooner would make a fine motorsailer with her midships fish well closed up and her machinery moved up into it out of the after cabin. She has an easily driven hull but would need her power in light weather, for she is short-rigged.

In any case, she is an able little vessel. She might well be named the *Simplicity*.

Bill Hand was in that minority of naval architects who always draw their boats going to the left. I suppose somebody ought to make a study of the correlation of this group with left-handedness. Funny how it's hard to compare a boat design heading to the left against one that is heading to the right. It just seems harder to catch her shape, somehow, force of habit being what it is.

This left-handed business notwithstanding, however, it can be said with safety that Mr. Hand could draw the best-looking short spoon bows (if that's not a contradiction) of anyone. To my eye, he put just the right rugged, handsome curves in the bows of his boats. Alden was good at it, but Hand was the master.

Whether or not you agree with that statement, this schooner does have a nice, high bow that leads into a most pleasing sheerline. Of course it is hard to judge the sheerline on paper. You really need to see it in three dimensions to be sure, for there are other factors at play in the overall appearance of the boat. The British writer Colin Mudie reminds us that a boat, when seen in the flesh, appears to have less sheer than is shown in her profile drawing — he

William H. Hand, Jr. (The Rudder, March 1927)

Mr. Hand's little auxiliary fishing schooner would also make a fine motorsailer or freighter. (The Rudder)

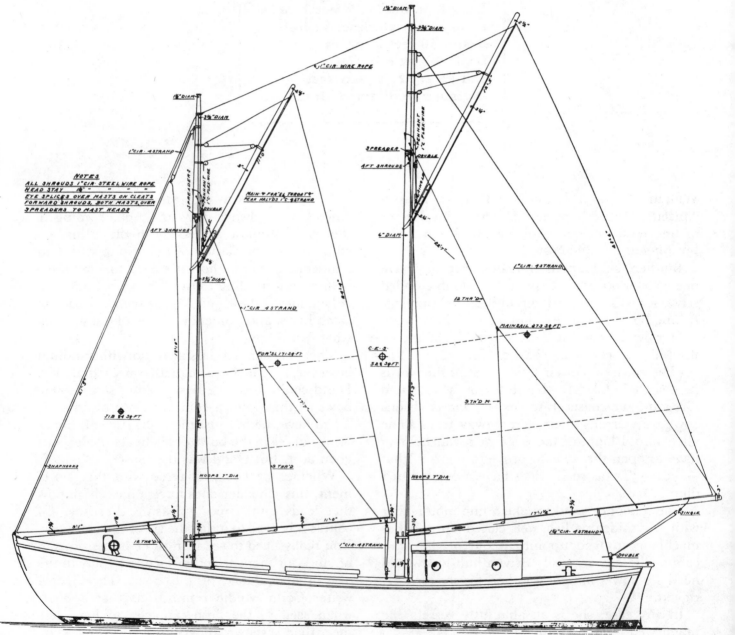

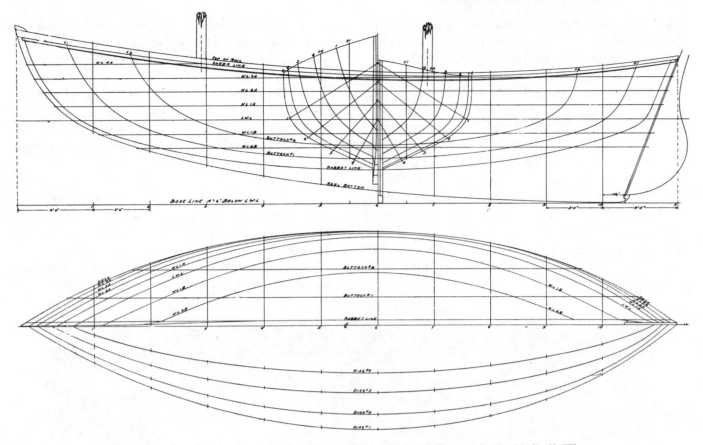

Everything about her lines is easy and moderate. She'd well deserve that word, "seakindly." (The Rudder)

says by three inches for 40 feet of length. When looking at the real boat, the sheer appears to be less pronounced than in the profile drawing, for the curvature of the deck edge takes the sheer-line farther away from your eye near the ends of the boat, Mudie says. I think he's right.

The schooner is 35 feet 3 inches long on deck, with a waterline length of 31 feet, a beam of 10 feet 2 inches, and a moderate draft of 4 feet 6 inches. Her sail area is a modest 528 square feet.

Her bow and buttock lines are extremely easy; she has a long, flat run for a double-ender.

Her sections show that she has a bit of flare all around the hull at the waterline that makes a boat look and be light on her feet and that gives her stiffness as she heels.

Her waterlines and diagonals show a hull that is quite symmetrical and that would stay well balanced when heeled. With her moderate draft and easy lines, her motion should hardly be violent or erratic. Of course, her moderate draft

would keep her from hanging on really well when going to windward.

Her rudder is certainly a simple installation and, being positioned way aft, would make her relatively easy to keep from broaching when reaching in a big breeze and sea, at the expense (as L. Francis Herreshoff reminds us) of the quicker turning that a rudder farther forward would provide.

Her sails are small, there being but 273 square feet in the mainsail, 171 in the foresail, and 84 in the jib. Her deep reefs look business-like; she can be snugged right down when it breezes on hard. With her narrow stern and overhanging boom, you'd want to leave the reef earings all rove off on the leech of the mainsail.

Her jib is self-tending on a club that is not quite full length. This arrangement lets the sail set better than does a full-length club. You can still rig lazy jacks on such a club — which, as a matter of fact, is a fine idea.

Her high-peaked gaffs look right and give her

sails a good shape. The foresail, with its leech leading aft rather than being vertical as on most schooner foresails, would set particularly well.

She'd balance under foresail alone for jogging along, or under jib and close-reefed mainsail, if preferred.

For running off, you'd want to rig preventers on the booms to keep the sails from jibing over when the person on the tiller forgets for a moment precisely which way the wind is blowing. Ah, but can't you see yourself as that person, chasing away before a fresh breeze, foresail hauled out on one side and mainsail on the other, jib strapped down tight to dampen the roll? The Old-Timer called it "readin' both pages."

She could easily take a 10-foot boat lashed upside down over the hatches between the masts. There is nothing like having a really good small boat with you.

In the house aft could be a couple of quarter berths, their forward ends doubling as settees, and then a galley in the forward end of the house. You could call such quarters cramped or snug, depending on your viewpoint.

All in all, I think this little vessel would make a fine singlehander or two-handed cruiser for long trips. She'd carry plenty of stores, water, and fuel, all amidships where the weight belongs.

Or you could live with the engine back aft and have yourself a nice little freighter.

Chapter 20

A Forty-One-Foot Chapelle Schooner

A beautiful, shapely hull has saved the life of many an old boat. Plenty of us have sufficient insanity to fall in love with a graceful vessel that has seen better days, and we're willing to commit exhaustive emotional and physical resources toward her rejuvenation and upkeep. I've never heard of a vessel being built to this outstanding Chapelle design, but if one had been, and I found her moldering away in some backwater, I'd be tempted to rescue her.

I know that when I'm feeling brave, I dream of sailing her. I used to think nothing of reefing a big, overhanging mainsail like hers, or sending up a yard topsail, or wrestling down a few acres of fisherman staysail, but now, even in a daydream, my strength and balance aren't what they were, not to mention my nerve. Yet I still take lots of imaginary sails in this schooner, still thrill to her easy roll and scend when she's reaching fast in a moder-

ate breeze and seaway, all her sails pulling and the foam hissing down her side.

I was shocked the other day to realize that I've never owned a boat with a full, deep keel. All my boats have been centerboarders, most with the board dropping through a keel of moderate draft, as on the Aria (three chapters back) or on this schooner. Funny how unconscious that choice has been for me. As I say, the mere realization of the fact is recent. I've considered buying many a deep-keeled boat, but, somehow, never have. The lines of this schooner are so satisfactory, with her seakindly shape and her ability to decrease her draft. She suits me. And I do think that she's exceedingly handsome.

The breeze isn't too strong this evening; maybe I'll just take her out for a reach across the bay and back in the sunset.

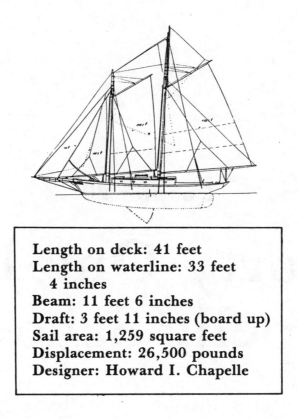

Length on deck: 41 feet
Length on waterline: 33 feet
    4 inches
Beam: 11 feet 6 inches
Draft: 3 feet 11 inches (board up)
Sail area: 1,259 square feet
Displacement: 26,500 pounds
Designer: Howard I. Chapelle

Many marine books are spoken of or written of using the word ''classic,'' probably more than really deserve to have such language applied to them. One book that does deserve such strong language is *Yacht Designing and Planning* by the late, great Howard I. Chapelle, published by W.W. Norton in 1936 and still selling well.

You don't think of a detailed explanation of a complex process as being particularly exciting reading, but this book, strange to say, is one of the most exciting Chap wrote. The reason is that the example he chose from among his own designs to illustrate points made in the course of guiding the reader from a mental concept of a boat to a finished design on paper ready to be built to is a very nice 41-foot, clipper-bowed, keel-and-centerboard, gaff-rigged schooner.

As you follow Mr. Chapelle along through chapters called ''Preliminary Design,'' ''The Lines,'' ''The Construction and Joiner Plans,'' and ''The Sail Plan,'' you see this grand schooner take shape gradually before your eyes and you are exposed to the considerable amount of thinking and figuring that backs up a set of plans for the design of a good boat.

Mr. Chapelle's schooner is, then, 41 feet long on deck, with a waterline length of 33 feet 4 inches, a beam of 11 feet 6 inches, and a draft, with the board up, of 3 feet 11 inches. She displaces 26,500 pounds and has outside ballast of 1,645 pounds in an iron keel. Her sail area is 1,259 square feet.

The schooner's lines drawings show how little she would disturb the water on her passage; her fine underbody is particularly well shown in the two perspective lines drawings. She has a sharp entrance with plenty of hollow and a long run.

Her stiffness comes from ample beam and the fact that she picks up bearing as she heels, particularly aft. With moderate outside ballast not hung too low, she'd have a very easy roll.

The generous overhang aft, besides adding much to her looks, allows her to pick up considerable effective sailing waterline length once she gets going.

All in all, the schooner has a very pretty set of lines, I think.

Mr. Chapelle gives full details on her construction. A few of them are: her keel is of white oak and makes up to 5½ inches by 6 inches; the frames, also of white oak, are sided 3 inches and moulded 1⅞ inches; the centerboard trunk is

Howard I. Chapelle. (Zayma Chapelle)

1¼-inch pine; clamps are 1½-inch by 5-inch yellow pine; she is planked with 1⅛-inch hard pine and sealed with ⅜-inch pine; the deck is 1½-inch by 4-inch pine; and the house is of 1¾-inch mahogany.

As to rig — well, it is almost enough simply to say that she is a gaff schooner. What more could any sailor want? Oh I know, there are other rigs with their various advantages over the schooner. I think the following snatch of conversation from H. Warington Smyth's *Sea Wake and Jungle Trail* put them in accurate perspective:

" 'But, Skipper, what really is the best all-round rig?'

"I invariably quote Joseph Conrad and say, 'For looks, the schooner; for speed, the cutter; for handiness, the yawl or ketch.' "

Of course the schooner rig, besides being the fairest of them all, has its practical aspects. It's an ideal rig for hard weather once you get the mainsail off. On the Banks, the fishermen used to turn their schooners into snug ketches by replacing the mainsail with a good-sized trysail.

This schooner has a sail area of 942 square feet in her four lowers (mainsail, 437; foresail, 265; fore staysail, 120; and jib, 120). Her topsail has 79 square feet and her fisherman staysail, 247, so with full sail she sets 1,259 square feet.

Notice her long, outside chainplates, the easiest kind to inspect, refasten, or replace.

She has preventer backstays on both masts, a sensible rig. You would set them up as necessary when on long boards, but you wouldn't have to use them when short-tacking.

Her gaffs are low-peaked and would require vangs. I'd even put one — or, rather, a pair — on the mainsail, leading one down each side to be set up on the weather quarter.

I'd want a second reef in the foresail and a reef in the fore staysail.

Her fore staysail is self-tending on a horse. The forward end of the club slides on a track, fishing schooner style, to keep the luff of the sail from binding when the sail is lowered.

It would be fun to send up a jackyard fore topsail when she's on the wind in a light breeze and you wouldn't have to tack for at least a couple of hours.

She has some real anchor gear on deck, a good hand windlass and an anchor davit each side. She's a bit dainty for catheads.

The tackle to lift the board slides on a brass track atop the port side of the house, belaying on its after port corner. The chain pendant would run in a pipe below and in a copper trough to protect the top of the house.

The schooner's deck plan shows brass filler plates around the edge of her deck out against the rail for salting her down. There are four of them forward and no fewer than 21 aft around her quarters and transom.

She has a very big cockpit formed by a coaming set on deck and a large, rather shallow footwell, of a size that will take a couple of folding canvas chairs if there's not a big crowd on board.

Her engine is under the bridge deck. It's offset to starboard with the shaft canted outboard to cancel out the turning moment of the off-center wheel. The water tank is under the bridge deck and there is a fuel tank on each side outboard of the cockpit well.

The house is quite high to give headroom in a rather shoal hull (6 feet at the after end of the house and 5½ feet forward). Mr. Chapelle just managed not to spoil her looks with this house by combining a fairly generous crown with a tiny bit of sheer to the sides of the house. He might have gone just a little bit further with both ideas.

Below, the schooner has lots of space for two or three people, being wisely not arranged to take a big gang cruising. The transoms in the

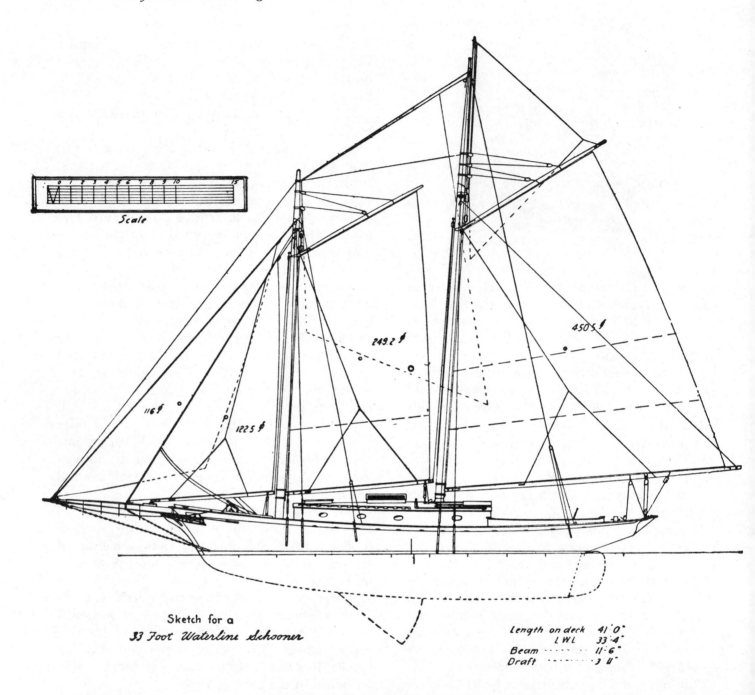

Scale

Sketch for a
33 Foot Waterline Schooner

249.2 ♀

450 ♀

116 ♀

122.5 ♀

Length on deck	41'0"
LWL	33'4"
Beam	11'6"
Draft	3'11"

Above: *Mr. Chapelle's preliminary drawing of the 41-foot schooner he used as the example in his classic book* Yacht Designing and Planning, *published more than 40 years ago and still a standard text on the subject. The sail areas given are approximate. (*Yacht Designing and Planning *by Howard I. Chapelle, W.W. Norton and Co.)* **Right:** *Her lines show a pretty hull with the moderate draft that makes for an easy motion at sea. (*Yacht Designing and Planning *by Howard I. Chapelle, W.W. Norton and Co.)* **Far right:** *Forward and aft perspectives of the schooner's lines. (*Yacht Designing and Planning *by Howard I. Chapelle, W.W. Norton and Co.)*

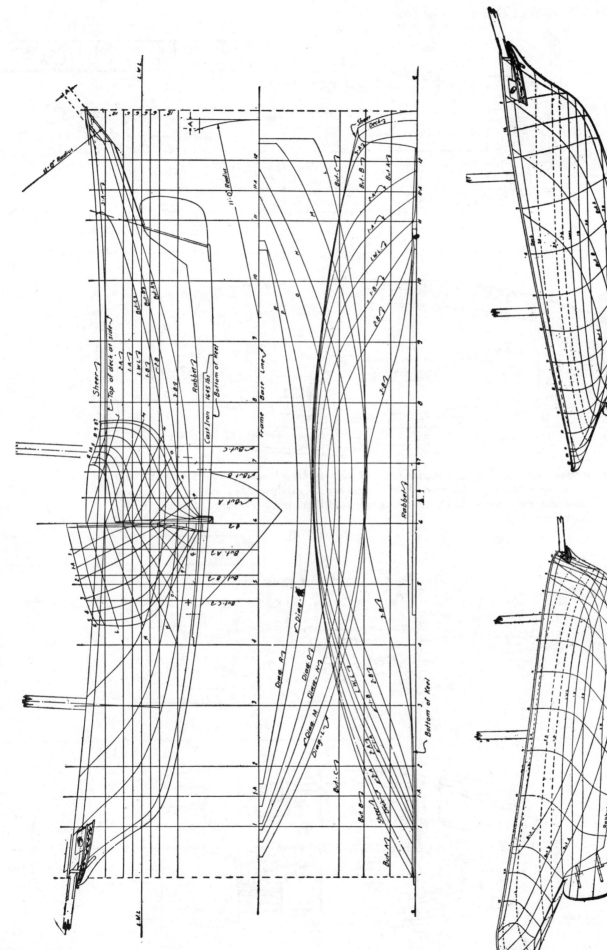
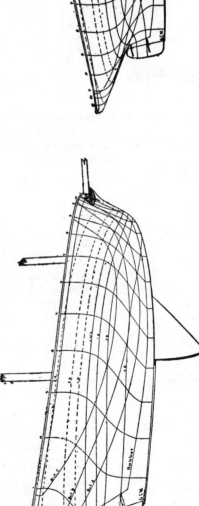

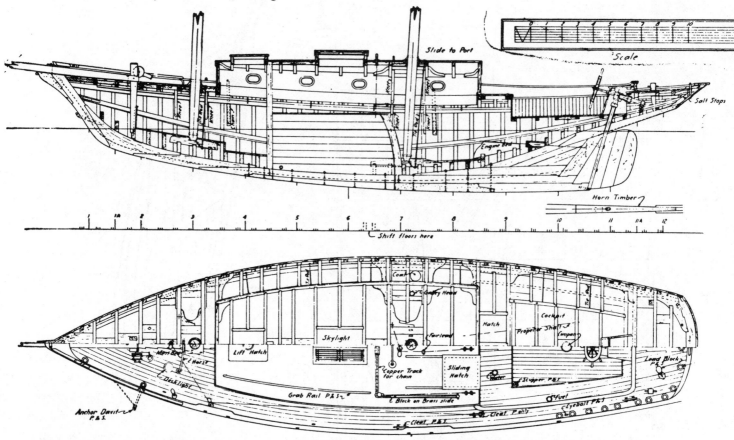

Above: *Mr. Chapelle's construction and deck plans of his schooner.* (Yacht Designing and Planning *by Howard I. Chapelle, W. W. Norton and Co.*) **Below:** *She is laid out with plenty of space for two or three people.* (Yacht Designing and Planning *by Howard I. Chapelle, W. W. Norton and Co.*)

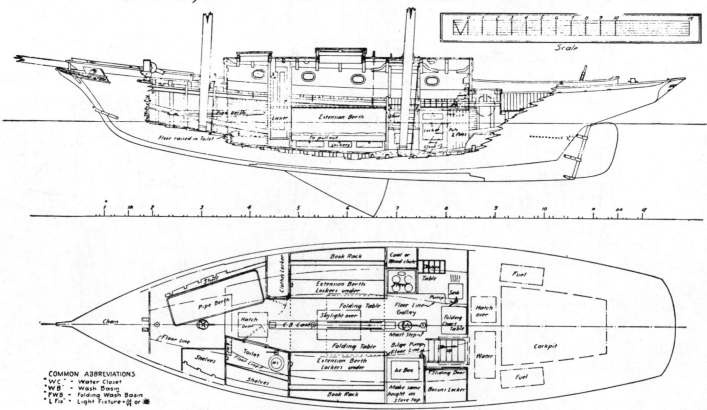

COMMON ABBREVIATIONS
- WC = Water Closet
- WB = Wash Basin
- FWB = Folding Wash Basin
- L Fix = Light Fixture

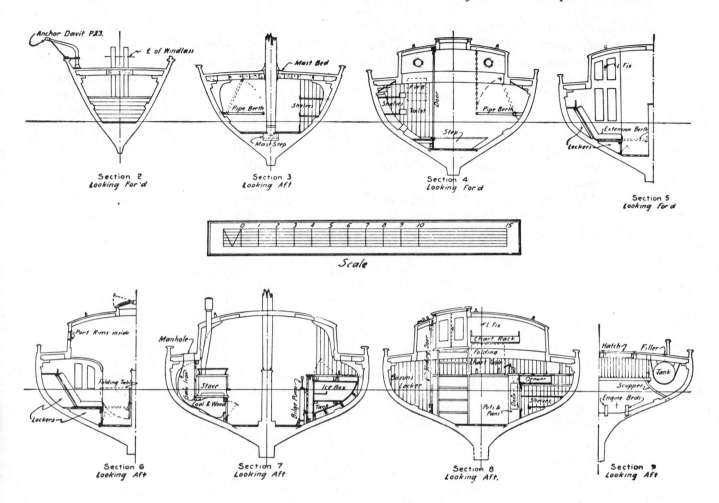

Above: *Sectional drawings help you visualize details of the interior arrangement.* (Yacht Designing and Planning *by Howard I. Chapelle, W. W. Norton and Co.*) **Below:** *Mr. Chapelle shows the reader of* Yacht Designing and Planning *how he makes a rough sketch and notes while the owner tells him his requirements for the design.* (Yacht Designing and Planning *by Howard I. Chapelle, W. W. Norton and Co.*)

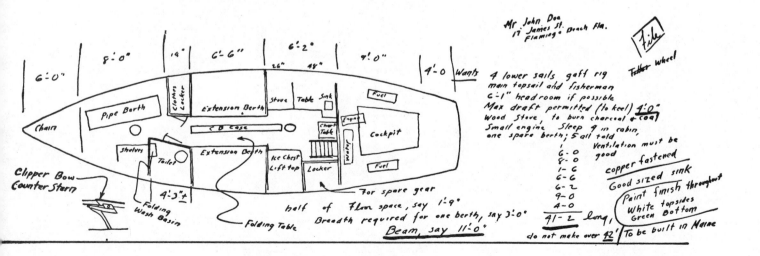

saloon slide out to form berths, and there's a spare pipe berth forward for a third hand. The centerboard trunk supports her cabin table.

In the after port corner of the cabin is a big locker labeled "Bosun's Locker." I would prefer to use this locker for foul weather gear and relegate the bosun's locker to the fo'c's'le, though, of course, there would be the usual ditty bag hanging just inside the engine room hatch in the bridge deck, handy to the watch.

She has a folding chart table at the after end of the cabin on the centerline. When it's folded back, you have full access to the sink.

To my mind this schooner would make a fine coastwise cruising boat. She'd be a lot of fun to sail and would be quite fast, especially once she freed her wind a bit. Don't discount her to windward, though, for she would foot fast six points off the wind with well-cut sails trimmed right, her topsail set, and her vangs in use. Yet, somehow, the way I see her best in my mind's eye is reaching in a fresh breeze with her four lowers set, wind just forward of abeam. A sea comes in under her — feel her lift and give and go down across the trough to the next one. Some fun, I say.

Chapter 21

The *Brilliant*

At a Yachting History Symposium at the Mystic Seaport, I chanced to sit next to Olin Stephens and took the opportunity to thank him for the pleasure his design of the Brilliant has given me over the years. Not that I've sailed in her, except in imagination, but I've spent much time poring over her plans and admired her many a time since I first saw her in Newport. Later in the day, Olin was on the speaker's platform and answered the question, "Which of your designs is your personal favorite?" by naming four vessels; one was the Brilliant. (The others were the Dorade, the Stormy Weather, and the Intrepid; when pinned down, Olin put the Stormy Weather on top.)

The Brilliant is now sixty years old. By 1993, she will have served the Mystic Seaport for forty years as a sail training vessel. She is still covering the miles in grand style, and she is still in impeccable condition.

Last summer, the school ship I was sailing, a Friendship sloop with lofty topsails, fell in with the Brilliant in Jericho Bay, Maine. She came running slowly down toward us in a light breeze, then jibed and paralleled our reaching course. I thought we might stand a chance against her, but then I overheard some talk on her deck, and hope vanished. Somebody had uttered the word, "gollywobbler." Sure enough, the huge sail soon went billowing to her mastheads and was promptly sheeted home to the end of her main boom. She pulled away from us like a train leaving the station; we saw nothing of her but her diminishing stern until we reached the harbor where she had anchored.

That night, there was a big, bright moon, and we made a drift round the harbor in Jim Brown's Scrimshaw (see Chapter 30). As we eased close by the Brilliant, gleaming in the moonlight, her bold, white bow and topsides were defined by the curve of her stem and the sweep of her sheer. Little flashes of light reflected from the varnish work about her deck and from the lower parts of masts that disappeared into the void above. It was the best sight of her I've ever had. She was ethereal, immensely powerful, mysterious . . . brilliant.

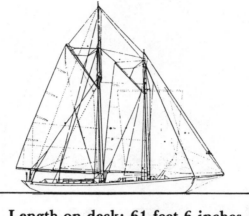

Length on deck: 61 feet 6 inches
Length on waterline: 49 feet
Beam: 14 feet 8 inches
Draft: 8 feet 0 inches
Sail area: 1,715 square feet
Displacement: 38 tons
Designer: Olin Stephens

It was a great thrill to me to sail with Pop in the yawl *Brownie* to Newport, Rhode Island, from our home mooring 40 miles to the westward in June of 1946 to see the start of the first postwar Bermuda Race. Older siblings used to talk about seeing such stupendous events — even including America's Cup races between the huge J boats — but I was always too young to view these historic occasions. Just when I turned old enough to go, the J boats were replaced by U boats.

So I was very excited when we came rolling in through the East Passage to Narragansett Bay with a boisterous sou'wester on our heels, bore up in smooth water round Fort Adams, and beat up through a big distinguished fleet of ocean racers and spectator boats to find a berth in Brenton's Cove. Busy as I was up forward getting halyards down off their pins ready to run, lashings off the anchor, rode laid out clear, and then jib hauled down and furled, still I saw out of the corner of my eye the wishbone boom of the great ketch *Vamarie,* the long, dark-blue hull of the latest Sparkman & Stephens creation, the *Gesture,* and the handsome white hull of a big, spotless, powerful-looking schooner.

As soon as we were anchored and furled up, I went rowing in the dinghy all through the boats. It was the white schooner that impressed me more than any of them. She was the *Brilliant,* and she just exuded the power of an able vessel, even lying at anchor.

Back on board, Pop told me something about her. He seemed chiefly impressed by her very fancy construction. He spoke of diagonal bronze strapping let flush into planking and deck. He said it was rumored her engine room was a single aluminum casting dropped into the boat up between the masts. No oil, gas, odor, sound, or vibration was supposed to be able to escape from the thing. The *Brilliant* was meant to have all the advantages of an engine with none of the disadvantages. Pop supposed that if the machine blew up, the explosion would merely lift the hatch off the top of the casting and the people having tea back in the cabin wouldn't even have their conversation interrupted. The prospect seemed to amuse him somehow, but I didn't like him poking fun at my glorious schooner.

But he was truly impressed with the *Brilliant.* He asked if I could see her seams, and I

Olin Stephens.

reported that they were certainly nowhere in evidence. I was particularly enamored of the swordfishing-type pulpit at the end of her bowsprit, and, all in all, was really quite jealous of her crew, though I didn't dare let on to Pop about that.

Next day the sou'wester increased, if anything, and we sailed out to see the start under just main and staysail. We were slam-banging along on the starboard tack watching all the big ocean racers come out and enjoying ourselves hugely, when along came the *Brilliant* converging on us from to leeward going dead into the wind under power with her mainsail up and slatting and her foresail being hoisted. Her big crew — apparently including her helmsman — was preoccupied with setting sail from her pitching deck, and on she came oblivious to the fact that a little sailing yawl was about to be splintered against her gleaming topsides. I thought Pop would probably yell to make them bear off, but he must have felt as I did that we

were just out fooling around watching while these guys were trying to get ready to go to Bermuda, because all he did was tack when we were 10 feet away from the big plunging schooner. Then, when they all looked over startled at our sudden appearance so close aboard, he fixed her helmsman with an icy stare and said, "Take a look around." I was embarrassed. Imagine treating the *Brilliant* like that.

Walter Barnum wanted a very strong offshore cruiser that could be driven in rough weather without fear of breaking gear or straining the hull. He went to Sparkman & Stephens for a design for such a vessel, and Olin Stephens drew the plans for the *Brilliant* in 1930. The boat was built in 1932 by Henry B. Nevins at City Island, New York, obviously to the very highest specifications. After World War II, she was owned by Briggs S. Cunningham. For the last 24 years she has been owned by the Mystic Seaport and has been used for sail training.

At Mystic, she makes 18 one-week cruises

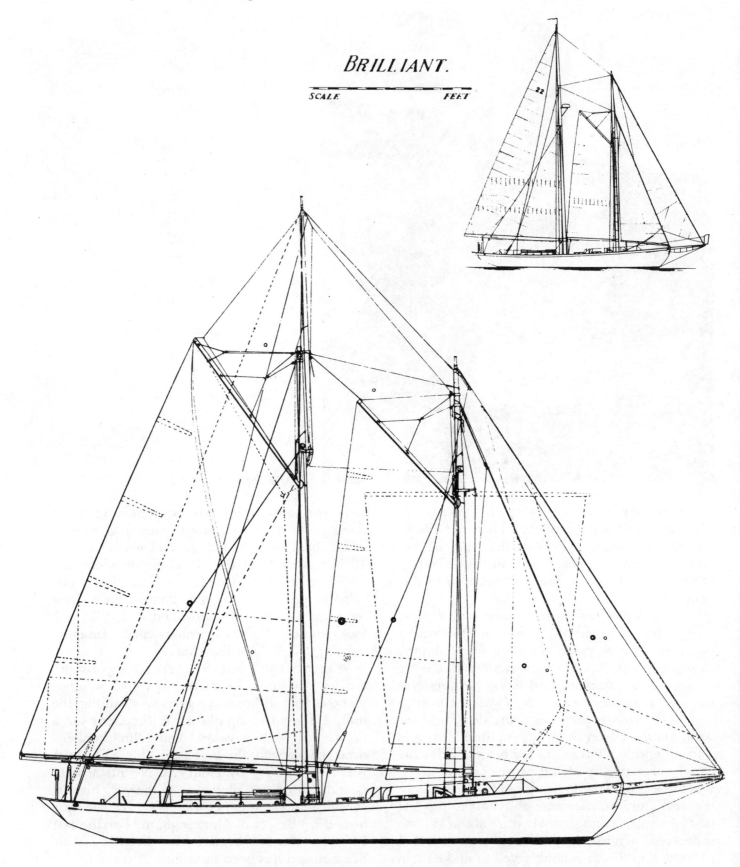

The Brilliant's *original gaff rig.* (Sailing, Seamanship and
Yacht Construction *by Uffa Fox*)

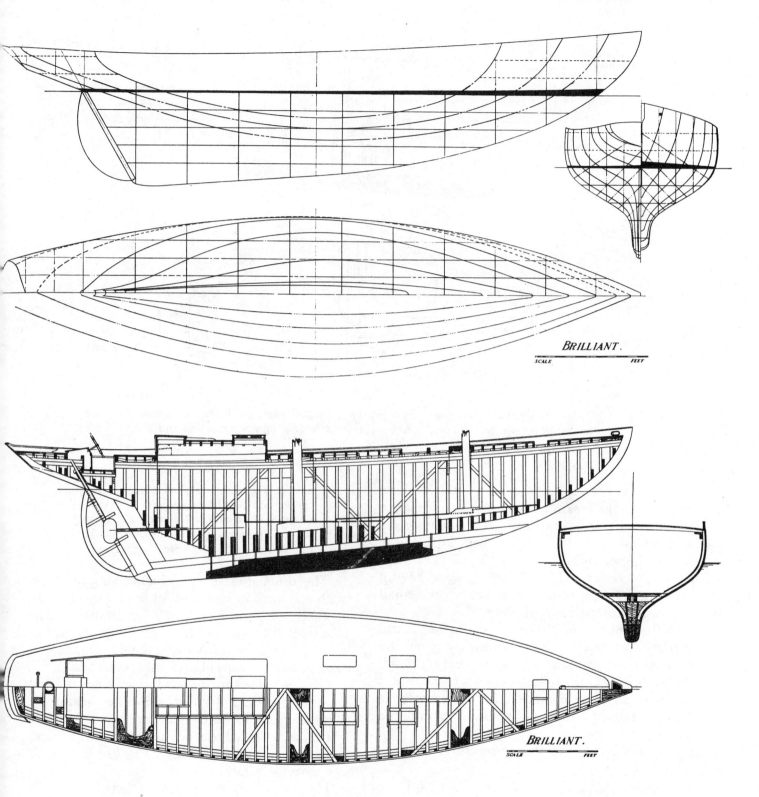

BRILLIANT.

BRILLIANT.

Top: *She has a very powerful hull, yet she is fine enough to be quite fast.* (Sailing, Seamanship and Yacht Construction *by Uffa Fox*) **Bottom:** *Her extremely high-quality construction is the work of Henry B. Nevins and lends awe to just about every conversation about her.* (Sailing, Seamanship and Yacht Construction *by Uffa Fox*)

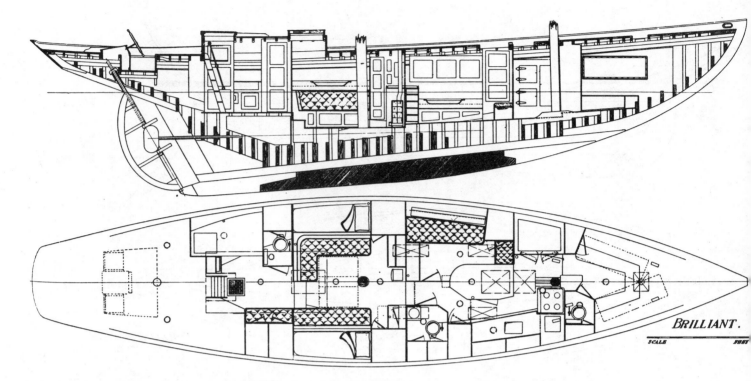

She has an interesting layout. The engine room is up between the masts, and back by the companion-way are all the essentials that need to be handy to the deck. (Sailing, Seamanship and Yacht Construction by Uffa Fox)

each summer along the southern New England coast. She has a skipper and mate and takes a group of 10 crew members, nine youngsters with an adult leader. At first her skipper was Adrian Lane, and for the last 19 years her skipper has been Francis E. Bowker, who, having been in coasters, thinks of her as a very small schooner rather than a big one.

Walter Barnum, Briggs Cunningham, and the Mystic Seaport have unstintingly given the *Brilliant* the very best of care, so that although she is approaching the half-century mark, she is in truly excellent condition and always looks very smart. It's still mighty hard to find the seams in her topsides.

Captain Bowker wrote me recently:

> At the present time, the *Brilliant* is hauled out at Mystic Seaport. We have set up on all the keelbolts. It was felt that, after all these years, her bottom should be caulked, but only a few places have been found that indicate any such care. Even the original seam compound remains undisturbed. Except for a piece of

oak in the wheelbox, no piece of original timber has ever been replaced. A man by the name of Murray was Nevins' master carpenter and for many years the *Brilliant* was known as "Murray's Masterpiece."

The *Brilliant* is 61 feet 6 inches long on deck, with a waterline length of 49 feet, a beam of 14 feet 8 inches, and a draft of 8 feet 10 inches. She displaces 38 tons and has 1,715 square feet of sail in her four lowers and 2,082 square feet with her main topsail and fisherman staysail.

Olin Stephens made her fine enough to have an excellent turn of speed; she is not beamy for a cruising schooner of her size. She has a fine entrance with a little hollow at the waterline, easy bow lines, and a long run. The diagonals are extremely fair.

Her rig is very nicely proportioned, her gaffs being well peaked up. She was given a mere Marconi mainsail about 25 years ago.

When shortening down, to get the best out of her you'd want to begin by reefing the mainsail. Beyond that, there are plenty of sail combina-

The Brilliant *on "The Nevins Yacht Elevator."* (Yachting, *June 1933*)

tions to choose from, right down to jogging along under foresail alone. Her main trysail would be a useful sail in hard weather, as would her storm jib and storm fore staysail.

The squaresail was used some in her early years, and it was found that perhaps its best point of sailing was with the wind one point abaft the beam when it wouldn't blanket the headsails.

She would have a big fisherman staysail reaching halfway to the deck for reaching in moderate weather and a huge gollywobbler to catch a light breeze.

Note the vang on the foresail. You'd probably want a club on the fore staysail to make it self-tending. And you might want to pair up the upper and lower backstays on the mainmast, leading them to one tackle.

I like the look of her flush deck with just the trunk cabin abaft the mainmast. She usually carries a boat on a cradle right side up between her masts, which somehow gives her a seagoing look. Some sailors say the drawback to carrying a boat right side up on deck is that it always gets filled with junk, but I say that one of the advantages of carrying a boat right side up on deck is that you immediately have a nice place for a lot of junk where it will stay put, out of the way.

Her cockpit arrangement lets you walk out to the sides of the well, and there is a big protected bridge deck.

Her engine room is, of course, ideal, about its only disadvantage being that a long shaft is required.

The *Brilliant's* arrangement below deck makes a lot of sense. Just inside the companionway, you have everything you need: a big chart table, a small head, and plenty of stowage for foul weather gear.

Next forward is the nice, big saloon with extra headroom under the forward end of the trunk cabin and two berths tucked well back out of the way.

Forward of the saloon is a stateroom with a good-sized head opposite. Then, wrapped around the engine compartment is a big, L-shaped galley with plenty of counter space. There's a fo'c's'le with two pipe berths. Mystic Seaport has added two bunks in the fo'c's'le.

When Walter Barnum got his cruising schooner, he decided first of all to see what she could do at ocean racing. The 1932 Bermuda Race was the last great race of schooner yachts. There were entered a number of John G. Alden's schooners, led by his latest, the *Malabar X*. There was the *Barlovento,* designed for Pierre S.

The Brilliant *driving to windward under full sail. (Mystic Seaport)*

Dupont III by Cox & Stevens. There was the *Mistress*, designed for George E. Roosevelt by Henry J. Gielow. There was the *Brilliant*.

And besides all these great schooners, there were such famous yachts as the *Vamarie, Dorade, Highland Light,* and *Jolie Brise*.

It was an eventful race. The *Brilliant* didn't particularly live up to her name, the *Malabar X* being the winner on corrected time. The *Highland Light,* Frank Paine's big cutter, set a new course record, and the *Jolie Brise* rescued all but one of the crew of the burning schooner *Adriana*.

In 1933, Walter Barnum sailed the *Brilliant* across the Atlantic to go in the Fastnet Race. That year's Fastnet turned out to be a slow, light-weather race that was won by the *Dorade;* the *Brilliant* didn't fare too well.

If the *Brilliant* didn't get the weather she needed to do startling things on the ocean-racing circuit, she certainly was proving herself to be a very lucky and well-sailed cruising boat.

Her transatlantic passage in 1933 from City Island to Plymouth was most remarkable. It was ably described by the *Brilliant's* navigator on the trip, the longtime, sparkling writer for *Yachting* magazine, Alfred F. Loomis. I don't want to tell you what he called his *Yachting* article describing the passage, because that would give away the fun.

Suffice it to say that Alf Loomis and a number of other sailors he described as "old-timers" (he, himself, was an ancient 43 at the time) were lured to sea by Mr. Barnum to help him waft the schooner *Brilliant* across the Atlantic on the wings of the predicted gentle westerlies so she could then be driven hard in the Fastnet Race. Off they went, but instead of gentle westerlies the breeze seemed to hang in the south from one point forward of abeam to one point abaft the beam and vary in strength from moderate to strong.

The breeze held like this for two straight days, and the crew was beginning to grumble to

Mr. Barnum that the cruise was not as advertised. Instead of fanning along upright, her people getting sunburned, the *Brilliant* was well heeled over on the starboard tack, romping along with wet decks, and her people either hunched in the cockpit in oilskins or well chocked off below against the roll.

At the end of the second day, Alf Loomis plotted in his position and remarked that they had sailed over 200 miles in the previous 24 hours. He said he had noticed, as a matter of fact, that they had also sailed over 200 miles the day before. The old-timers, out for a pleasure cruise, looked at each other and looked at Barnum. The latter addressed his ancient crewmen somewhat thusly: "Boys, set the genoa jib and be damned quick about it." And then: "All right, boys," from the depths of the sail bin, "we'll put a couple of topsails on her."

So they drove the *Brilliant* under mainsail, foresail, fore staysail, genoa jib, main topsail, and fisherman staysail.

Mr. Barnum said they ought to take the big jib off her when it got dark, but, strange to relate, it never did get dark on that particular night in the middle of the Atlantic — at least it must have stayed light — because the old men left the big sail right on her.

And the breeze held. The *Brilliant* averaged over 200 miles a day for five days in a row. And one of those days was a paltry 160 miles. On the sixth day she did 214. On the seventh, 202. Now she had done 1,448 miles in seven days, and she had done over 200 miles each day for the last five days — 1,077. She ended up averaging over 200 a day for nine days, and in 10 days did 1,976 miles, for an average speed of 8⅓ knots. Her best day's run was 231 miles, not quite 10 knots.

She had light weather at both ends of the transatlantic passage but still was land to land, Block Island to Bishop Rock, Isles of Scilly, in just short of 16 days, and City Island to Plymouth in 17 days, 18 hours. Some sailing for a heavy cruising schooner!

To put the *Brilliant's* achievement in perspective, it is interesting to look at some other sailing records.

On a whole different scale, the 185-foot, three-masted schooner *Atlantic,* designed by William Gardner, averaged over 10 knots from Sandy Hook to the Lizard, 2,925 miles, in winning the transatlantic race in 1905. In 1980, the 58-foot French trimaran *Paul Ricard* sailed this same course at an average speed of more than 12 knots. The 73-foot ketch *Windward Passage* averaged over 10 knots in 1971 in both the 800-mile race from Miami to Montego Bay, Jamaica, and the 2,225-mile race from Los Angeles to Honolulu. Francis Chichester in the *Gipsy Moth V,* a staysail ketch 41 feet 8 inches long on the waterline, sailed singlehanded 1,081 miles in five consecutive days in the Atlantic in 1970. Alain Colas in the *Manureva* (ex-*Pen Duick IV*), a 69-foot trimaran, sailed singlehanded around the world in 1973 covering 4,500 miles in 22 days on the passage from the Cape of Good Hope to Cape Leeuwin, his best day's run being 326 miles. At any rate, the cruising schooner *Brilliant* is rubbing elbows with some pretty fast company. One of her crewmen in the 1932 Bermuda Race, Graham Bigelow, whom Alf Loomis called "The Old Gray Poet of Norfolk," wrote:

> "Fannies wet all day and night,
>   *Brilliant* sailing like a kite.
> Get that damned club topsail set,
>   Just to make us curse and sweat.
> Set the guinny on the sprit,
>   Sheet her down and watch her split.
> Gulf Stream squalls we drive right through.
>   *Brilliant,* here's to you!"

When Adrian Lane was the *Brilliant's* skipper and Biff Bowker was her mate, they told me the *Brilliant* was about the finest schooner anywhere on the East Coast. I wasn't about to argue with them. She's impressed me with being just that since the first time I saw her.

Chapter 22

The *Susan*

The Susan *was the last, the smallest, and, in some ways, the best of Murray Peterson's wonderful schooners. She is certainly the most affordable. When they saw her plans published, a number of prospective builders inquired about large-scale plans. Happily, these requests could be forwarded to Murray's son, Bill.*

Bill Peterson believes a dozen Susans have been built since the original was launched. Arden Scott, a sculptress in Greenport, Long Island, built a lovely Susan, and, soon after rigging her, sailed her in a Gloucester schooner race and won. Sadly, my friend Nelson Bevard was prevented from finishing his when his company moved him far from salt water.

It only makes sense to try to sail a sistership of a boat you are considering building before committing all those resources to the project. If that is impossible, the next best thing is to try her out in your imagination.

Let's say we are thinking of building a Susan and have ideas of going voyaging. One important trial I'd want to give her would be working to windward at sea in a fresh breeze that gradually increases to gale force. Care to come along? Bring your foul-weather gear.

The breeze is fresh, and she's full and by under all plain sail: full mainsail, foresail, and jib. We already have our foul-weather gear on, because the whitecaps are gathering force as it breezes up, and the spray has started to fly. We're driving her a little; the rail is well down, and now, in the strong gusts, she's wetting the top of the bulwarks, even between seas. Big whitecaps are everywhere, and the seas are building. If this weren't a trial, we'd already have a single reef in the mainsail. Now that we've found she can lug her sail when asked to, let's go all the way to a second reef in the mainsail. There. That puts her back on her feet and slows her down enough so she's not jumping at the seas.

On it comes. Thirty knots now, a moderate gale, seas heaping up, foam blowing down them in streaks. We're driving her too hard again. So we pull the jib to weather, parbuckle the club to the fore shroud, and ease the mainsheet to get her comfortable. Tie the third reef into the mainsail. Now we run her off, sails sheeted in to slow her down, douse the jib and put a good, snug furl on it in the relative quiet. Say, these seas are building, aren't they? Some elevator ride up here on the bow.

And then we put her to it, by the wind again. Foresail and triple-reefed mainsail. Must be blowing nearly forty now, a fresh gale. She staggers a bit, the occasional steep one all but stops her, but she's still making to windward. Bravo! But, enough. In mainsail. We put two reefs in the foresail, smothered in spray once, as a breaker slaps her side. Now, trim the little, double-reefed foresail in flat, lash the wheel hard alee, and let's tumble below. Ah, so quiet and snug down here. Let it roar. We've another reef to go, if need be. And we've bare poles. Into a lee bunk with a thriller. Some fine little vessel.

Length on deck: 28 feet 6 inches
Length on waterline: 22 feet
**   10 inches**
Beam: 9 feet
Draft: 4 feet 1 inch
Sail area: 460 square feet
Displacement: 6½ tons
Designer: Murray G. Peterson

The coast of Maine is as elegant and complicated a piece of geography as anyone could want. Some folks wax enthusiastic over its islands, some over its big, protected bays, and some over its long, beautiful rivers. There are a lot of fine places for people who are addicted to boats.

There is one really great spot that I have been lucky enough to be introduced to. It reminds me a lot of the cove on the Pawcatuck River in Rhode Island where I fooled around in little boats a "few" years ago. This Maine place is a cove just far enough up a river to be quiet from the sea. There's even a ledge that goes just under at high tide to protect the cove from the river. The ledge discourages strangers, but behind it is just enough swinging room for a few boats.

Ashore on the point is, first of all, a big stone dock with a nice old boathouse on it. It used to be a fish shack in bygone years.

Up the grassy slope from the boathouse is a lovely, sprawling house-and-barn, the first part of which was built before the Civil War. All around are woods, except for that big grassy slope.

Tucked away upstairs under the eaves of the fine old house is a paneled room reached by its own narrow, twisting staircase. Small windows look out onto the cove. There are big drawing tables, plenty of drawer space for boat plans, shelves of the best books about boats, interesting guns, paintings of handsome vessels, a rigged model of Slocum's *Spray*.

This is the home of the Peterson family. This is the room where Murray G. Peterson designed his schooners. Here William Peterson, Murray's son, carries on his late father's work, making available his father's plans and providing expert advice and assistance in the construction of Peterson-designed vessels.

This is where I recently saw some handsome bronze fittings for a 28-foot schooner designed by Murray Peterson and being built in British Columbia by a good friend of mine, Nelson Bevard. Bill sold Nels a full set of working drawings for the handsome little vessel and will provide construction advice and help. What a good thing for Murray Peterson's son to be doing.

And what a fine vessel is this schooner, the *Susan*. Mr. Peterson designed her a dozen years ago when he was 60 years old. Wrapped up in

Murray Peterson.

the design for this schooner is a lifetime of experience and thinking relating to just this type of boat. Mr. Peterson's specific idea for the design was a boat that would be easily driven in a light breeze and that would also be very seaworthy.

The *Susan* was beautifully built in Camden, Maine, by Malcolm H. Brewer. Her planking is 1-inch cedar on 1½-inch-square oak frames 9 inches apart. She is 12 years old and hasn't leaked yet.

Murray Peterson sailed the *Susan* a lot and got more pleasure out of her than from any of the dozen other boats he had owned during his lifetime. She is still moored for six months of each year in that cove behind the ledge, and Bill and his wife and mother, for whom the boat is named, often sail in her, standing down the river, and letting her feel the ocean swell. She's well cared for and well sailed.

The *Susan* is 28 feet 6 inches long on deck, with a waterline length of 22 feet 10 inches, a beam of 9 feet, and a draft of 4 feet 1 inch. Her schooner rig has 460 square feet of sail. Her displacement is 6½ tons.

She's the biggest 28-foot boat I ever saw. Approaching her in a dinghy, you notice a certain slab-sided look amidships that makes her seem rugged rather than clumsy. From right astern, her transom looks absolutely massive. You'd swear you were looking at a 60-foot schooner rather than at a 28-foot one. If anything, the illusion is heightened when you step on board. Because of her high freeboard, heavy displacement, and the wide deck space allowed by her small houses and protected by her 7-inch bulwarks, she gives you the feel of a much bigger vessel than she really is.

The *Susan* has short ends and high sides; she's very dry for a 28-foot boat. Murray Peterson gave her a rugged spoon bow rather than his usual clipper bow, because he felt that the form of the clipper bow would be too restricted on a boat less than 30 feet long.

She certainly has a perky sheer. Her draft has been kept moderate. She has very easy bow and buttock lines for such a short boat and a well-formed run.

Her sections are easy from the turn of the bilge to the bottom of the keel. She has a

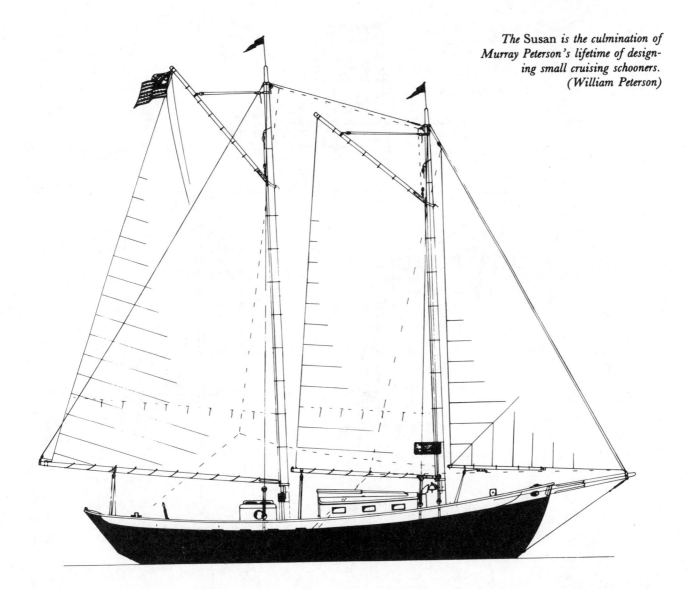

The Susan *is the culmination of Murray Peterson's lifetime of designing small cruising schooners.*
(William Peterson)

reasonably fine, straight entrance. There is lots of bearing aft. Her rudder is well aft and nearly vertical.

Henry Bohndell of Rockport, Maine, made her sails and rigged her. Bill Peterson says that not even a serving has let go in 12 years.

The single headsail makes good sense in such a small schooner. The *Susan* has a good-sized overlapping jib to set in light and moderate weather. Her tall, narrow foresail with its rather long gaff needs, of course, a vang.

Murray Peterson drew up a number of different rigs for this design, of which I show a jib-headed cutter and a gaff-rigged knockabout with a topmast. Partial as I am to two-masted rigs with their great versatility, and partial as I am to bowsprits with their utility and grace, I

really like the looks of that gaff-rigged knockabout sloop. It's the fastest of the three rigs shown. And see how the absence of a bowsprit emphasizes the husky, able look of the *Susan's* hull.

That topsail would be more fun to play with than a barrel of parrots and would really help her along in a light air. Think of the huge balloon jib you could set sheeting to the end of the main boom! Naturally you'd need, to go with it, a topmast preventer backstay set up to the weather quarter to hold things together.

I'd want a third deep reef in the mainsail.

I can hear all three of these rigs crying out for nicely curved gallows frames for their main booms.

Mr. Peterson designed a 6½-foot pram for

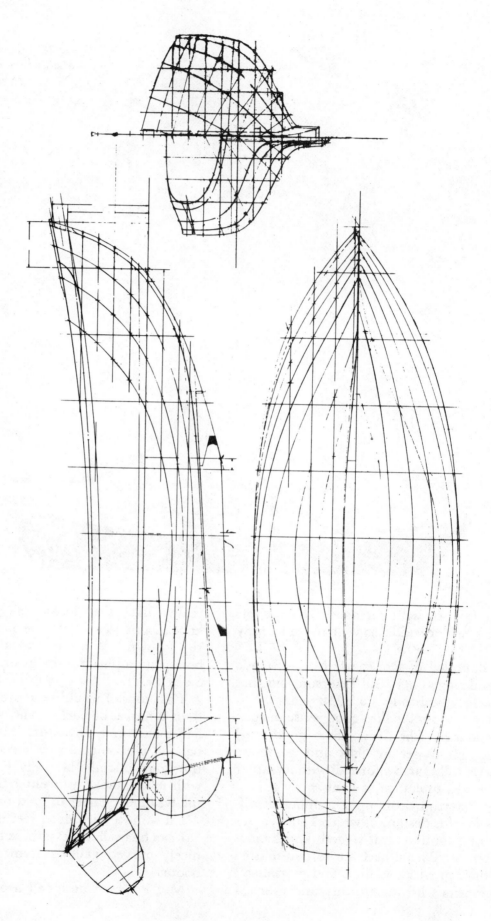

She has a husky, rugged hull and seems like a much bigger boat than she really is. Mr. Peterson said she sailed better than he had any right to expect. (William Peterson)

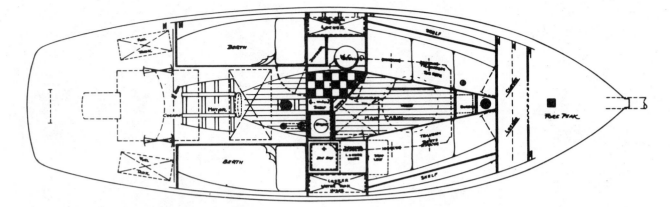

Above: *Her snug forward and after cabins give unusual privacy in such a small boat. (William Peterson)*

Left: *Her galley, with the companionway steps tucked away in the corner. (William Peterson)*

Below: *On deck, she seems like a big vessel. (William Peterson)*

The Susan *takes a handsome picture, whether at anchor . . .*

or with a big bone in her teeth. (William Peterson)

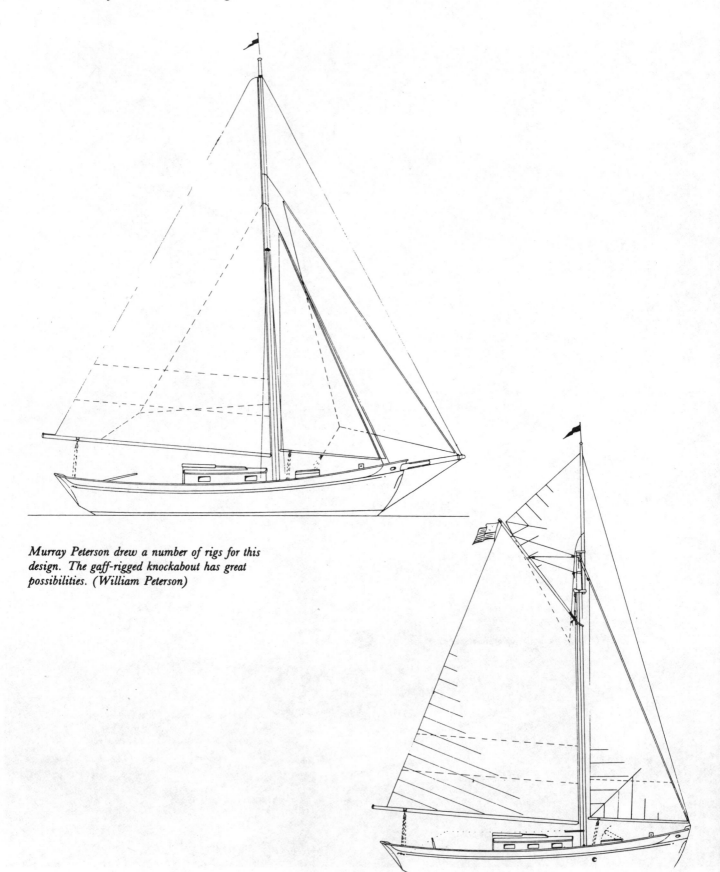

Murray Peterson drew a number of rigs for this design. The gaff-rigged knockabout has great possibilities. (William Peterson)

the *Susan*. She stows upside down on deck, leaning up against the forward house.

The pram is a shapely and burdensome little vessel. In the barn attached to the old house up beside that ledge-protected cove, Bill Peterson recently built a pair of these nice prams.

The *Susan* has no coaming around her cockpit well. I think I'd want one.

You go down the companionway at the after end of the forward house on a most ingenious ladder. The corner between the galley and the head has simply been filled in with triangular steps. They take up very little space yet are quite handy.

Murray Peterson loved engines and knew how to work on them. In his designs, he gave you plenty of room to get at the engine. While the engines in his boats were always ready to run, it was hard to persuade him to spoil a quiet sail by starting her up.

The *Susan's* engine, a 15-h.p. Volvo Penta diesel swinging a two-bladed propeller, sits right out in the middle of the after stateroom, which therefore must double as an engine room. Some folks would object to such an arrangement and would quickly box in the engine so as to pretend it wasn't there. But a nice engine is not a bad thing to look at, and if it's right in the middle of your bedroom you'll probably take good care of it. On the other hand, with such a handy little sailing vessel as the *Susan*, you could just leave the engine out altogether, given a small measure of patience in the crew.

You get to the after stateroom by ducking through the head. It's the kind of arrangement that seems cramped at first but that you quickly get used to.

The schooner has a pair of fuel tanks aft in way of the cockpit well and a pair of water tanks amidships outboard of the galley on the starboard side and outboard of the head on the port side. The latter tanks would seem to take up rather valuable space, and the design has been modified to put tanks under the after berths.

The forward cabin is a snug little nest. Its small house lets you stand up in the right places and gives six feet of headroom.

The cabin table has leaves that make it a perfect circle, and it can be unscrewed from its base and stowed away when not wanted.

There are lots of lockers in this little vessel, including a big hanging locker going right across the boat just forward of the foremast.

Murray Peterson said the *Susan* was a "lucky" combination of design factors and said that she sailed better than he had any right to expect. Well, there certainly may be some luck in this design, but there certainly is also in it the culmination of the work of a man who devoted a considerable portion of his great talents to designing small schooners.

I think the *Susan* is an ideal cruising boat, no matter which rig you choose.

Chapter 23

The Rozinante

Late in life, L. Francis Herreshoff had his friend O. Lie-Nielsen build him a Rozinante. The mental picture of Skipper Herreshoff beating up through the Marblehead harbor fleet in his lovely, nimble vessel was, alas, never to be realized. Herreshoff died before the Rozinante was launched.

She is now owned by Michael Reid. He is an ideal owner for her: He is an excellent woodworker, with the skill and patience to build furniture; he is a careful seaman with a conservative approach to learning his own limitations and those of his boat; and he loves the beauty and simplicity of this great creation of L. Francis Herreshoff.

The Rozinante obviously needed some work when Reid acquired her. He restored and refinished with great care, and then went beyond the obvious to perfect parts of the boat that were merely doubtful. He now knows his boat, and he knows that she is in good condition throughout.

Mike wanted to try the adjustable springstay arrangement that the Arete has, so one gray, late afternoon when his boat was anchored in a Maine cove, I gave him a hand lowering the mizzen mast, rerigging the stay, and restepping the mast. He had the job well planned, and it went quietly, methodically, and uneventfully.

Sailing a boat like the Rozinante is new to Mike. He's feeling his way, learning all he can from mentors, taking few chances, gradually extending the range of the waters he's willing to explore and of the weather he's willing to encounter. Mike loves to cruise in the Rozinante. He has kept her extremely simple, and he enjoys being at anchor, sitting in her cockpit at sunset or below in the evening with an oil lamp, absorbing the beauty of his little vessel.

My own feelings for the Rozinante are more exuberant. I had such fun sailing the Arete that when I wrote about her, I got carried away at times. As I reread this chapter, some phrases strike me as glib, such as talk of a raised pinky (not the schooner), or of a false mizzenmast tripling as steering aid, binnacle stand, and boom crutch. No matter. Let 'em stand. I still get pretty excited thinking about her.

I was right about that lasting impression. It's now ten years hence, and, when I remember sailing the Arete, I do think first of that delicate, pointed stern slipping through the water.

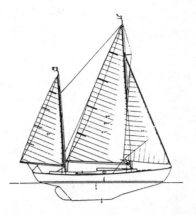

Length on deck: 28 feet
Length on waterline: 24 feet
Beam: 6 feet 4 inches
Draft: 3 feet 9 inches
Sail area: 348 square feet
Displacement: 6,600 pounds
Designer: L. Francis Herreshoff

Ted Sprague and I made each other a deal that neither one of us could refuse. Ted keeps a Rozinante in Rockport, Maine, but until he retired, he had to put bread on the table by working at his engineering job out in Ohio. I learned via boatyard gossip that he was to be separated from his boat for the summer, and since I have always wanted to sail a Rozinante, it wasn't long before I was on the phone to Ted, making him the sacrificial offer of looking after the lovely little lady for the season. Ted is a thorough boatman and knows well that it is far better for a boat to be used, kept clean, and kept ventilated than to sit forlornly on a mooring with no one to wipe away her tears. At any rate, fortunately for me, Ted said I could be the caretaker for the Rozinante canoe yawl *Arete*. Wow!

When I think back 10 years from now on the rare experience of sailing the *Arete*, I know very well the lasting impression that will leap to mind. It will be looking aft at that delicate, pointed stern slipping through the water. If you would have a boat, my friend, get one with a pointed stern.

There. As far as I am concerned, the preceding paragraph says enough about the Rozinante to put her right into the Hall of Fame. Nothing more need be said about the Rozinante, particularly in light of the fact that she is a heroine in that wonderful book, *The Compleat Cruiser,* written by L. Francis Herreshoff, her designer. But you know how publishers are. They always want more. All right, Mr. Publisher, here come more details about the great Rozinante and what she can do. But please, please let's not any of us lose sight of that lovely stern slipping along through the water. It represents peace.

The Rozinante brings to mind a violin, in a general sense because she is so perfectly designed and made for her intended purpose, and in the literal sense because of the lovely wood in her and because of her very delicate and finely tunable rigging. Underway, you find yourself tiptoeing around making gentle adjustments to things. It took me a long time to realize she wasn't going to break.

Mr. Herreshoff referred to her type as a canoe yawl, yet her rig is clearly ketch. He explained all this in the first of his series of articles about the Rozinante that was published in *The*

L. Francis Herreshoff on the roof of The Castle with Marblehead harbor in the background. (Muriel Vaughn)

Rudder and reprinted in his book *Sensible Cruising Designs:* "This little yacht is a small double-ender of a type that used to be called canoe yawls, and in the 1890s was a very popular type in England for cruising some of their delightful waterways like the Clyde, Firth of Forth, Humber, Mersey, and of course the Solent in days gone by. The canoe yawl is sort of a descendant of some of the sailing canoes that were used in these waters for cruising during the previous decade. The name 'canoe yawl' simply means a boat with a sharp stern that is larger than the usual sailing canoe, or about the size of what was called a yawl boat in those days. Admiral Smyth in his *Dictionary of Nautical Terms,* 1867, describes a yawl as 'a man-of-war's boat resembling the pinnace, but rather smaller; it is carvel-built, and generally rowed with twelve oars.' The term 'canoe yawl' in its day had nothing to do with the rigs these pretty vessels used, for among them there were sloops, ketches, yawls, luggers, and cat yawls . . . ."

Mr. Herreshoff goes on to say that a canoe yawl "should be a good sea boat and a fast sailer under a small sail plan." And, as a matter of fact, those are exactly my next most lasting impressions, after the stern of the Rozinante. I was

amazed at her ability to cope with rough water and always surprised that her seemingly tiny working sails could get her along so well.

One of the many pleasant things about the Rozinante is that you can see and enjoy the shape of her while on board, because she's open all the way through. If you don't pile too much gear in the ends of her, not a good idea anyway, you can see from the cockpit right up into the shape of her bow and right back into the shape of her stern, as she carries you dancing along.

The boat is 28 feet long on deck, with a waterline length of 24 feet, a beam of all of 6 feet 4 inches, and a draft of 3 feet 9 inches. Her sail area is only 348 square feet. Her displacement is 6,600 pounds, and her lead keel weighs 3,360 pounds.

She has very fine lines throughout, with a nice hollow at the waterline both in the bow and at the stern. Her sections are really fairly straight, especially forward, for such a shapely hull.

The sterns of the various Rozinantes I have seen look quite different from each other. The knuckle in the sternpost has to be shaped exactly as called for in the lines drawings, and the rake of the sternpost has to be set precisely as Mr. Herreshoff drew it, else the looks of the boat will be spoiled. On a couple of the Rozinantes I have seen, the knuckle is a bit too pronounced and the sternpost doesn't have quite enough rake. These boats lack the superb grace of the design as represented by Ted Sprague's *Arete.*

She has a very nice sheerline. I didn't measure, but I have a hunch that the *Arete* has just a tiny bit less sheer in her stern than Mr. Herreshoff drew. Both from on board the boat and from alongside in a dinghy, her stern doesn't seem to spring up quite as much as expected.

I will give only the essentials of the Rozinante's construction, since the details are given by Mr. Herreshoff in *Sensible Cruising Designs.* The planking he specified is either ¾-inch mahogany or ⅞-inch pine or cedar. Frames are steam-bent white oak, 1¼ inches by 1¼ inches. The wood keel is 12 feet 4 inches long by 2 inches thick and 14 inches wide, of white oak, yellow pine, or Philippine mahogany. Stem and sternpost are 4 inches thick by

2¾ inches wide at the inner faces, of white oak or hackmatack, or could be laminated of either white oak or Philippine mahogany. Floor timbers are 1½ inches thick, varying up to 8 inches deep, of white oak. Deck beams are 1 inch by 1½ inches, but 1½ inches by 1½ inches for three extra-strong beams, two at the forward and after ends of the forward deck hatch and one at the after end of the cockpit, the first beam abaft the mizzen mast, to be of oak, ash, or elm. Clamp is 1 inch by 2¼ inches "or more," of spruce or Douglas fir, "if possible in one length." Shelf is 1 inch by 1¼ inches of the same material as the clamp. Deck is tongue-and-groove strips ¾ inch thick by 3 inches wide, of fir, spruce, soft pine, cypress, or California redwood, covered with canvas. Cockpit coaming and house sides are each 19 feet long and ¾ inch thick of mahogany or oak (the former is far superior for this use, in my opinion). House beams are ⅝ inch by 1⅛ inches of oak, ash, or elm. The top of the house is ½ inch thick tongue-and-groove of pine, spruce, or Port Orford cedar, covered with canvas. Cockpit floor is teak slats, 1 inch wide by ¾ inch thick, spaced to leave an opening of ¼ inch between slats. Cabin sole is ¾ inch thick of soft pine, cypress, California redwood, "or other suitable wood." Cockpit seats are ¾ inch thick by 12 inches wide by 6 feet 6 inches long of soft pine (the *Arete's* seats are mahogany, which is elegant).

The deck and top of the house on the *Arete* are not covered with canvas. They are covered with an entirely different kind of material, one without the ancient tradition that canvas enjoys. Now it may surprise you to learn — it certainly surprised me! — that the use of this upstart replacement for canvas was condoned by L. Francis Herreshoff. In the chapter on the Rozinante in *Sensible Cruising Designs,* he wrote, "Fiberglass decks are said to be very good if painted with a non-skid paint." It really says that, right on page 83!

The *Arete* was very nicely built by Smith and Rhuland down in Lunenburg, Nova Scotia, in 1969. One departure the builders made from the plans is noticed quickly on coming aboard by all true Rozinante aficionados: there is a nicely rounded cap along the top edge of the cockpit coaming. This is an improvement, for you inevitably walk on that edge at times, and it also gives you a nice handhold when standing up in the cockpit facing to weather with the boat well heeled over.

A glance at the Rozinante's construction plan shows what a simple boat she is. True to her canoe yawl heritage, she's really just a big open boat partially decked over. With her stripped-out simplicity and her lack of an engine, her cost, Mr. Herreshoff estimated, would be about five-eighths that of the normal cruising auxiliary of the same size. One of the drawbacks to the design is the narrowness of her side decks in way of the cockpit. You can see in the construction section drawing just how little boat there is outboard of the cockpit coaming. Sitting on the weather side of the cockpit, you can't see the lee rail except at the bow and stern, and this mars somewhat the very great enjoyment of watching this boat work her way through the waves. Also, if she's being pressed and you wonder if she finally may have her lee rail down, you have to get up and lean over to leeward to see. (She seldom has.)

The mooring, kindly loaned to the *Arete* for the summer by my neighbor, Dr. Dana Sheldon, was out in the Sherman Cove part of Camden Harbor, where the views of hills and bay are spectacular but where considerable surge works in across the ledges when the wind is in the south. Working around on the *Arete's* deck was a bit precarious at first. She has a quick little roll and jump at times, and it does take time to get used to her narrowness. You keep thinking there will be more deck out there on which to catch your balance than there really is. Once, I actually stepped out over the coaming — onto nothing at all. Thank goodness for that cap on the coaming edge! I came to the conclusion that the most likely time to fall off the *Arete* is when she's at the mooring.

And her tiny, narrow stern deck is a bit precarious for working on the mizzen. A good, stout mizzen topping lift is important, because now and again you find yourself lurching against the boom when you're furling the sail and she's jumping a bit.

Then there is the problem of getting out onto that afterdeck from the cockpit. The *Arete's*

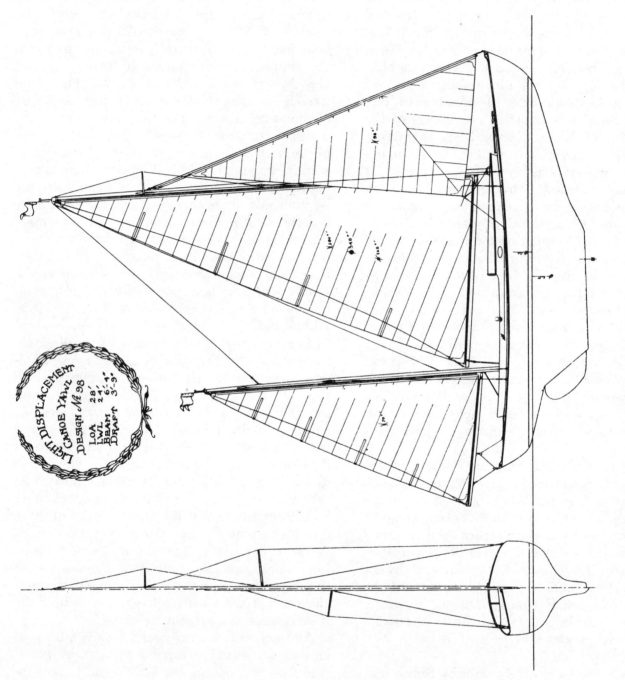

LIGHT DISPLACEMENT
CANOE YAWL
DESIGN № 98
LOA   28'
LWL   24'
BEAM 6'-4"
DRAFT 3'-9"

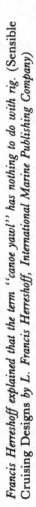

Francis Herreshoff explained that the term "canoe yawl" has nothing to do with rig. (Sensible Cruising Designs by L. Francis Herreshoff, International Marine Publishing Company)

The Rozinante has a delicately balanced set of lines. (Sensible Cruising Designs by L. Francis
Herreshoff, International Marine Publishing Company)

main backstay doesn't go to the mizzen mast as shown on the plans, but rather comes down to a two-legged bridle running to chainplates on the rail just abaft the mizzen shrouds. At times the mizzen mast, its shrouds, and the backstay bridle seem designed as a most effective obstacle course to keep you off the stern of the boat. I finally got pretty good at wriggling through and under, and by the end of the summer all that rigging hardly slowed me down at all.

There is no place on board a Rozinante to stow a dinghy. On such a small, narrow vessel you just have to put up with towing a boat. Why can't some genius design an inflatable dinghy that's truly easy to blow up — and deflate — and really rows well?

The big, deep cockpit of the Rozinante is fantastic. Its convenience and security more than make up for the boat's lack of deck space amidships. Just to begin with, it's a fine, secure, sheltered place in which to work at the mooring. Spread out tools and materials to your heart's content, or use the place for a sail loft down out of the wind. Mr. Herreshoff said the Rozinante's cockpit could take six comfortably for sailing; well, I'll go four, but when I use that word "comfortably," I mean people really have room to stretch out or move around a bit without falling over one another.

The thwart across the after end of the cockpit just abaft the mizzen mast is very nice to sit on and steer when she's not heeled over too much. When Weldon described the Rozinante to his friends in *The Compleat Cruiser,* he said this thwart was placed three inches higher than the cockpit seats so that the helmsman could see over the heads of his crew. In the *Arete,* the thwart is only one inch higher than the seats, but it is surprising how much even that small difference makes. In any case, it's good to have a choice of steering seats so you can sit facing forward or to leeward, just as you please.

The cockpit coaming slants outboard at an angle of eight degrees. Mr. Herreshoff designed the cockpit seats to rise coming inboard by that same angle so that the seats and coaming would form a right angle. The *Arete's* seats are nearer to level than that and are most comfortable, but I think they would be even better as the designer decreed.

The cabin doors are stowed away when not in use on slides under the forward ends of the cockpit seats. There's a hook at the back to keep them from sliding back out when the boat heels; Mr. Herreshoff designed a wedge arrangement for this same purpose that would be even handier than the hooks, which require a bit of kneeling down and looking and feeling back up under the seats to secure. About my biggest criticism of the *Arete* is that the lower pintles on her cabin doors should be longer so when you put the doors back on you can start the lower gudgeons on their pintles first, and then line up the upper ones, rather than having to line up both at once. I got really frustrated at times doing this in the dark in the Sherman Cove surge. I tell you it was a terrible hardship. The whole thing was probably the builder's fault rather than the designer's, for Captain Nat Herreshoff knew this trick, and I feel sure it wasn't wasted on his son.

The *Arete* has a big diaphragm pump permanently installed in the bilge at the forward end of the cockpit, discharging through a gate valve fitted at the waterline on the starboard side. This is a wonderful rig. The handle to the thing stows in clips under the after end of the starboard cockpit seat, so that if he needs to, the helmsman can be pumping the bilge in five seconds without leaving the tiller. The pump would not move as much water as a bucket, but it would certainly help out a lot, and would clear the bilge below the sole quickly.

For ground tackle, the *Arete* has a pair of yachtsman's anchors, one of 25 pounds and one of 15 pounds. Pete Culler used to say to put down your heavy anchor and sleep peacefully, and that is just what we did. Both anchors were stowed under the seats in the cockpit with stocks folded and together with their rodes if we weren't doing a lot of anchoring, and if we were, the 25-pounder was lashed on deck away forward with its stock hanging over the rail and snugged right up into the bow chock.

Mr. Herreshoff gave no companionway hatch to the Rozinante, saying it would cost $150 to build (a couple of decades ago), "and I would duck my head many times for that sum." The *Arete* has one, and I must say it's a very nice arrangement in the Rozinante. It makes a fine place to stand and watch her go.

The top of the *Arete's* companionway hatch,

and also of her forward deck hatch, are made of a thick, strong, transparent plastic. Aesthetically, these hatches leave much to be desired when compared with varnished mahogany, but they do let a tremendous amount of light below, and the transparent forward hatch, in particular, transforms what would otherwise be a dim forepeak into a bright place where even missing sail stops can be found. The place where my open canvas bag of oilies and boots was stowed happened to be right under the forward hatch, and it was somehow comforting in fine weather to be able to glance down there and see foul weather gear at the ready as I walked past. I guess I would prefer to keep the transparent hatch forward but to have a nice mahogany slide aft where you need the additional light less and where you see and use the hatch more.

The glass ports in the sides of the house look nice and let you look out from below. And, sitting on the weather side of the cockpit with the boat heeled over, you can look into the cabin and down through the lee porthole to watch the foam from the bow wave flash by. This makes up a little bit for the lee rail being hidden behind house and coaming.

Below, the after end of the *Arete's* cabin is taken up with considerable structure. At first it seemed to me that too much of the cabin was given over to this galley paraphernalia, but I later came to appreciate what is a considerable amount of solid storage and work space in so small a boat. On the starboard side is a big, deep icebox that kept cubes for five days in the Maine summer. There was also a flat for the usual two-burner kerosene stove. On the port side was a nice little sink with a wobble pump drawing water from a big (maybe as much as 20 gallons) water tank beneath it. On each side were counter space, lockers, and drawers. With all the food and cooking gear stowed away for a cruise, you still had one whole big, deep drawer in which to stow ship's gear, a first-aid kit, and a few simple navigational instruments.

Mr. Herreshoff designed a comfortable chair in one after corner of the cuddy. It was made like a canvas beach chair with the canvas forming seat and back in one piece and following roughly the contour of the hull. A neat arrangement, and one that I think would be an improvement in the *Arete,* for she has no truly comfortable place to sit and read below. For use north of Cape Cod, Mr. Herreshoff said, she ought to have a small coal-burning stove in the other corner. I heartily agree with this, and we sorely missed such a wonderful contrivance on at least a couple of occasions.

Forward, the *Arete* has the so-called double bunk of the Rozinante design. I never have figured out why everybody calls this a double bunk, what with the mainmast growing right up out of the middle of it. Anyway, it's most comfortable, whichever side of the mast you choose to sleep on.

The *Arete* has a W.C. under the bunkboards. It's a neat, out-of-the-way installation, but we found it so out of the way that we seldom used it, even after I cut handholds in the bunkboards (with Ted's kind permission, of course) so we could reach through to open and shut the intake and discharge valves. The bucket was far more convenient than the W.C. And, for males, even more convenient than the bucket was the lee rigging, main shrouds in moderate weather to take advantage of the mainsail as a curtain, and mizzen shrouds in heavy going because of the security of standing inside the coaming on the cockpit thwart (one advantage of the narrow side deck).

The fellow in the construction drawing smoking his pipe and doing his chores up in the fo'c's'le under the forward hatch looks more comfortable than he really is, I suspect. She's fairly cramped up in there.

It takes time, even in a small, simple boat like the Rozinante, to learn the best positions for doing things. It wasn't until near the end of the summer that I learned where to sit when getting lunch underway on a rough day. What you do is you put a cockpit cushion on the sill between cuddy and cockpit and brace your knees on the lee cabinet. You're secure, you can reach everything in the galley, and you can easily pass the results of your labors out to those eager hands.

My first impression of the *Arete's* spars and rigging was that everything was too light, but I was thinking in terms of the length of the boat rather than in terms of her displacement and sail area. The sails are small, for she is so easily driven that little power is needed to move her. Everything on the boat is so diminutive that you find yourself handling halyards and sheets daintily between thumb and forefinger (you can raise the pinky or not, as you wish).

Her mainsail has an area of 180 square feet, the jib has 98, and the mizzen, 70.

Quite complete details of spars, fittings, standing rigging, and running rigging are given by Mr. Herreshoff in *Sensible Cruising Designs*. To give an idea of the scale of things, the mainmast is 4½ inches by 3½ inches at the deck. Hardly massive. The rectangular spars are not as good looking to my eye as are round spars, but they are certainly less bulky.

The strut on the after side of the mizzen mast steadies the spar, which has no partners, since it stands in the open cockpit.

I'd be sorely tempted to raise both booms on the Rozinante by about three inches. The main boom does a little more head knocking than it ought to, and raising both booms would improve visibility to leeward. When steering from the thwart, I found myself peering to leeward through the crack between the foot of the mizzen and the boom.

Mr. Herreshoff's sail plan for the Rozinante shows the springstay making to a turnbuckle aloft on the mizzen mast. On the *Arete,* the springstay led to a rope tail rove through a fairlead on the side of the mizzen mast at the same position as Mr. Herreshoff's turnbuckle and then down to a cleat near the foot of the mast. This is a great rig. It was almost as much fun to play with that springstay as it is to play with the vang on a gaff. On the wind in a breeze, if the mizzen was luffing along lazily, taking a bit more strain on the springstay would flatten the sail right out and put it to work.

The halyards and sheets are all in the cockpit — with the exception of the jib sheets, which belay awkwardly on the outside of the outward-slanting coaming. Mr. Herreshoff shows no winches on the boat, of course, but the *Arete* has a small pair of jib-sheet winches mounted on the outside of the coaming, and I must say they are most handy. Perhaps a good rig would be that fancy kind of winch, right on the top of which you can belay the sheet. It's an awkward reach to the cleats on the outside of the coaming when she's driving along well heeled over and you go to cast off the lee jib sheet to tack.

The main sheet comes right to a cleat on the forward side of the mizzen mast, which just couldn't be handier. Its height on the mast produces just the right angle for the sheet so that no traveler is needed. The mizzen sheet comes in through a hole in the after end of the cockpit coaming and belays next to the tiller.

The *Arete's* jib may have been a bit shorter on the luff than the jib Mr. Herreshoff drew on the Rozinante's sail plan. At any rate, I let the tack of the sail up about eight inches off the deck, which made the sheet lead right, kept the sail a little drier when punching to windward, and, above all, improved visibility on the lee bow.

The *Arete's* only light sail is a small spinnaker, but she is not rigged with spinnaker gear. We set it a couple of times tacked down to the stemhead as a ballooner, but it was more of a conversation piece than anything else. We seldom felt the need for light sails. On the wind or reaching, the working jib seems to be plenty, and she is able to get along quite well with it. Well off the wind, we found that you ought to either head up high enough to just fill the jib, or else run right off wing and wing. Running before it with the jib blanketed and main and mizzen on the same side, the mizzen just about completely kills the mainsail. A good sail for the boat would probably be a balloon jib hanked onto the stay to pole out for running. Then you'd want to take in the mizzen.

We found the *Arete* would carry full sail to windward comfortably until it was blowing perhaps 18 or 20 knots. Then we'd take in the mizzen, and with that much breeze, she'd still have just the tiniest bit of weather helm under jib and mainsail. Then, if it kept breezing up, somewhere between 20 and 25 knots depending on whether we were feeling lazy or ambitious, we'd reset the mizzen and take in the mainsail. This is a rather drastic reduction of 110 square feet; if you were racing her, you would instead reef away, say, 50 square feet of the mainsail.

But jib-and-mizzen turns the Rozinante into a wonderfully easy-to-handle cruising boat that will sail well — including going to windward — in 20 knots of breeze or more. At 40 knots if it kept breezing up, you'd want a further reduction, and this could be made by reefing away, say, 25 square feet of the mizzen. For that, you'd want earings and reefing laceline all rove off, so that the sail could be reefed without leaving the cockpit. (I am going on about all this because the Rozinante is such a wonderful seaboat it is a shame to leave her tied up in heavy weather.) Then, for that really hard chance, it would be good to have a storm jib with an area of, say, 65 square feet. Under storm jib and reefed mizzen, she would be showing only 110 square feet of sail, and I think she'd be among the last boats of her displacement to be kept from working to weather in frightful wind and sea conditions.

Yet another advantage of Mr. Herreshoff's ketch rig in his canoe yawl is that she lies to very handily head-to-wind with the mizzen sheeted flat and nothing else drawing. I don't mean this as a heavy weather tactic. *In extremis,* she'd be better off running under bare poles dragging most of the rope on board (from amidships on each side, not from that delicate stern). But in any normal weather, if you want to stop for lunch or a nap, just take in jib and mainsail, sheet the mizzen flat, and let her lie quietly head-to-wind. Or, if singlehanded, when you come flying into a harbor and want to catch your breath before anchoring, round up, drop the jib, let the main sheet run, sheet the mizzen flat, and let her lie head-to-wind while you stow the jib below and get the anchor all ready to let go. All you need is a little clear space to leeward, for of course she'll go slowly astern. Or, when picking up the mooring, as soon as it's aboard, sheet the mizzen flat and she'll go straight astern until she takes up on the pendant instead of sailing all over the place. Or, when getting underway from an anchor when singlehanded, set the mizzen and sheet it flat, pick up the anchor and get it all washed off and stowed away while she goes slowly astern, then put on the rest of the sail and fill away. That mizzen transforms a prancing thoroughbred into a docile farm horse with the feed bag on.

The Rozinante's tiller arrangement is strange and peculiar. The tiller doesn't swing freely back and forth but instead hits the mizzen mast. You have to lift it a couple of inches to get it to clear the mast. And you have to reach behind the mast even to get your hand on the

thing! It all seems quite awkward — at first. But then you begin to get used to it and rather than trying to push the tiller through the mizzen mast, you get in the habit of automatically lifting it to clear. And you begin to realize that 99 percent of the time the boat is sailing along with a bit of weather helm so that the mast doesn't interfere at all! And you get used to reaching aft for the tiller.

Then, little by little, you begin to take advantage of that mizzen mast. If you want the tiller lashed amidships (as when lying to under the mizzen), rather than reach for a piece of line, you just wedge the end of the tiller down against the after side of the mizzen mast. And if you want her to steer herself for a couple of minutes while you go do something else, you just leave the tiller up against the weather side of the mast and go about your business. (If you have a Rozinante and want to astound friends who aren't used to her, just walk away from the helm. The tiller will fetch up against the mizzen mast and the boat will just keep right on going, but your friends, not realizing that this is going to happen, either leap for the tiller or look at each other as if to say, ''Why did we come sailing with a crazy person?'')

And then, unconsciously, you begin using that mast as a benchmark while steering. You find yourself reaching for it with your thumb and automatically gauging exactly the amount of helm you have on, using your thumb against the mast as a measuring stick. And that thumb quickly becomes an amazingly sensitive rudder angle indicator. By now you're ready to install false mizzen masts in way of all tillers. Such a spar might even triple as a binnacle stand and boom crotch.

The *Arete* had the 10-foot oar that Mr. Herreshoff recommended stowed away below as shown in the construction drawing. Her oarlocks on the cockpit coaming are perhaps 18 inches farther aft than the position shown by Mr. Herreshoff. The rowing position worked fine, however; there was plenty of room to stand up and pull facing aft, of course, and you could also stand up and push, bracing your back against the mizzen mast. You can move her along at 1 or 2 knots, 1 knot being a steady pace for

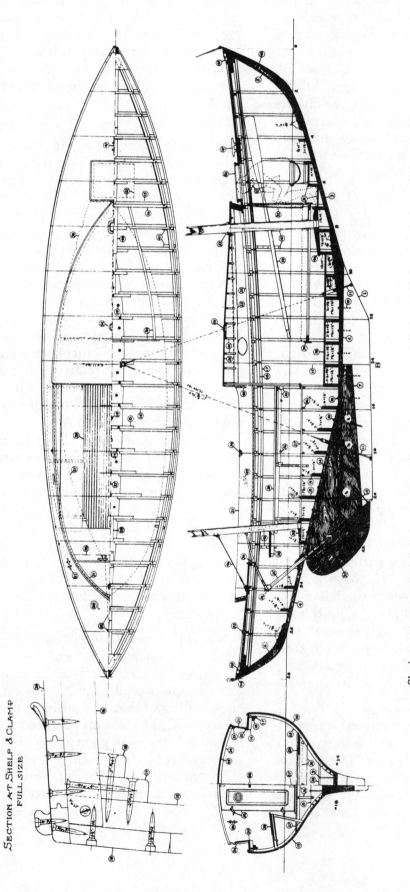

SECTION AT SHELF & CLAMP
FULL SIZE

She is not a roomy vessel, but she has a long waterline for her displacement. (Sensible Cruising Designs by L. Francis Herreshoff, International Marine Publishing Company)

distance and 2 knots being a sprint that most people couldn't maintain for more than a few hundred yards. The tiller arrangement comes in handy for rowing, because once you get her going, you can keep her going at a comfortable cruising speed with the tiller up against the mizzen mast on the opposite side to the oar, and that will keep her going pretty straight. This takes some practice, and it doesn't really work if you're trying to maneuver the boat in close quarters around a harbor, in which case a second person to steer is almost a necessity for good control. For any serious rowing of the Rozinante, though, I think the oar should be the longest possible contraption that will stow below, namely, something like 14 feet. That would mean it ought to have plenty of weight in the handle for balance, but such an oar would be quite superior, I think, to the 10-footer, which is a bit scant for such a big boat.

But the really easy way to move the Rozinante under oars, we discovered, is to tow her. With any kind of a decent pulling boat, you can add a full knot to the Rozinante's speed under oar by using the dinghy as a tug and towing the mothership astern. And with a short towline of about 20 or 25 feet, maneuverability in cramped quarters, such as coming alongside a dock, is excellent, for as master of the towboat, you can pull, twist, and nudge as the occasion demands. Towing a boat with a dinghy, even a boat much bigger than the Rozinante, tells you an awful lot about her: her weight, how she turns, her windage, how she carries her way. Towing the *Arete* certainly demonstrated — even more forcibly than ghosting along in a light air or driving through a big head sea shortened down to jib and mizzen — just how very easily driven is the Rozinante's hull. You can't believe you're towing a 24-foot-waterline boat.

The *Arete* has a 4-h.p. Johnson long-shaft outboard that stows neatly under the port cockpit seat and mounts on a simple bracket that fits into a bronze track, one of which is bolted to the outside of the planking just below the rail amidships on each side. We didn't use the motor much, but the few times we did, it seemed very easy to put on and take off, and it shoved her along easily at about 5 knots. We never discovered how much breeze it would push her in-

to, because if there is any wind at all, you can't resist sailing a Rozinante.

I had the *Arete* underway 30 times during the summer. Francis Herreshoff wrote of the handiness of the Rozinante for evening sailing, and that certainly proved to be true. We had a lot of afternoons of gentle to moderate to fresh southerlies on Penobscot Bay that summer, and it became a most pleasant habit to leave the office a bit after five, having picked up a crew or not, as the case might be, row out to the *Arete* on her mooring in Sherman Cove, tumble aboard, make sail, and be underway in five minutes, feeling her heel over and gather way to just fetch out through the spindles between Sherman Point and the ledges. Once in the Bay, we'd pick out just which hole in the islands would make the best sail full and by on the starboard tack. The late afternoon breezes were so constant in direction that it almost always turned out to be "let her go about so, below East Goose Rock to miss that sunker in there, then sharpen up a bit to weather the end of Lasell Island, and then let's shoot past 10 feet off the lee side of Goose Island and see if we can surprise the seals on the other side. Then we might as well let her go for Pulpit Harbor over on North Haven."

The people in Pulpit Harbor must have thought we were nuts. We'd keep sailing in there at six-thirty or seven in the evening and, instead of anchoring, spin her around and sail right back out again. Coming back across the Bay, we'd generally head up just to weather of Saddle Island and then have a nice reach for Camden. Some of the sunsets behind the Camden Hills were kind of pretty.

I expected the *Arete* to sail very well in light and moderate weather, but I did not realize how very handy, able, and dry she would be in a big breeze and sea.

I would not call her an extremely fast boat, but she is certainly quite fast. Of course we had a few brushes with other boats. She didn't quite hold a Scheel 30 to windward in a light breeze, but she sailed even with her on a reach. She worked away from a Tartan 30 on the wind in a moderate breeze. In a faint breath and perfectly smooth water, she wouldn't quite hold an Oxford 500 on the wind. On all these occasions, the other boats had big genoa jibs.

Sailing with Bill Peterson's 28-foot schooner *Susan* (described in Chapter 22), designed by his father, Murray, the *Arete* was a bit faster going to windward in a fresh breeze but was slower running in the same breeze and much slower running when the breeze eased up. But my excuse for being so badly beaten by the *Susan* running up the Damariscotta River is twofold: I should have had her wing and wing longer, as Bill rightly had his schooner, and we were towing a dinghy that was by then half full of water and had to be snubbed right up under the stern to keep her under control, where she was certainly making more waves than was the *Arete*.

I guess my conclusion as to the Rozinante's speed is that she is faster than most boats of her length, but not faster than all. Somehow that statement doesn't seem very helpful. Let's try another comparison: The fastest boat of the Rozinante's length that I ever sailed in was the *Aria*, my old Buzzards Bay 25-footer designed by Francis Herreshoff's father. (The *Aria* was described in Chapter 17. There is no doubt in my mind that the *Aria* would sail rings around the *Arete*, but the *Aria* was designed as an out-and-out racing boat. I never thought of the *Aria* as being at all hard to handle, but the Rozinante, by comparison, with her three little toy sails, is absurdly easy to handle.

I guess the most instructive sail I had in the *Arete* was the day Dana and Dorothy Sheldon and I went out for a couple of hours in the afternoon when it was blowing a gale out of the north-northwest. It was calm enough in the harbor, but out on the bay you could see little else but good-sized white breaking crests. We gave her the jib and mizzen and ventured forth. She poked her nose out around Sherman Point and began climbing over the steep head seas, still protected by the hills from the full strength of the wind. We laid her up close-hauled on the port tack and slanted out into the worst of it to see what she would do.

Well, she did just amazingly well. A couple of crests broke maybe six inches over the bow, but this foamy stuff washing aft was breakwatered away by the pointed forward end of the house. There was a bit of spray flying back over the cockpit now and then, but that was far more the exception than the rule. In the hardest gusts,

she put her lee rail perhaps just under, but it was clear she wasn't about to be overpowered with that amount of sail in that amount of breeze, and she was never in danger of shipping water into the cockpit to leeward. Best of all, she drove to windward at as much speed as you wanted in that sea, and she had the power to keep accelerating in the hardest gusts of all.

We all agreed it was difficult to estimate the strength of the wind that day, because it wasn't steady. It was what you think of as blowing 35 or perhaps 40 knots, but that really means that it probably never blew less than 15 or 20 and gusted to 35 or 40. Probably some of the short bursts were a bit heavier.

It was grand going, but my agreement with Ted had been one of caretaking, not testing to destruction, so before long we tacked and hightailed it home. Off the wind, she was as docile as a lamb and steered no harder than she ever does.

Another interesting time was beating out past Whitehead Island at the south end of the Mussel Ridge Channel on a sail from Camden to Friendship. It was blowing 25 to 30 knots; we had her under jib and mizzen. We had just picked up a nice fair tide. "Nice" is probably the wrong word, because that current did a good job of heaping up the head seas as it poured out of the Mussel Ridge. The roughest water lasted only 500 yards, and Bob Howard and I were about to congratulate ourselves on getting through it in one piece when a couple of seas must have combined into one and along came a high, steep, freaky-looking thing. The *Arete* climbed it with equanimity, but then her bow fell down into the huge gaping hole on the far side of it and her stern pounded down on the back side of it with a jarring crash. As the stern dropped away from Bob, leaving him hanging onto the coaming six inches above the cockpit seat, he shouted, "Some . . ." And as he caught up with the seat again, out came, " . . . boat!" At the same time, I was thinking, "Some wave!" But Bob was right. The boat certainly was more remarkable than the wave. It took me a little time to realize what had happened. Usually when the bow of a boat dives into the ocean and there's a great crash, it means her bow has pounded. But the *Arete* didn't pound

The Arete *working out of Camden's inner harbor. (Bill Page)*

her bow; she dove into that hole beyond the big sea, finally fetched up on its bottom, pitched back the other way, and whaled the backside of the receding sea with her stern. In the old days, she would have been saying, "Take that! you sunuvabitch," but in this enlightened era, I suppose she was saying something like, "I am very upset with you because you display your power like that and toss me about and I become quite anxious." Either way, old ocean ain't going to do nothin' but just keep on heapin' up and rollin'.

I never had the *Arete* running in a heavy following sea. Her stern is so fine you wonder if it would always lift in time. Ted Sprague says he hasn't run her off in really rough water either, but as an experienced inlet runner, he wonders how she'd do in such conditions. My guess is she'd do just fine, but it's only a guess.

But now we come to the real crunch of thinking about this wonderful Rozinante as a boat for sailing in rough water. Francis Herreshoff wrote, "Best of all a canoe yawl can be about the safest vessel that can be had since her design is based on those most seaworthy open boats ever known — whaleboats. Rozinante is a partly decked-over whaleboat with a ballast keel that will make her non-capsizable." Clearly this statement is made in the context of coastwise cruising and daysailing, not offshore pas-

sagemaking, yet still it may be a bit too strong. After all, the Rozinante is basically an open boat carrying around a big chunk of lead. If a large quantity of water enters her cockpit opening, she will sink like a stone. The question is, of course, what is the risk of that happening on a boat that is to be sailed coastwise, not across oceans? That question leads to the related one, "What is the likelihood of being caught out?" Will the Rozinante ever be caught so far from shelter that she cannot escape the wrath of a rising gale before the seas get really big and dangerous? Well, I for one am willing to take that risk, because if I find myself in that situation, I will have made so many consecutive errors in judgment — not to mention having lost sight of the very purpose of cruising — that I will deserve to lose the vessel and drown.

Keep the Rozinante within striking distance of protected water and she will, I believe, stand as much wind and sea as she will encounter.

Now, through all these words, I hope you haven't lost the feeling of the *Arete's* lovely, pointed stern, slipping away and away through the water. When you leave her to row ashore in the dinghy, examine that stern. Get its shape really in your mind. And then pull up ahead and look at the Rozinante from right forward. Can it be that that little slip of a skinny thing has carried us so far? She has.

Chapter 24

A Fast Ketch

After Francis Herreshoff's design of this lovely double-ender was published, O. Lie-Nielsen used to come calling at my office to try to sell me on the idea of having him build her for me. He had admired the design for years and was itching to see her take shape in his boatshop. He knew I'd fallen in love with the boat and hoped I'd tell him to order lumber. I had to explain about the purchasing power of a sailor operating a small book-publishing company, a publisher with no rich uncle.

Lie-Nielsen's visits always triggered a recurring daydream: As in the last sentence of the chapter, I'd be standing at the ketch's wheel, working her to windward in a fresh breeze. She's one of those boats that wants to eat up to weather. When I see the water darken just beyond her windward rail, and feel her heel to the gust and accelerate, I can ease the wheel up a spoke, let her lay her nose maybe a full point closer to the wind without slowing down at all, then meet her and put a spoke or two of weather helm back on to head her off as the puff passes. The soapsuds are hissing down her side and frothing rapidly away astern, trailing a bit to leeward. She's prancing easily over the seas and using the wind in a magical way, as if intent on reaching its very source. I think this one might just be another lottery boat.

Length on deck: 55 feet
Length on waterline: 44 feet
Beam: 10 feet 6 inches
Draft: 7 feet 6 inches
Sail area: 1,000 square feet
Displacement: 15 tons
Designer: L. Francis Herreshoff

Vessels have surely been raced from the beginning. What sea captain worth his salt, whether he be in command of an elegant clipper ship or a crude dugout, wouldn't want to test his craft against the competition?

Yachts designed strictly for cruising get raced too, of course, on both a formal and an informal basis. Some of the greatest feats of race-winning occur when the master of the losing yacht in a match race never realized a race was on. Later, the winning skipper tells his friends, "Why, you should have seen the good old *Vindicator* sail right past the *Sally Ann* this afternoon! It was if the *Sally* was hove-to." He fails to mention that the *Sally Ann* was under reduced sail in a moderate breeze, her gang concentrating on a couple of mackerel jigs astern.

Races are organized for cruising boats with limits on light sails and crew carried, specifications on minimum accommodations, or various combinations thereof. Such restrictions generally produce good cruising boat racing for a few seasons before some sea lawyer figures a good way round it all and cleans up. Then you have to start all over again.

Cruising boats should be raced on occasion. It's good for boat, skipper, and crew to have to drive the boat occasionally at her maximum speed over a prescribed course, including windward work. It's particularly beneficial for a cruising boat to race in hard weather, for it is under such conditions that you learn things about your boat that you wouldn't learn if you were cruising under the same conditions. It's a good thing to know just how much driving she really will stand. Better to find the weak points in hull and rig racing round the buoys in a breeze than up against a lee shore in a hard chance.

L. Francis Herreshoff devised a rating rule for the racing of cruising boats in 1931 for the Corinthian Yacht Club at Marblehead, Massachusetts. The rule was based on a given sail area for each class, such as 500 or 1,000 square feet. He designed a lovely 55-foot double-ended ketch as an example of what his rule might produce for the 1,000-square-foot class.

Mr. Herreshoff's rule provided for the standard rig and propeller allowances of the day, and he included penalties for excessive overhangs, low freeboard, narrow beam, lack of bulwarks, and small cabinhouses.

Francis Herreshoff's restricted sail area cruiser is 55 feet long on deck, with a waterline length of 44 feet, a beam of 10 feet 6 inches, and a draft of 7 feet 6 inches. She displaces 15 tons.

The sail area of 1,000 square feet is computed using 100 percent of the fore triangle, 281 square feet. The jib shown in the sailplan has an area of 300 square feet;

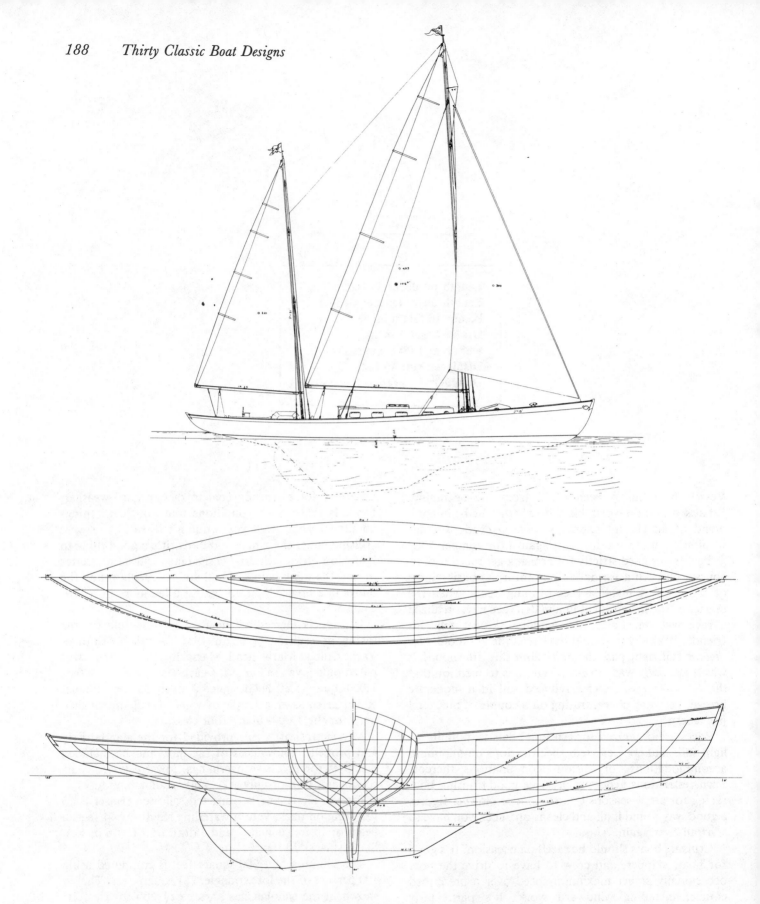

The sailplan and lines of the 1,000-square-foot restricted sail area cruiser. (Sensible Cruising Designs *by L. Francis Herreshoff, International Marine Publishing Company)*

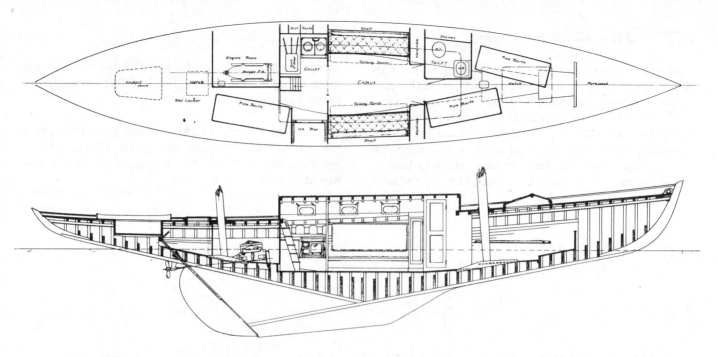

The 1,000-square-footer's interior arrangement. (Sensible Cruising Designs *by L. Francis Herreshoff, International Marine Publishing Company*)

thus, taken with her mainsail of 495 square feet and her mizzen of 221 square feet, her sail area is actually 1,016 square feet with the slightly overlapping headsail.

Under his own rule, Mr. Herreshoff's cruiser takes a slight penalty for too narrow a beam. The editor of *Yachting* at the time, Herbert L. Stone, thought that a loophole in Mr. Herreshoff's rule was the lack of reference to displacement, and that boats too light to make comfortable cruisers might be its unhealthy product. He also commented that Mr. Herreshoff's design had too little accommodation for her length to become a popular type.

The vessel is, at any rate, a sort of huge canoe yawl. There are many similarities between her and the *Rozinante*, a real canoe yawl designed by Mr. Herreshoff 25 years later. The big ketch has a very easily driven hull. Long and narrow, she would be fast and weatherly.

Her bow is certainly more rugged than her drawn-out, dainty stern, yet her profile looks in fine balance. She is quite cut away forward, her rudder is quite far forward and its post well raked, so there would probably be times when she'd be a bit hard to steer.

Look at her lovely, long, flat run. Is there enough lift in her stern to cope with a nasty, steep, following sea? Yes, for her waterlines are quite full aft. She has a sharp entrance. Her hull lines exude speed.

She has easy bilges, considerable flare above the waterline, and deep-slung ballast; she'd have low initial stability, but it would be hard to get her rail under.

She'd have a relatively easy motion for such a deep, narrow boat.

The ketch rig of this vessel divides her 1,000 square feet of sail into easily managed parts, with her mainsail just under the 500-square-foot maximum decreed by Uffa Fox as the biggest sail one person can normally handle.

She could carry bigger jibs, but would seldom need them. Her running backstays could have an alternate forward lead for short tacking.

Francis Herreshoff said this boat would be very easy in a seaway and would be capable of being driven to windward with very little sail. Having sailed his *Rozinante*, I'd certainly agree. This big ketch would be some seaworthy. She'd stand a tremendous lot of breeze under jib-and-jigger and could work to windward under a storm jib and reefed mizzen in really frightful conditions.

The ketch's hull speed would be close to 10 knots; and she would turn in, I believe, a very high average lifetime speed, which is the kind of speed really wanted in a cruising boat.

The pram shown stowed athwartships across the sailroom hatch looks a bit awkward; perhaps she'd be better atop the house over the skylight. Such an arrangement would leave lots of deck space aft; between the after end of the house and the forward end of the cockpit you could spread around a few low deck chairs and chaise longues and things.

That separate sailroom would be a joy, as would the

separate engine room, which houses a Scripps F-4. This boat would be quite fast under power. Note the propeller coming out above the deeply buried rudder.

The ketch's accommodation plan is quite normal, with galley aft, saloon amidships, and head and bunks forward. Her five bunks are all slung on hinges, so you could sleep reasonably level however she was heeled. That quarter berth would be a nice place for the next person on watch, tucked back out of the way but still quite handy to the deck. There's 6 feet of headroom under the house.

Racing or cruising, this Herreshoff ketch would be a wonderful boat. Standing up to her wheel and just watching her beat her way to windward in a breeze would be quite an experience.

Chapter 25

The Doughdish

The Doughdish is the greatest small daysailer ever, but with all her fine qualities, the best thing about the Doughdish for me is that she brought me together with Bill Harding. Since his invitation to come and try out the boat (the resulting sail is described in the chapter), we've become good friends. We've sailed together in the Ben My Chree, *the great, 26-foot daysailer designed by Francis Herreshoff that Bill rediscovered and has reproduced as the Stuart Knockabout, and we've sailed in the first of the reproductions. Whenever I'm cruising within striking distance of Hospital Cove, by sea or land, I make it a point to anchor off Bill's dock and go ashore*

for a yarn or pull into his driveway for a gam. He made a new mainsail for the Goblin, *a sail we had a lot of fun designing. Now we're fussing over just the right reaching jib for her.*

Bill reports he has now built 304 Doughdishes, so he's approaching the number built by the Herreshoff Manufacturing Company itself. You still don't get a topping lift on your Doughdish, unless you insist on it. Bill says as long as he has two arms, he doesn't need a topping lift. But I still say. . . . Well, you can read what I say in the chapter.

Length on deck: 15 feet 10 inches
Length on waterline: 12 feet 6 inches
Beam: 5 feet 10 inches
Draft: 2 feet 6 inches
Sail area: 140 square feet
Displacement: 1,500 pounds
Designer: Nathanael G. Herreshoff

Bill Harding hoisted the jib on his Doughdish with the mainsail still in stops, and I was just about to shoot him a questioning glance when he sheeted the little sail flat, spinning the boat round and running her off the wind. I hadn't even seen him cast off the mooring.

We loosed the mainsail and set it. Bill motioned me to the tiller, and off she went on a broad reach out of Hospital Cove, Cataumet, Cape Cod, with full sail set to a fluky southerly that was gentle to fresh at times and mostly moderate.

The first thing I noticed is that you can see all around in this boat, for the boom rises at a jaunty angle.

The second thing I noticed was that she feels like every other Herreshoff I have ever sailed: fast, responsive, and a thoroughbred in every way. The Doughdish has the usual Herreshoff weather helm, and in this case the boat is so tiny it's light as a feather.

She is pretty to watch go through the water when you're not on board her, as I learned when Bill dropped me off on the stern of a moored sloop out by Scraggy Neck so I could take some pictures.

Then we set out into Buzzards Bay, and I realized a lifelong dream: sailing in a Herreshoff 12½-footer — in the very waters for which the boat was created.

This dream had endured some hard times. To be sure, Pop was a great enthusiast of the 12½-footers, but

another of my mentors, Ed Cabot, used to heap great scorn upon them. The poor little boats were always the butt of his Buzzards Bay racing stories, and he could say Doughdish so quick it had only one syllable and you had a hard time believing in a boat with such a no-count name. But of course Ed used to race in the E class, the big Herreshoff 15s, and those great racing yachts would sail rings round a measly little 12½-footer. My dream was sustained one rough day, when we came upon a 12½-footer in the middle of Buzzards Bay reaching happily along under full sail with six grown-ups on board.

Some of the E boat racers thought their boats too much of a handful for their children learning to sail. Robert W. Emmons and others went to Nathanael G. Herreshoff in 1914 and asked him to design a smaller boat, more suitable for their children but still able to cope with the strong winds and big, steep chop of Buzzards Bay.

For Nat Herreshoff and the Herreshoff Manufacturing Company at Bristol, Rhode Island, 1914 was quite a year. A New York Yacht Club syndicate wanted him to make sure once again that the America's Cup stayed on the west side of the Atlantic; he kept the big mug here with a 75-foot-waterline cutter, the great *Resolute*. A wealthy yachtsman wanted a huge cruising schooner;

Herreshoff designed one and the yard turned out the 115-foot-waterline beauty, the *Katoura*.

And that same year the Wizard of Bristol was conjuring different versions of his two-year-old *Alerion*, a 22-foot-waterline sloop with whose creation he was well pleased. In 1914 the Herreshoff yard produced a near sistership, the *Sadie*, and two classes of larger modifications: four Buzzards Bay 25-footers and three Newport 29s.

Nat Herreshoff thought the *Alerion* type would do well too for this "Buzzards Bay Boy's Boat," as he called the little 12½-foot-waterline vessel on her sail plan (1914 was pre-E.R.A.). She is the sort of boat a boy might draw while looking out the schoolroom window on a spring day, with her nicely curved bow, raked transom, strong, simple sheerline, and high-peaked rig. The 12½-footer has as handsome a hull as you can find.

Bill Harding thinks Captain Nat may also have been inspired by the keel catboats in which he had learned to sail. And the 12½'s stern is quite reminiscent of the pretty transoms of the Bahama sharpshooters. I doubt that there is any Bahama connection, though. Probably Captain Nat gave the Buzzards Bay Boy's Boat her lovely, raked, wineglass transom, rather than the short counter sterns of the other *Alerion* types, just to get maximum room, carrying capacity, and stability in such a short, beamy boat.

We went out into the Bay full and by on the port tack. It wasn't one of those real rough-and-tumble Buzzards Bay days when the sou'wester whistles and the seas heap right up, but the southerly had worked up its own lesser breed of chop, and there were some decent waves for a small boat. She would thrash into a series of them, taking all your attention for a minute. Then when it calmed down you would look back over the lee quarter to see if all that commotion had stopped her, and lo, she's still charging along, just seeming greatly to enjoy the whole business. We knocked her off a point and, of course, she really loved that. A little container ship came out of the canal and rumbled past to leeward. Efficient looking. Plain, to put it kindly. I wouldn't want to have to steer her. The pilothouse is so far forward that the jackstaff on the bow would be right in front of your face. The only way to gauge her swing would be to look aft. Her steep bow wave was a lee sea for us, so we bore off a few seconds to take it on the bow.

After we headed up again, we decided we had time to go to Marion before turning back. Being in a small boat, we could cut inside Bird Island, so rather than having to jam her right up on the wind, we held our close reach. She went along just fine. Bill and I were enjoying ourselves hugely.

Nathanael Greene Herreshoff. (Captain Nat Herreshoff *by L. Francis Herreshoff, Sheridan House, New York*)

When the 12½-footers came out of the Herreshoff yard, they were called simply the "Buzzards Bay Class." The first one, contracted for on October 30, 1914, at $420, was Herreshoff Hull Number 744, the *Robin*. The dimensions given on the company's record of contracts are: length on deck, 15 feet 6 inches; waterline length, 12 feet 6 inches; beam, 5 feet 10 inches; and draft, 2 feet 5 inches. This record is handwritten; as near as I can make out, the name of the *Robin*'s owner is Stewart Duncan.

Eighteen more boats in the class were put under contract on November 14, 1914. These 19 boats were delivered for the 1915 season.

They caught on. A few more were built every year, another 38 boats having been added to the class by 1924. By this time the price had more than doubled, to $900. In the next seven years, the class really took off; by 1931, another 154 boats had been built. There was another big building spurt between 1935 and 1943 that produced 146 boats. This made 357 Buzzards Bay Class 12½-footers turned out by the Herreshoff Manufactur-

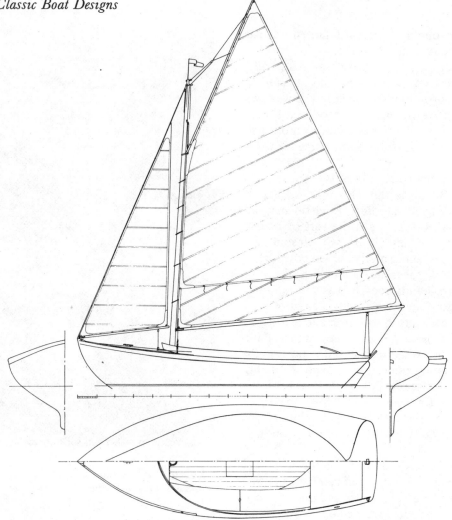

Plans of the Herreshoff 12½-footer Doughdish. (Doughdish Inc.)

ing Company. The price per copy had climbed to a high of $1,100 in the late Twenties and then dropped back to a Depression low of $790.

The first 12½-footer built with a marconi rig was Hull Number 901, D.W. Flint's *Wanderer Jr.;* she came out in 1924. The company began calling the marconi-rigged 12½-footers Bullseyes. By then scornful E-class racers were calling the gaff-rigged 12½s Doughdishes. To this day, Bullseye implies a marconi-rigged 12½-footer and Doughdish implies a gaff-rigged boat. Buzzards Bay sailors have kept to the gaff rig, while more fashionable racing classes in places like Marblehead and Fishers Island have fancied the marconi.

The boats may have been designed for boys to learn to sail, but girls, men, women, and old-timers of both sexes couldn't keep their hands off them. The

12½-footers were raced from the beginning, racing being thought to be good training for the young and good experience for the not-so-young. To say nothing of fun for all. Along the way, a single-luff spinnaker was added to the boat's basic equipment. In 1937, the Beverly Yacht Club had a fleet of 75 of these boats racing.

The last 12½-footer turned out by the Herreshoff Manufacturing Company was Hull Number 1518 in 1943. In 1947 and 1948, the Cape Cod Shipbuilding Company built 30 of these 12½-footers. The Quincy Adams Yard built 10. Occasionally you still hear of another 12½-footer being built. Just a few years ago McKie Roth built one for Andy Nixon at North Edgecomb, Maine.

Cape Cod Shipbuilding later came out with a fiberglass version of the Bullseye. They used the basic design of the 12½-footer, but the idea was not to duplicate the

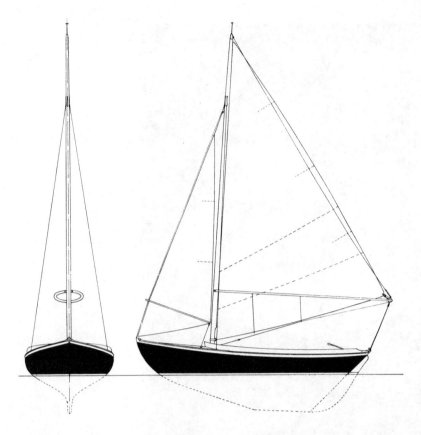

*About 1935, the Herreshoff Company came out with a "modernized" sailplan
for the Bullseye with wishbone booms on both sails.*

wooden boats. The Cape Cod Bullseye has less displacement than the original, has a cuddy molded into the
deck piece, and has aluminum spars. Some 700 of these
boats have been built. Willard Wight has several for day
charter in Camden, Maine, and every fall the locals race
them in the harbor before he hauls them out. I crewed in
one of these autumnal extravaganzas on a very blustery
northwest day and was well impressed with the ability of
the Cape Cod Bullseye to stand some heavy gusts. You
just can't beat a good design.

Bill Harding estimates that some 250 original wooden
12½-footers are still in commission. Many of these
boats are a half-century old; all are over 25. The biggest
concentration is still in Buzzards Bay.

The H Class Association was formed in 1972 for the
purpose of ensuring that the 12½-footers would keep
on racing. The association held its first regatta in July of
that year, and the next day Bill Harding got the idea of
making a fiberglass reproduction of the 12½-footer that
would duplicate the wooden original just as closely as
possible. It seemed the only way to keep the class going
indefinitely. To many Buzzards Bay sailors, a bay
without Herreshoff 12½-footers would be no bay at all.

Bill Harding teamed with Peter Duff, of Edey and
Duff, builders of the Stone Horse and other fine vessels,
to develop the construction details of a foam-core
fiberglass 12½-footer and to produce the boat. Naturally, they called their reproduction the Doughdish and
their company Doughdish, Inc. Bill runs the business;
Peter builds the boats. The company's headquarters is
at Bill's sail loft (Harding Sails) in Marion, Massachusetts.

For a model, Bill took the lines off his own Herreshoff 12½-footer, one built in 1936. He also measured
quite a few other boats to satisfy himself that his boat
was typical.

The given dimensions of the Doughdish are: length on
deck, 15 feet 10 inches; length on the waterline, 12 feet 6
inches; beam, 5 feet 10 inches; and draft, 2 feet 6 inches.
Her displacement is 1,500 pounds, with 735 pounds of
outside lead ballast. Her sail area is 140 square feet.

After a season of reproduction Doughdishes racing
with originals, the class organization accepted the
reproductions into the class. Doughdishes seem to sail
about even whether they are built of wood or foam-core
fiberglass. (The Doughdish beats a fiberglass Cape Cod

The Doughdish on her trailer. (Doughdish Inc.)

Bullseye in a breeze, but the Bullseye is a little faster in gentle going because of her lighter displacement.)

A reproduction Doughdish looks just like the original except that she has no frames visible inside and no seams visible inside or out. Bill Harding still has his 1936 12½-footer. She has been well cared for and is in excellent shape, but her hull is nowhere near as fair as that of her replica on the next mooring.

Bill Harding and Peter Duff have done a very satisfying thing in keeping alive one of the greatest small boat designs ever.

As we sailed along, Bill kept looking admiringly at the little boat he knows so well. He has sailed in a 12½-footer, just as we were doing, hundreds of times, but I could tell he still was fascinated to watch her go. "I couldn't live without one of these boats," he said. When he's not sailing a 12½-footer or making sails for one (or for some other boat), he likes to carve half models of 12½-footers. (His shop is right off his kitchen, so the models are handy to work on.) Bill says he never gets tired of carving that hull shape and of going over their form with a piece of sandpaper.

Bill Harding is a good sailor. In between watching that his little vessel was being sailed all right, he would stare hard around the horizon so as not to miss anything going on in his home waters. He would tend his peak halyard as the wind breezed up or eased off, or as we changed our point of sailing.

Once past Butler Point, we let her go off on a broad reach up into Marion. A big, handsome catboat came out making stately progress to windward. Bill the sailmaker noted how flat her big gaff mainsail looked in profile but how drafty you could tell it was after she went by and you could see the sail edgewise.

The boat population in Marion is 10 times what it was last time I was in there, some few years ago, to be sure. I was impressed by the general ugliness of the fleet, emphasized by the loveliness of the little boat we were sailing. We did find a Newport 29 hauled out at the head of the harbor and the Herreshoff Fishers Island 31 class sloop *Torch* on a mooring without her mast stepped yet (she was the *Scorpion* when she came out in 1930).

On a mooring up near the head of the harbor we found a green Herreshoff Fish class sloop that I used to

The Doughdish lifting along on a fast reach. (Doughdish Inc.)

see out cruising years ago. The Fish is a 12½-footer blown up to a waterline length of 16 feet. Bill luffed the 12½-footer right alongside the cruising Fish boat. She was as I remembered her except for the open cockpit, which I had thought was watertight. Her cabinhouse comes fairly well aft, so her cockpit is much smaller than that of a standard Fish boat. It's surprising to come upon a boat like that all of a sudden after not seeing her for 35 years.

We beat back out through the moored boats and worked up under the weather shore well out toward Blake Point before putting her about on a final starboard tack for home.

The Doughdish's Airex hull is ¾ inch thick; the material gives her a very strong, tough hull. She's generally less vulnerable in case of accident than is a wooden 12½-footer; and should she be damaged, is more easily repaired. One of the reproductions got ashore on Wing's Neck and pounded on the rocks for quite a while. Most of the damage she sustained was superficial, and she was repaired for $150.

The Doughdish has fiberglass decks and bulkheads. The decks are finished nonskid. The wood in the boat is teak. The beautiful stuff is used on the inner facing of the transom, the cockpit sole, the long cockpit seats, the nicely shaped coaming, the rail, and the wide sheer strake, molded to the traditional Herreshoff shape.

About 600 pounds of net positive flotation is built into the ends of the boat in the form of expanded foam behind the bulkheads. (The original 12½-footers had air chambers fore and aft for flotation.) So if she should swamp in a hard chance, she will keep you afloat until you can get her bailed out with a bucket or two. Two buckets take up the space of one bucket, but unless you are singlehanded, they bail twice as much water. Buckets are a great investment under any economic conditions.

The 12½-footer has a seaworthy hull. Her motion in rough water is corky but not uncomfortable, because all the lurches are damped out by her heavy keel. She won't pound or slap.

She can be wet because she's really very small, yet is

Hard at it. (Doughdish Inc.)

so seaworthy that you don't think twice about taking her into rough water — until the spray begins to fly. She is certainly drier than most boats her size.

The Doughdish's gaff rig is low and seamanlike. She has dainty Sitka spruce spars. Single shrouds lead from a cone-shaped masthead fitting that also takes the peak halyard blocks. She needs no backstays. A mast collar holds the mast up against the forward bulkhead while you set up the rigging, after which there is no strain on the collar.

The stemhead fitting is a neat bronze casting that makes the stem looked raised in profile like that of the original boat; it forms a sort of little breakwater for the eye for the headstay and jib club gooseneck.

The sails have no battens. They are nicely made of

Dacron, many of them tan, by, of course, Harding Sails.

The mainsail has one shallow reef. Usually I don't have time for shallow reefs, but I have to remember that this is a racing boat. I would have another deep one for the hard chance I hope always to avoid. I would judge that when sailing to windward the Doughdish would be helped by a reef when it breezes up to 18 or 20 knots.

She has one of those "self-tending" jibs that you have to push another inch to leeward every tack before you're really satisfied with its trim. The 12½-footers originally came with a storm jib, but the working jib is small enough so that such a sail is probably not necessary.

The Doughdish's running rigging is all sensible and

seamanlike as to size, purchase, and hardware — except that the boats have no topping lift on the main boom. And after all my preaching about what good and faithful servants topping lifts are! Ask a topping lift to hold the boom up out of the way for a minute or an hour and he jumps right to it. Tell him you no longer need him and he slacks right away without complaint, being careful not to spoil the set of the sail he serves. Why would anyone fail to ship such a crew? The Doughdish does have a nice little boom crutch, which is useful when the mainsail is furled.

Our starboard tack took us full and by back between Butler Point and Bird Island. Then we could crack off just a bit and head back for Cataumet, bearing off a little extra to let the tide set us up under Scraggy Neck. The breeze increased a little, particularly after we passed Scraggy Neck and began beating up into Hospital Cove. In fact, the day began to feel decidedly raw. True, we were a bit damp around the edges, for although the boat is so maneuverable you can run her bow right off with a cross sea, rendering it harmless, the occasional little wave would shoot up the side with glee to let its top blow in over the coaming. The veed coaming makes a good breakwater, but it's not always high enough.

Oar and spinnaker pole lash up under the cockpit seats out of the way. Bill says the way to row a Doughdish is to push with one oar and steer. Under the cockpit sole, Bill carries the little bronze Herreshoff anchor that came with his 12½-footer of 1936 vintage. There is a small stowage compartment worked into each bulkhead.

Some of the early 12½-footers had a thwart across the cockpit about a third of the way aft, and the side seats ended at the thwart. I think that would be a fine rig. You could shift your weight anywhere across the boat to trim her just right when running or in a light breeze. You could sit facing forward or aft as well as to the side; and the forward end of the cockpit would be unobstructed for sailhandling or scrunching down out of the wet. It might be intriguing to try a little spray hood over the forward end of the cockpit.

Steering, you can sit on the after end of either cockpit seat or also sit up on the stern deck facing forward if she's not heeling over too much. I always wondered if on a lazy run in a 12½-footer you would lollygag about all the way aft using the transom as a backrest. You wouldn't; it's not high enough. (Besides, your crew would have to go way up forward to keep the boat in trim.)

The great thing about the cockpit of the 12½-footer is that it has no centerboard trunk. All the boats this size I have ever sailed in have had them. I used to get yelled at when racing because I couldn't hurdle the thing and trim the jib at the same time. I am here to tell you that sailing in a little boat with no centerboard trunk is some kind of luxury.

It was nice to beat up into Hospital Cove in smooth water. Ahead of us, on high ground, was the nice old family cottage that Bill winterized for living in year-round. Below it, at the edge of a sandy beach, was the little boathouse where the Doughdish spends the winter.

We got in and tied up in time for a late lunch. The forecast had promised us rain all day, but since we hadn't paid any attention, it didn't get started till ten minutes after we got ashore.

I think it's just grand that the small Herreshoff classes — the 12½-footers, the Fish class, the Herreshoff 15s, and even the *Alerion* herself — are again available in well-built reproductions. Of all of them, the Doughdish is the most faithful to the look and feel of the original boats turned out by the Herreshoff Manufacturing Company.

If I had any sense at all, I'd trade my soul for a Doughdish and put her by for my old age. Put her by?

Chapter 26

The *Nimbus*

In thinking about the Nimbus *over the last few years, I have found myself wondering if the 35-foot version of the type wouldn't be a much better boat. She would be just that much faster, with her 6-foot, 8-inch longer waterline; Richard Henderson told me that he had trouble passing the 35-footer in his Kelpie, an Ohlson 38 that has won plenty of races. I think the bigger version would be easier to handle than the smaller, with more space and a steadier motion to outweigh the increased size of her sails. She has a watertight cockpit that makes her far safer in a knockdown. She has enough space below for a workable cruising cabin for two, something you can't really say for the* Nimbus.

A couple of years ago, Kathleen and I even looked at the 35-footer when we were thinking of living aboard. She was certainly cramped for a home afloat (and Peter Van Dine had no such criterion in mind when he designed her), but even so she was a little tempting to me, because she is so beautiful. Something I noticed when we were on board her, however, is that her cockpit seats are set too low; you can't see forward over the house when sitting at the tiller. Whether this mistake occurred in the design or in the building, it should be fairly easy to correct by raising the seats and, if necessary, giving her a higher coaming.

On the imaginary cruise in the Nimbus *used as an example in the Introduction to this book, I was tempted more than once to trade her in for the 35-footer.*

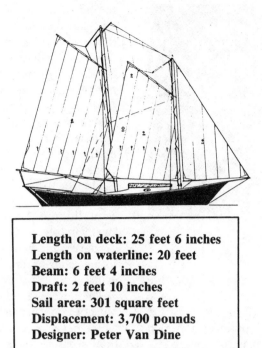

Length on deck: 25 feet 6 inches
Length on waterline: 20 feet
Beam: 6 feet 4 inches
Draft: 2 feet 10 inches
Sail area: 301 square feet
Displacement: 3,700 pounds
Designer: Peter Van Dine

Drew McManus, down on Cape Cod, used to have an interesting approach to boat ownership. He'd buy a new boat every spring, keep her in pristine shape while sailing her all summer, put her on the market in the fall, sell her in the winter, and be ready to repeat the cycle. Once he'd swallowed the initial capital investment, he didn't spend much of anything on boating, he had the enjoyment of boats in near-perfect condition without having to do a lot of maintenance work, and he got to try out a lot of different boats over a period of years.

I was Drew's customer for a 25-foot Tancook whaler designed and built by Peter Van Dine of Annapolis, Maryland, which enabled him to buy one of Phil Bolger's Dovekies (see *Still More Good Boats)* built by Edey & Duff.

Thus began what was for me a three-year affair with a lissome lady with whom I had no right to be hooked up. It's only now that we've been separated for a couple of years that I can bear to tell you about her.

The *Nimbus* is one of 12 sisters, all built by Peter Van Dine. He also designed and built a big 35-foot version of the type. These are rather close replicas of the Tancook whaler, the local fishing and fetch-and-carry boats of Tancook Island, Nova Scotia, well known for their beauty, speed, and seaworthiness. Peter researched the type carefully, came up with a hull shape that a Tan-

cook Islander would have been proud of, molded his hulls in fiberglass and built everything else in the boats of wood.

I thought *Nimbus* ("a rain cloud," but also "an atmosphere, as of romance, about a person or a thing") was a fine name for the little vessel, for more than one smallish fishing schooner has carried it honorably and, besides, the word was nicely painted on a pair of handsome oak quarterboards well secured to her topsides near the stern.

Of course I fell in love with her very fine, very pretty, slippery-looking hull. She has a perfect sheerline, a perfect hollow to her after waterlines, and a perfect curvature in her topsides. Her stem profile is just a little too straight to my eye; I always wished her clipper bow was more accentuated. She has quite a bit of drag to her keel, but enough depth of forefoot so a head sea didn't shove her bow off. She has very easy bow and buttock lines. Her entry is not as hollow as I expected for a Tancook whaler, yet she never stopped when hitting a sea and is just full enough forward not to root at all off the wind. She has lovely wineglass sections and flare in the topsides all around her waterline, which is important to the stability of a narrow, shoal hull. This flare all around the waterline also gives her a light and airy appearance in the water.

Peter D. Van Dine. (Robert de Gast)

The *Nimbus* is 25 feet 6 inches long on deck, with a waterline length of 20 feet, a beam of only 6 feet 4 inches, and a draft of only 2 feet 10 inches, with the centerboard up. She displaces 3,700 pounds, of which 1,600 pounds is ballast. Her sail area is 301 square feet in three working sails, plus another 100 square feet in the fisherman staysail.

Her ballast consists of steel punchings set in cement. The hull is all of a piece above this ballast, so she could pound on the bottom a bit without leaking.

Her outboard rudder is wood and its pintle-and-gudgeon arrangement — just a pin through two adjacent eyes; one lagged into the sternpost, the other into the rudder — is the only crude thing on the boat. It is just a little sloppy and lets the rudder stand out from the sternpost a little too far for really good looks. I was interested that one of her many admirers picked up on this minor flaw in her otherwise-perfect appearance and commented on it right away.

Her centerboard is asbestos cement covered with fiberglass; it is very light and easy to handle.

The little vessel was built by Peter Van Dine to a very high standard. Her molded fiberglass hull is extremely fair. Her deck is white cedar, strip-planked and painted; her cabin sides and coaming are white cedar finished natural. She has a nice oak toerail and a fairly heavy oak rubbing strake. Her cabintop is foam-sandwich fiberglass, well crowned and plenty strong.

The bulkhead between cabin and cockpit is vertical tongue-and-groove stuff. We never did succeed in getting this bulkhead fully watertight, which it certainly should have been.

Taking care of the *Nimbus* was a cinch. I'd have her plucked out of the water by a harborside crane in the fall and dropped onto her trailer. She'd come home to the backyard for an immediate bottom scrub. Get her all cleaned up and trundle her off to a boatyard shed for the winter. As soon as the snow had melted, back she'd roll into the driveway for the spring "fitting out." This consisted of wiping off her bottom with a rag and giving her two coats of the cheapest red antifouling I could find; auto-polishing the topsides; painting the deck (one tablespoon of pumice per quart for a perfect nonskid surface, formula courtesy of Peter Van Dine); touching up the cockpit paintwork; and scraping and giving two coats of varnish to the rail and rubbing strake.

The rig would have been given a going-over during the winter. Her nice, hollow, varnished spruce masts were slid into the cellar through the usual tiny ground-level window, and the rest of her wooden spars, blocks, deadeyes, and belaying pins were lugged downstairs too, so the cellar became a rigging loft, and the smell of varnish gave a lift to more than one January thaw.

There were seven spars to varnish, counting the tiller, but not counting the foresail, jib, and fisherman clubs, which never needed attention during my ownership, for they seem to be protected from weathering by their respective sails. Of course, the fisherman was stowed below when it wasn't set. The gaffs were two diminutive, interchangeable sticks. The masts were beautifully made; I was always going to stuff a bunch of tinfoil up the hollow of the mainmast for a radar reflector but never got around to it.

Her mainmast is not quite as tall as a Tancook Islander might have made it, which hurts her looks a little and kills a little of the advantage of the fisherman, but I must say the slightly shorter spar made putting up her rig just that much easier. I could just do it alone.

The foremast could simply be manhandled into a vertical position and lowered through the deck into its step on the vessel's backbone. Then set up the forestay and the foremast's single shrouds.

Now came the tricky part, for the mainmast steps on top of the centerboard trunk and has no bury to hold it up while you set up the rigging.

I'd lay the mast in the cockpit with the masthead out over the stern. Reeve off the deadeyes and lanyards on the shrouds so they'd be slack while the mast was going up, but would hold it aft and athwartships once it got up. The most convenient line leading from the foremast head to haul the mainmast up to a vertical position was the fisherman staysail throat halyard. Make one end of it fast to the eye in the free end of the springstay, the eye that was to go over the head of the foremast. Stand back in the cockpit where I could steady the mast, and heave away, raising it up, steadying it from swinging outboard, and, when above 45 degrees or so, lifting its heel

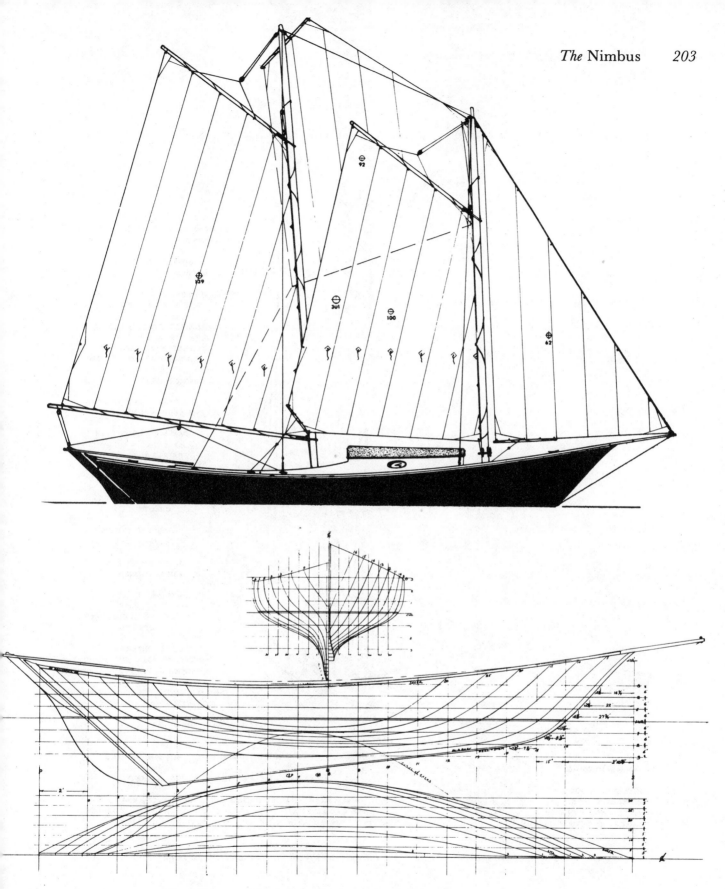

The sailplan and lines of the Tancook whaler Nimbus. *(Peter D. Van Dine)*

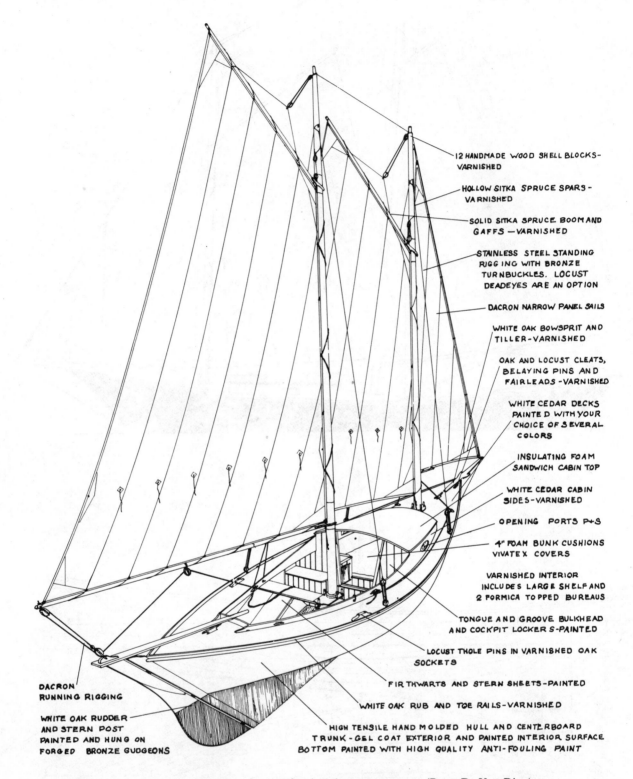

12 HANDMADE WOOD SHELL BLOCKS - VARNISHED

HOLLOW SITKA SPRUCE SPARS - VARNISHED

SOLID SITKA SPRUCE BOOM AND GAFFS — VARNISHED

STAINLESS STEEL STANDING RIGGING WITH BRONZE TURNBUCKLES. LOCUST DEADEYES ARE AN OPTION

DACRON NARROW PANEL SAILS

WHITE OAK BOWSPRIT AND TILLER - VARNISHED

OAK AND LOCUST CLEATS, BELAYING PINS AND FAIRLEADS - VARNISHED

WHITE CEDAR DECKS PAINTED WITH YOUR CHOICE OF SEVERAL COLORS

INSULATING FOAM SANDWICH CABIN TOP

WHITE CEDAR CABIN SIDES - VARNISHED

OPENING PORTS P+S

4" FOAM BUNK CUSHIONS VIVATEX COVERS

VARNISHED INTERIOR INCLUDES LARGE SHELF AND 2 FORMICA TOPPED BUREAUS

TONGUE AND GROOVE BULKHEAD AND COCKPIT LOCKER S - PAINTED

LOCUST THOLE PINS IN VARNISHED OAK SOCKETS

FIR THWARTS AND STERN SHEETS - PAINTED

WHITE OAK RUB AND TOE RAILS - VARNISHED

HIGH TENSILE HAND MOLDED HULL AND CENTERBOARD TRUNK - GEL COAT EXTERIOR AND PAINTED INTERIOR SURFACE BOTTOM PAINTED WITH HIGH QUALITY ANTI-FOULING PAINT

DACRON RUNNING RIGGING

WHITE OAK RUDDER AND STERN POST PAINTED AND HUNG ON FORGED BRONZE GUDGEONS

A perspective drawing showing her interior arrangement. (Peter D. Van Dine)

into the mast step on the centerboard trunk, then continuing to heave right up until the springstay was up against the foremast head and the main shrouds came tight. Then all that remained was to get to the foremast head to slip the eye of the springstay over the masthead. I cheated on this in Camden Harbor, for there was a little staging coming off the harbor wall to take a gangway down to a float, and at low tide from this staging, my foremast head was right in front of my eyes.

When I was trying to make up my mind whether or not to buy the *Nimbus,* I used to worry about the mainmast being stepped on top of the centerboard trunk. What a crazy scheme, I thought. So I decided to call up Peter Van Dine to try to get him to agree that such an arrangement didn't make any sense. "I was wondering about the mainmast being stepped on the centerboard trunk," I said to Peter on the phone to open the discussion.

"Yes, wasn't that lucky?" Peter said. "It just happened to work out that way." In the conversation that followed, it dawned on me that with fiberglass construction, the centerboard trunk is a strong girder rather than a source of leaks. All you have to do to convert it to a mast step is give the top of it some support athwartships, which Peter did with a thwart right across the boat in way of the mast step.

The standing and running rigging on the *Nimbus* is all too small, in my opinion. Oh, it's plenty strong — at least no *rigging* carried away on her in my experience — but it's so tiny it hurts your fingers to catch hold of a shroud to steady yourself when she's jumping a bit, or give that last little swig on the foresail sheet to flatten it in. A little more diameter all around wouldn't do her any harm.

When I started sailing her, I found myself once again worrying about that mainmast stepped on top of the centerboard trunk. All in the world that was holding the spar aloft was the springstay and two shrouds, a triangle of single wires. If any one of the three should carry away, the mast would suddenly be swinging around by the other two. So I doubled up, by rigging a second springstay right alongside the first and by rigging a pair of preventer backstays, making down to eyebolts in the deck with lanyards, about 18 inches aft of the shrouds.

The shrouds made down to eyebolts in the deck, the lower deadeyes being secured to the eyebolts simply with a none-too-hefty bolt through the eye, which thus took a bending strain. Peter Van Dine warned me about this arrangement, saying that on second thought it ought to be beefed up with bigger eyebolts. Good idea, I thought, and I think I'll change those crossbolts that take the bending strain from bronze to stainless steel for greater strength while I'm at it. But I didn't get around to doing this simple job.

She has a nice little flat bowsprit that is really too small to work out on. I put a downhaul on the jib.

Her sails are vertical-cut without battens and are made of heavy Dacron. They set beautifully.

The loose-footed foresail with club is hard to furl until you learn to lower the gaff right down onto the housetop, which you can then use as a table to help you get the thing under control. Yes, the foresail club bangs the mainmast a couple of times when you go about, and it would bang your head too, so you just have to stand from under.

The sheet arrangement on a loose-footed foresail — even one of only 100 square feet, as in this tiny schooner — is a dilemma. You want it simple, so that there won't be a whole lot of blocks and ropes thrashing around the mainmast when you tack; but then you want it powerful, so you can flatten the sail right in on the wind in a breeze without breaking your back.

The two-part sheeting arrangement that Peter Van Dine came up with is so absurdly simple that at first I couldn't see how it worked (and so, of course, was sure it *wouldn't* work), and I must say it took me and everybody else who came aboard the boat quite a few tacks before we could operate the sheet without thinking hard about just what to pull on.

The foresail sheet on the *Nimbus* is a single line, the ends of which are made fast to the cockpit coaming, one on each side. The line runs through a bull's-eye on the club at the sail's clew. That won't work, will it? There's no hauling part. Ah, but there *is* a hauling part. It's the slack weather bight of the sheet, which is brought round to leeward of the mainmast, hauled aft, and belayed. The rig is so utterly simple it's mystifying, but once you work with it enough to see through the mysterious simplicity, it works like magic.

No vangs are needed on this vessel's short gaffs, for the leeches of both mainsail and foresail lead aft far enough to keep most of the twist out of the sails. Too bad. I love vangs.

The fisherman staysail is a great sail. On any kind of a reach from a light air to a gentle breeze, it gave her an exciting extra bit of speed. Camden's my kind of place to sail out of, because no matter which way the wind is blowing, as soon as you get out into Penobscot Bay you can steer anywhere from northeast around through southeast to southwest, and pick yourself out a nice reach out and back. One day, doing just this, we found ourselves sailing fast in a gentle breeze under all plain sail in company with a modern 32-foot sloop, also under working sail. We were going just about even. Down comes his working jib, and up goes a big overlapping reacher. Oh no you don't, we said, and up went the fisherman to pull her rail down and make her fly just that much more. Thanks to that beauty, we didn't have to watch that guy's stern. (And they talk about the excitement of the America's Cup.)

With all this gear and rigging on the little vessel, it was tempting to add more. Up went a main topsail with both jackyard and club, and here again we could have used a bit more mainmast, for even with a fairly long jackyard extending the head of the sail past the masthead, we could only eke out 30 square feet in the thing. This sail is a good deal more trouble than it's worth, and I must admit we never fussed with it enough to get it just right. Still, it gave us something to occupy our minds on a calm day.

The *Nimbus* has a set of tholepins back in the middle of the cockpit out near the rail on each side. She also has a nicely carved sculling notch fastened to the side of the sternpost just above the rail. Shaw & Tenney made me a fine pair of 12-foot oars for her. There's room for only one person at a time on the oars. You can stand up and push, rowing with both oars, but it seems like an awful lot of work for the progress you make. Better to row with just one oar and compensate for the turning moment with the rudder. With one oar you can stand up and push, or sit on the thwart in way of the mainmast on the side opposite the tholepins you are using and pull. Rowing with one oar gives a bit more speed than sculling, but sculling was far superior for maneuverability. We'd always scull in or out of Camden's inner harbor if there was no breeze.

The best way to move her in a calm was to tow her with a dinghy. Now you have rowing comfort, maneuverability, and the easy power of two light oars. You could tow her up to twice as fast as you could move her with an oar from on board.

Peter Van Dine has put small electric motors in some of his boats, but the *Nimbus* didn't have one, for which I was grateful. It's as much work carrying batteries around as it is to scull, row, or tow, and not nearly so satisfying.

The cockpit of the *Nimbus* is divided in half by the thwart at the mainmast. This thwart gives her a nice small-boat look, somehow. The forward half of the cockpit is sort of a standing room with a locker built into each forward corner, so you get two individual seats. We protected this area with a simple white canvas dodger, so these seats stayed dry in rain or spray underway or at anchor.

With the dodger struck you could stand in this forward part of the cockpit leaning your back against the mainmast, or move right out and plant your thighs against the coaming. From this latter position you could easily reach right over the side into the water without any fear of falling overboard, which always gave me a feeling of security in case somebody *did* fall overboard. Most boats have no such secure place from which you can reach the water in a stance from which you can apply lifting power.

My wife, Priscilla, complained that there were too many strings and things in the cockpit. She was right, of course. Right in the middle of the best part of the place were centerboard trunk, thwart, and mainmast, and there were plenty of halyards round the foot of the mast. Then there was the foresail to be trimmed through, around, and in what little space remained. I made a minor concession by leading the inboard end of the hauling part of the main sheet up through a snap hook on the main boom to at least get *that* out of the way a little. If this rig caused too much bend in her skinny main boom in a hard breeze, we'd just take the sheet back out of the hook and let it be in the way.

I reasoned that if you have no engine in a boat, you ought to have plenty of ground tackle. I wheedled a nice 15-pound yachtsman's anchor out of Drew McManus (part of his scheme was to transfer his own collection of gear from boat to boat), added a 25-pound, three-piece yachtsman's anchor made by Paul Luke, and gave each a 200-foot rode. When not in use, the anchors stowed in the big locker under the cockpit seat way aft and the rodes stowed under the side benches in the cockpit.

I tracked down a handsome and accurate box compass that mounted just beautifully on the center of the thwart just abaft the mainmast. It could easily be seen from the whole after part of the cockpit and was up out of the way where nobody kicked it.

I succumbed to a plastic jerry can for a water tank. This practical but ugly device I hid away in the big locker under the cockpit seat aft. Above this seat, still farther aft under the very stern deck was another locker with an open front. In there went the tholepins, foghorn, spare line and small stuff, and the chart in use at the moment, all immediately to hand from the helm. In there, too, I hid the key to the padlock on the cuddy boards. As a test, I told our youngest son that the key was somewhere on the boat outside the cuddy and asked him to see if he could find it. It took him about 30 seconds.

The little schooner has a small sump running down into her "deadwood," with the suction hose of her bilge pump running down to its bottom. The pump is a diaphragm affair permanently installed in the bilge right under the cockpit floorboards. The discharge hose runs

Peter Van Dine's boat making the most of a light breeze on Mill Creek, just off Chesapeake Bay. (Peter D. Van Dine)

into the top of the centerboard trunk well above the waterline. So to pump the bilge you lift a floorboard, reach back into that same open locker in the stern for the handle of the pump, stick it in, and start pumping. No pump to get out, no hose to lead overboard, no hull valves to open. Of course, I also had a big horse bucket on board in case she ever shipped a sea.

There's a little lanyard on the tiller that lets it swing out just about to the rail and no farther. I could tell at a glance it was too short and would restrict maneuverability. The first time I got her underway, I made sure it was let go; I wasn't about to ram somebody in the inner harbor just because I couldn't put the helm over as far as I wanted to. Of course, it didn't take long to realize that she never could use any more helm than the lanyard allowed anyway, so I put it back the way Peter Van Dine intended in the first place and was perfectly happy with it forever after. She turned majestically for such a little boat, even with the board down, but once you got used to her she was very easy to maneuver.

She has two basic steering positions: down on the big after seat when she's not heeling too much, and up on the side deck with your feet on this seat when she is. The latter position seemed a tiny bit precarious if she was jumping, but my preventer backstays came just right to hang onto.

Probably the best seat in the boat is on the lee forward locker, back up against the house, leaning against the lee coaming too, feet down on the cockpit floor or up on the thwart, or knees out under the lee deck. Sitting here with the boat heeled and sailing fast, you are really close to the water hissing by. Great stuff. And she is a fine self-steerer, so even alone I used to take this seat and look aft just watching her go. Of course I had to jump up and look ahead every other minute to keep from hitting anything.

The entry to the cuddy was through a small doorway that could be closed off with three vertical sliding boards. She has no companionway hatch. I'd like to have had one so I could have stood in the hatchway to watch her go, but I was also grateful for the simplicity of the arrangement and for the fact that it is really watertight. She has a lovely oval porthole in each side of the house, closed by Ralph Wiley-type, clear plastic rectangles on the inside. Somehow, they always leaked a little.

At the after end of the cuddy is a nice flat on each side with locker under. The starboard one I took over for a bookshelf, office, and stowage for the compass in harbor. The port one I left clear for cooking or a chart table as the occasion demanded. I thought seriously of putting one of those tiny solid-fuel stoves on the port flat, but then realized that if I got a good mantle lantern it would heat the tiny cabin and provide a bright light for reading in the bargain. This worked fine.

After considerable research, I combined a backpacker's canned butane stove with a sturdy Sea Swing gimbaled potholder. I could mount this on the cockpit coaming in time of peace, or down in the cuddy in time of war. Most of the cooking seemed to get done in the cockpit under the dodger.

Forward of the flats she has a double berth. It's tight quarters, and you play kneesies with the foremast. There was always plenty of light stuff to be stowed forward on the bunk: fisherman staysail, dodger, bedding. Quarter-folded charts went under the mattress.

I put a low camp chair on board. The place for it was on the big stern seat, right aft in the cockpit. With the little vessel anchored at the end of a day's sail, I'd put up the dodger to keep out most of the cool breeze, unfold that baby and set it up right at the after end of the cockpit, put something on the stove ready to light off, unroll a sleeping bag on the bunk and get the lamp going down below, set the riding light even though the sun hadn't quite set, and then settle back in the canvas chair to watch the harbor against the backdrop of all these little niceties on board. There's a snugness about a boat this size. Some evenings I'd get so carried away with it all that I'd forget to break out the demon rum.

For a 25-foot boat the *Nimbus* is mighty cramped, for she is narrow and shoal of hull. She makes a wonderful singlehanded cruising boat and a fine daysailer for two. Two can go cruising and four daysailing, but it's crowded.

And my goodness, won't she sail! This is a fast and able little vessel. She is extremely well behaved and docile, very steady on her helm, and just always seems to want to do the right thing by you, even reaching off when it's rough and blowing hard, a time when many fore-and-afters get rambunctious.

Peter Van Dine had mentioned to me that he trimmed the jib in for close-hauled and left it right there whether he was on the wind or off the wind. I knew better. Yet I found that off the wind, the close-trimmed sail holds her head off so beautifully that she will steer herself on a broad reach, and I couldn't see that easing the jibsheet and holding her off with the tiller made her go any faster. I never trimmed the jib the last two years I owned her.

For maneuvering in close quarters, the rig was jib and mainsail. With this rig you could tack without touching a thing but the tiller (the jib is self-tending), and, if things got really tight you could turn her sharply by backing one or both of the sails at the ends of her.

She would lie-to nicely with just the mainsail set and strapped in tight and the tiller snugged amidships by its lanyard, the boat making way dead astern.

She'd carry full working sail up through a moderate breeze. When you start getting some fresh gusts, slack the foresail sheet a bit to put some belly in the luff of the sail. This eases her without changing her balance at all. She'll still steer herself if you want. When there are more fresh gusts than anything else and it looks like breezing on, take in the foresail. If it keeps breezing up, take in the jib, reset the foresail, and let her jog under foresail while you ease the mainsail right off and reef it. Might as well put the second reef in and be done with it. Then away she goes with foresail overlapping what's now a smaller sail aft.

This is the basic rig of this type of boat. When it's blowing hard and rough, she just loves to get back to the ancestral rig of the Chebacco boat: overlapping sail forward, smaller balancing driver aft, no headsail. She'll go through a lot this way, and if things get even worse, you can reef away some of the foresail. Or, if you need a breather, hand the mainsail and lash the helm hard down, leaving her to jog along under foresail alone, looking after herself, making a bit of headway and a bit of leeway, rudder keeping her head up and foresail keeping her easing along on the same tack.

We had her lee rail well under a few times when we were too lazy to shorten down promptly, but she would heel so far and then stop with the wind spilling out of her sails. Thanks to her fairly wide side decks, I never had the feeling she'd ship water over the lee coaming when driving hard, unless in a seaway. And of course, you shouldn't be out driving hard in an open ballasted boat in a seaway.

She had a fine, easy motion for such a light boat, though she could be a bit lively going to windward if there was a steep, nasty chop. It was always fun to watch her high, skinny bow lift to a sea, and of course, there's just nothing like the refinement of watching a pointed stern slip through the water.

It was fun to watch her go on any point of sailing in any conditions of wind and sea, but probably the best was close-hauled under jib, foresail, and mainsail in a moderate breeze, rail down, lifting and settling to an easy sea. You'd sit on the weather deck, balanced between backstay and the lightest of tillers, watching her parallel schooner's masts, sails laced close to them, send her prancing along. Oh, my goodness.

Three of us took her out racing on Penobscot Bay on a crystal-clear northwest day. Never trust a northwester. We were up against a trio of J-24 types, one of which was actually a J-24. We did not expect to stay with these

The Nimbus *working up through the fleet in Camden Harbor at the end of a cruise. (David P. Jackson)*

hotshots, with their spinnakers and hiking sticks, but we figured the day would be instructive. We weren't disappointed.

It was blowing fresh at the start, and the first leg put the wind abaft the beam. The speed demons went off with genoa jibs, and we went off with full working sail, no fisherman staysail. We held one of them, but the other two set spinnakers halfway down the leg and took off.

The second leg was a dead run, and the breeze eased to moderate. The spinnaker boys were long gone, but we wung out the foresail, pulled up the centerboard, and worked out ahead of our nearby competitor, with his poled-out genoa.

The last leg was a long beat home. No sooner did we harden up than it breezed back up to fresh, then strong, then more. Very quickly a short, steep sea built up, and things began to happen on board the *Nimbus*. The first thing that happened on board was that we watched our rival sail by to windward, outpointing and outfooting us. Schooners are reaching fools.

The next thing that happened was that one of those little bronze crossbolts that I had failed to replace gave up the ghost with a loud ping. We had just tacked and the new weather shroud on the mainmast disappeared. At the time, I was just in the process of setting up the new weather preventer, and had rove the lanyard and put on a half hitch. There was just time to clamp down on the thing and put on a couple more hitches. Thank goodness for preventers. We tacked again to bring the mess to leeward, retrieved the main shroud, and lashed it back onto its eyebolt.

Then we set about shortening down in earnest, for the nor'wester was starting to blow viciously right out of a clear sky. I suppose it would wreck the environment or something, but I really wouldn't care if it never blew out of the northwest again. On board the *Nimbus,* we had no leisure for such philosophy. We were busy jogging along under foresail with jib and main sheets eased, getting the jib down and half furled (a wet and lively job), and putting the second reef in the mainsail. That finally done, we got underway again under foresail and double-reefed mainsail. All the competition was way the heck up to windward someplace. And still she was a bit overpowered in the gusts. The hell with it, let's reef the foresail. That stopped her for another little while, and then we proceeded on our deliberate way, battering into just the wrong size sea for her.

I didn't like the jib furl and made the mistake of going out on the bowsprit to do something about it. Just as I finished, there was a bigger lurch than usual, another ping, and no more forestay. So we eased her up again, everything thrashing. Set up the jib halyard to the stemhead, proceeded on our way, and cleared away the jib below. The fitting at the bowsprit end had let go thanks to my weight on the bowsprit coming down as she dove and fetched up, the force being a good deal sideways, since she was well heeled over.

So we limped toward the finish, the breeze finally easing gradually so we shook the reef out of the foresail. Later that same day, we crossed the finish line, not bothering to take our own time. Within 48 hours, she had heavier eyebolts all around for the shrouds and stainless steel crossbolts to hold the lower deadeyes to them. I replaced the bowsprit end fitting without changing its size and henceforth stayed off the bowsprit when it was rough. No part of the rig gave any more trouble.

If the *Nimbus* left a little to be desired on her one round-the-buoys race, she proved to be a superlative vessel on her one "big" cruise. I went off for nine days singlehanded.

Thinking about this trip beforehand, I dreamed of two or three days of smoky sou'westers to take me Down East, say to Cutler, and then a week of working her back up to the westward. Yes, sir, I was really going to take her out and drive her. Far horizons.

Then, as the time to start drew nigh, I smartened up. It ain't really distance I'm after; I just want some time to enjoy the little vessel and have a good look round. Maybe I'll see where she goes without beating, like a gentleman. Well, that's what I did, and she went all the way to Swan's Island and back, sailing a circuitous route of about 100 miles.

The funny thing was that after shifting from a hectic plan to a serene one, it took me three days to calm down on the boat. You should have seen me thrashing around out there, losing my temper at every little thing. But by the end of the third day, the solitude had me standing back looking at myself. It was an absurd picture that I saw: *Homo sapiens* with the rare opportunity to go off cruising singlehanded in a lovely little vessel, roaring around the deck kicking stuff and swearing. Kind of silly. I stopped.

Slowed right down, took things one at a time, and gained a level of confidence in handling the vessel that was new to me.

It was just as well. The next day brought a moderate gale from the northwest. I got underway from my snug, deserted cove and headed southeast. Started under foresail and double-reefed mainsail. Before leaving the shelter of the last island and heading out into Jericho Bay, I rounded up in the lee and took the mainsail off her. Then away she flew, under just foresail. The seas began to build a bit as we got out from under the weather shore, and she loved it. Not so the tin canoe I was towing. I was just about to shorten up her towline drastically when she took a sheer up to windward, realized she'd gone wrong, and tried to get back astern. In the process she built up a huge bow wave on the towrope side, and, all in slow motion, this bow wave rose up over her side and filled her. She capsized and then dragged disconsolately along, apparently not caring which side was up.

No matter. I had my new-found Peace of Mind. I rounded up and got her jogging along under the foresail with the helm down. Put over two big red plastic fishing floats on the lee side for fenders. Brought the slowly revolving canoe alongside to leeward, got her upright, and lashed her alongside. Took my station at the lee side of the standing room just forward of the mainmast, horse bucket in hand. Bailed out the canoe, being grateful for all her flotation taking up space that thus couldn't be filled with water. Let her aft again, but snubbed her painter right up to the sculling notch, lifting her bow up out of the water a bit and giving her to understand that as long as it was at all rough she'd be bound in that ignominious position so she couldn't go a-wandering. Then filled away and let the little schooner romp some more.

At the end of that day we came smoking into Burnt Coat Harbor on Swan's Island. The breeze had eased to fresh, and we beat into the harbor under the somewhat unlikely rig of foresail and full mainsail, jib furled. She certainly carried plenty of weather helm, but was traveling fast withal.

I picked my berth where there'd be plenty of swinging room and shot her into the wind. Let the foresail sheet go so that sail couldn't fill with wind any more. Strapped the mainsail right in tight and lashed the tiller amidships. Now she might go ahead or she might go astern, but there was no way she could fill away and sail. I went forward while she had plenty of headway, untied the anchor from its cruising position on the bow, and let it dangle off the bowsprit. Waited for her to stop, and just when she started astern let go the anchor. Watched her get good sternboard, and when she had drawn out plenty of scope, snubbed her hard. The hook held. Dropped the foresail right down onto the cabinhouse. Veered some more scope right out, the boat again going straight astern and the anchor again holding hard when she was snubbed, the rode showing a nice flat angle with the water. There she lay, mainsail still set.

Then something made me look up at a certain point ashore. I was being stared at by a row of a half-dozen Swan's Island lobster fishermen. One of them waved, and I waved back. I never once got the *Nimbus* underway in the three years I had her without receiving at least one verbal compliment on what a fine-looking little vessel she was, but this silent noticing by a bunch of pros was the finest tribute she got.

Chapter 27

The *Island Belle*

Years ago, when I read Maurice Griffiths' rapturous prose about sitting in the cockpit of his grounded-out cruising boat, watching the tide come in gradually to fill all the tiny rivulets in the mud around his vessel, I had difficulty empathizing with his enthusiasm. I'm learning. Just the other day, I beached my double-paddle canoe at the edge of a Maine tickle and watched the coming tide first surround, and then engulf, a craggy rock. I was enthralled as the rock's ramparts were threatened, and then overwhelmed, and its crevices became rivers, its pockets, pools.

The Island Belle *would be a fine vessel from which to watch such tidal changes. Imagine bringing her into a protected cove that could only be entered at high tide and where she would ground out safely at low water. I know just the place, off Winter Harbor, Vinalhaven, Maine.*

It would be prudent to spend a tide anchored outside the cove and enter it first in the dinghy near low water to find the best spot to moor the three-master so she won't come down on any rocks when the tide goes out. Using prominent boulders and trees—man has yet to make his mark on this cove—we sketch ranges for the place where we want the vessel to lie, and we determine two additional sets of ranges where we want to drop her anchors, one 100 feet ahead and one 100 feet astern.

At high tide, in the calm of sundown, we bring her in, towing her with the dinghy under oars, so as not to break the spell of silence in this landlocked haven. She passes easily over the rocks that barricade the cove when there is less water.

We tow her to the nearest set of marks, where the stern anchor is carefully lowered, then across the middle set of marks and on to the third, where the bower is dropped. Now she is hauled back on the stern anchor until she's again on the middle marks, right where we want her, anchors equidistant. Both anchor lines are swayed taut and belayed. Ah. The Island Belle *and her crew are hidden away from the world in peace.*

Now, for three days, maybe a week, we become attuned to the cycles of nature. Along with the great blue herons who live here, we know last light and first light; we know moonrise and moonset; we know height of tide and the instant of its turning without reference to tables. We delight in watching the place drain out to reveal the mysteries of its bottom; and we delight in watching it fill again, so that every irregularity is covered by a perfectly level plane. We like, especially, to watch by moonlight as the tide steals in and covers the glistening mud with brilliant water. We experience many times that wonderful moment when the vessel breaks the hold of the ground and floats free.

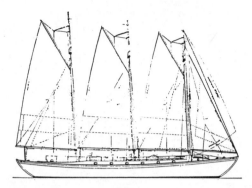

Length on deck: 59 feet
Length on waterline: 48 feet 6 inches
Beam: 12 feet
Draft: 3 feet 9 inches
Designer: Wirth M. Munroe

It would be nice to know the Truth about which designers of good boats had what kinds of influence on which other designers of good boats. Sometimes the influence of one designer on another is obvious; a number of designers got their start in the office of John G. Alden and couldn't help but be influenced by his ideas of what makes a good boat. Other times the influence is apparent, say, in the resemblance of the boats of a number of young designers to the designs of William Garden, for example. Yet it's difficult to know whether that resemblance is a matter of conscious copying, unconscious copying, or mere coincidence. Probably the young designers themselves don't always know.

This influence and adopting of ideas from designer to designer is a Very Good Thing. The whole premise of this series of books is that good boat designs of the past are worth study and emulation. If I were to try to design a boat, I would certainly keep firmly in mind the works of the Wizard of Bristol, Nathanael G. Herreshoff.

What got me going on this whole business of one designer influencing another is the *Island Belle,* a development of the Presto-type sharpie given the bow and stern of a whaleboat and a three-masted-schooner rig by her designer, Wirth M. Munroe.

It's not just that Wirth Munroe was the son of Com-modore Ralph M. Munroe, the developer of the deep, ballasted, round-chined, flaring-sided sharpie that took its name from his *Presto* (see Chapter 2), but also that Commodore Munroe and Nathanael Herreshoff became friendly with each other late in their lives and compared notes on boats. Then L. Francis Herreshoff, Nathanael's son, designed the *Marco Polo,* a double-ended, three-masted schooner the same size as the *Island Belle* at about the same time (just after World War II) that Wirth Munroe was designing the *Island Belle.* Probably coincidence, but, as I say, it would be nice to know the Truth.

At any rate, it's interesting to compare the *Island Belle* with the *Marco Polo* (see Chapter 16). The *Island Belle* is 59 feet long on deck (4 feet longer than the *Marco Polo),* with a waterline length of 48 feet 6 inches (3 inches less than the *Marco Polo);* a beam of 12 feet (2 feet more than the *Marco Polo);* and a draft of 3 feet 9 inches (1 foot 9 inches less than the *Marco Polo).* I don't have a displacement figure for the *Island Belle,* but she is undoubtedly lighter than the *Marco Polo.*

The *Island Belle* was designed for all-round cruising. Like the other Presto boats, she was to be a good gunkholer that would also be safe offshore in rough weather. The *Marco Polo* was designed specifically for

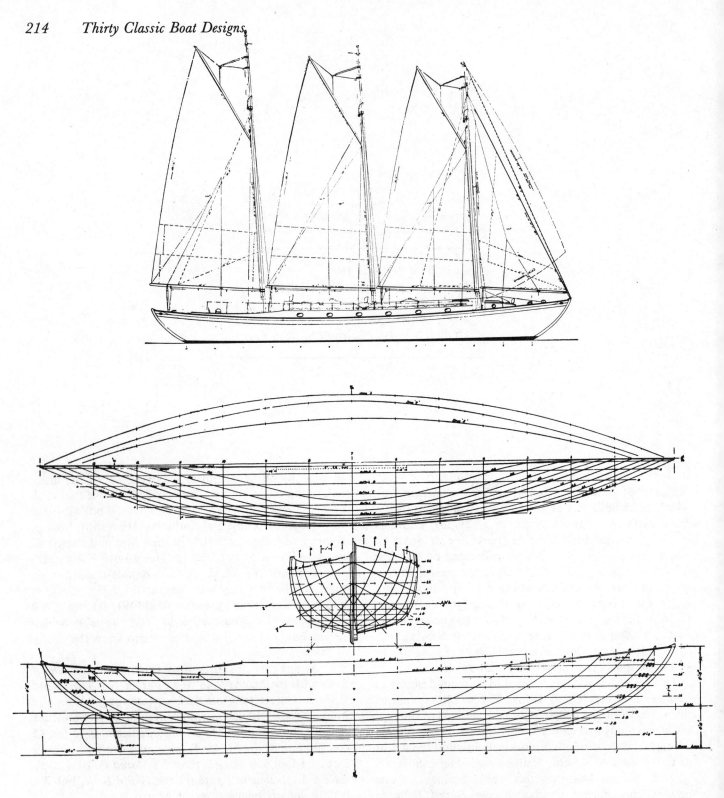

The Island Belle*'s sailplan and lines. (The Rudder, December 1947)*

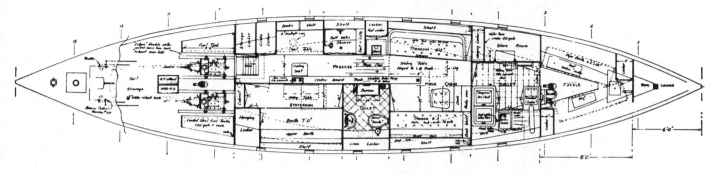

The Island Belle*'s cabin plan.* (The Rudder, *December 1947*)

Strutting along on the wind with her original rig.

long ocean passages. The *Marco Polo* has a big engine to help her on her way in light weather. The *Island Belle* would certainly sail faster than the *Marco Polo,* and the *Marco Polo* would be more seaworthy in a hard chance.

I do have to say two more things before we take a detailed look at the *Island Belle.* First, a big thank you to Joseph C. Dobler of Manhattan Beach, California, who put me on to Wirth Munroe's whaleboat-Presto-sharpie-tern-schooner in the first place; and, another big thank you to Dean A. Worcester of Crownsville, Maryland, who owned her for 21 years and wrote me many interesting details about her.

The *Island Belle* has the pretty profile of a whaleboat.

Yet she is deeper and narrower than a whaleboat, with less flare and more freeboard than those open rowing and sailing beauties. Wirth Munroe's hull has very fine lines; she would reach her hull speed of close to 10 knots relatively easily.

Her high, slightly flaring topsides would give her stability once she begins to heel. One of her owners wanted to increase her stability for offshore racing; so, under Wirth Munroe's direction, he shifted her ballast from inside to outside. This gave her a keel that increased her draft to 4 feet 6 inches. Her designer felt the change improved the vessel.

She originally had a big centerboard just off-center to port, so the trunk avoided the mainmast (and probably jammed stones, should she take the bottom). Her rudder is protected by the keel; I'd want it a bit longer for maneuverability.

The three-masted rig keeps the sailplan low (to go with what is, after all, a fairly tender hull) and the sails small. The area of the mizzen is but 333 square feet. She'd have a good turn of speed despite her moderate, much-divided sail area, thanks to her fast hull.

Of course the divided rig means you have four sheets to trim every time you head up or off, or if the wind shifts. And you have ten spars to keep varnished. If you like varnishing spars (as I do), you'll love the *Island Belle.*

Her tall mastheads give a good lead to the peak halyards and allow the sails to be well peaked-up, yet have their gaffs clear the springstays between the mastheads (the springstays don't show in the sailplan, but they were part of the design and were rigged on the vessel).

When she got her keel, the *Island Belle* was given a marconi mizzen with a permanent backstay leading down to a boomkin. She also got a bowsprit. And the shape of her gaff sails was changed, increasing the lengths of the luffs and thus squaring the gaffs more. This change would have been disastrous without vangs. Wirth Munroe did not approve of these modifications to the rig.

John Moll's drawing shows her modified rig.

Her tall mastheads would allow a pair of big fisherman staysails, each with a club at the peak of the sail to extend the head, Tancook whaler style. Just imagine her flying along on a reach in a light breeze with those babies set! She'd turn a few heads, wouldn't she?

I'd prefer her two headstays to be side by side for ease in shifting jibs, and particularly for ease in tacking with the overlapping jib.

She has lazyjacks all around, which makes great good sense.

When shortening down in the *Island Belle,* you'd take in the mainsail first. If it blew harder, you'd find she would balance under foresail and mainsail. Dean Worcester liked to sail her under mizzen and forestaysail in heavy weather. She'd heave-to, like a two-masted schooner, under foresail alone. Or, she could reach or run like a scalded cat under storm jib and mizzen trysail.

Her raised deck gives her a strong hull and a lot of unbroken deck space, and will keep her relatively dry. The secret to good looks with a raised deck is to keep the bow higher than the deck, and the stern at least as high. That way, the hull dominates the raised deck rather than vice versa. You'd want the *Island Belle*'s raised deck protected by higher lifelines than are shown. Think of

all the boats you could stow up on there; I visualize at least a peapod (with a little double-paddle canoe tucked inside) and a sailing dinghy.

There's a lazarette way in the stern reached by a deck hatch. Sails stow beneath the cockpit sole (that's where we'll put those fisherman staysails).

Her engines straddle the mizzenmast. She originally had a pair of Kermath 2-113s, each turning an 18-by-16-inch feathering wheel. It's hard to argue with the reliability given a vessel by two engines. And if you want to drive her with both sail and power, you have the nicety of a lee propeller well submerged.

She has two 100-gallon fuel tanks outboard of the engines. She carries 190 gallons of fresh water: 140 in a pair of 70-gallon tanks, one under each transom in the saloon; and 50 in a tank in the galley on the port side.

When you come down the main companionway, there is an oilskin locker handy to port. In the passageway leading forward there's a big chart table, with its seat folding off the centerboard trunk, and a 6-inch deadlight in the overhead right above it. Next comes a saltwater shower and a heating stove; I'd want some sort of connection between these two appliances.

To starboard is a double stateroom with 7-foot lower and upper berths and a folding table. The head connects to both stateroom and saloon and has its own little bureau.

In the saloon there is a nice desk and chair and a hinged sliding table attached to the port side of the centerboard trunk.

The galley has a big storeroom to port with a hinged table off its door. There is a ladder so you can go out the galley hatch, or at least climb up for a breath of fresh air and a look around before the coffee boils.

The fo'c's'le has its own head and two pipe berths.

For some reason, I visualize the *Island Belle* running off in fairly thick weather in Ipswich Bay north of Cape Ann before a moderate gale from the northeast. She's under foresail alone and making knots, and her people are keeping what Frank Bullen in *The Cruise of the Cachalot* called a "brilliant lookout," for they know that if they get a sounding of 20 feet before they see the bell buoy marking the entrance to the Essex River, they'll have to haul their wind, work her offshore round Cape Ann, and feel their way into Gloucester. They wouldn't sound their way in on a lee shore in this weather if they didn't have plenty of confidence in the vessel's ability to beat back out.

But it's not all that thick, and soon after a sounding of 25 feet, a wet, oilskinned arm is raised toward the "horizon" ahead, and, sure enough, there's the big buoy, clanging and swaying, fine on the starboard bow.

Then it's just a matter of picking a way in past the buoys that mark the shifting channel, running in past the tower on Two Penny Loaf, reaching the welcome calm of Essex Bay, and jibing up the river with, fortunately the last of the flood. When the final twist of the stream has been followed, she's eased alongside, docklines are made fast and hauled taut, and the crew tumbles below to see about a fire in the stove, some dry clothes, and maybe even a toast to the vessel.

Dean Worcester wrote: "This boat is exceptionally well balanced under many combinations of sail and sails herself admirably. She is easy to single hand, and my wife and I would take her most anywhere without additional crew. We cruised from Maine to Key West, always with great confidence in her sea kindliness."

The *Island Belle,* long since renamed the *Rebel,* was going strong until just recently. A boatyard fire in 1983 destroyed her.

Chapter 28

The *Magpie*

I've stopped envying waterfront estates with gazebos commanding fine views, for I've realized that a boat's wheelhouse is a gazebo with a 360-degree water view that you can vary at will. Now, I envy wheelhouses. When I get that "wheelhouse urge," I often turn to the *Magpie*.

I should have known I was smitten with this vessel when I first wrote about her, because I bothered to make my favorite additions. I stuck a swordfishing pulpit on the end of her bowsprit, put a crowsnest at the mainmasthead with ratlines leading up to it, fenced in the outside steering station and added a wind deflector, and gave her a fisherman staysail. As my infatuation has continued, nay, grown, I have gone on improving her, as you can see by the drawing at the end of the chapter. She now has a little triangular riding sail on the foremast, a squaresail, a second reef in the mainsail, lifelines, and a high, side-opening booby hatch over the after companionway.

Her rig has become quite refined, I think, for a motorsailer. Reaching in a moderate breeze, with her 300-square-foot fisherman staysail added to her mainsail and headsails, she can spread 880 square feet of sail. Running in the trades—I have big plans for the *Magpie*—she has a nice rig of 600 square feet, with mainsail (mislabeled in the sail plan as 226.5 square feet, but really 326.5) and the 270-square-foot squaresail. In hard weather, she can be shortened down to double-reefed mainsail, riding sail, and forestaysail, a snug rig of 360 square feet. And for heaving-to in a gale, you have, always at the ready, the 100-square-foot riding sail, luff hooped to the foremast, foot held by a stout boom, and trimmed with, say, a four-part tackle. That little sail represents security.

Now the *Magpie* has almost all the things I really like in a boat for comfortable, long-range cruising: wheelhouse; outside steering station with outstanding visibility; bowsprit with swordfishing pulpit; crowsnest; schooner rig; square yard; big engine room. The only thing missing is the great cabin with stern windows. Let's see, if we raise the afterdeck to the height of the bulwarks. . . .

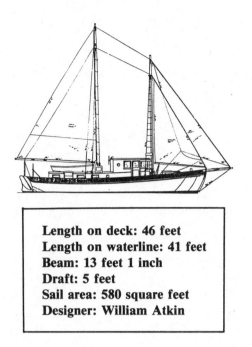

Length on deck: 46 feet
Length on waterline: 41 feet
Beam: 13 feet 1 inch
Draft: 5 feet
Sail area: 580 square feet
Designer: William Atkin

We hear a good deal these days about "sail-assisted power vessels." With the coming of the external- and then the internal-combustion engine, sailing vessels got an assist from power; as engines delivered more horsepower more reliably, sail was vanquished. Now, with the price of fuel so high, sail is coming back to curb the thirst of engines.

Of course, these developments are not sharply delineated. The motorsailer has been with us for some time, and who's to say whether a powerfully engined vessel with a short rig is a sailing vessel with auxiliary power or a power vessel with auxiliary sail?

Well, William Atkin considered the *Magpie,* one of the many cruising boats he "designed especially for MoToR BoatinG," definitely to be a powerboat. He gave her a schooner rig to help her on her way, steady her, and reduce her fuel bills, probably in that order of importance when he designed her nearly 50 years ago. Today, the last reason might well be first.

As usual, Mr. Atkin produced a handsome, purposeful-looking vessel. She has nicely balanced, short ends, with plenty of shape to her transom and outboard rudder, and a lively sheerline. Her buttock lines are very easy; she has a good run. She has a reasonable amount of lateral plane, and her beam has been kept moderate. The waterlines are fairly full forward.

The *Magpie* is 46 feet long on deck, with a waterline length of 41 feet, a beam of 13 feet 1 inch, and a draft of 5 feet. Her freeboard forward is 6 feet.

Her heavy hull would take some driving to keep her going. She'd be steady on her helm and would certainly heave-to steadily.

Billy Atkin gave no displacement figure for the *Magpie* in his write-up of her design, but judging from her scantlings, she ain't no lightweight. He specified: keel of white oak, 14 inches by 14 inches; oak frames, 2 inches by 2 inches on 12-inch centers, with every fourth frame doubled; 1½-inch white pine planking, sheer strake to be mahogany; clamp and shelf each 2-inch by 2-inch fir; floors at every other frame, 2-inch by 8-inch oak; ceiling, ¾-inch white pine or fir; deck beams, 2-inch by 2½-inch white oak; deck, 1½-inch white pine; pilothouse ¾-inch mahogany staving.

The only fancy specification was for diagonal brass straps, ¼-inch by 6 inches, on top of the house in way of the mainmast.

She was to have 5 tons of inside ballast consisting of cement laced with boiler punchings poured between the floors and leveled off even with their tops. Some builders would shudder, but Billy Atkin loved the stuff:

In putting in cement ballast be sure the wood surfaces are absolutely free from oils and paints. The cement will then cling to the wood and there can be no danger of

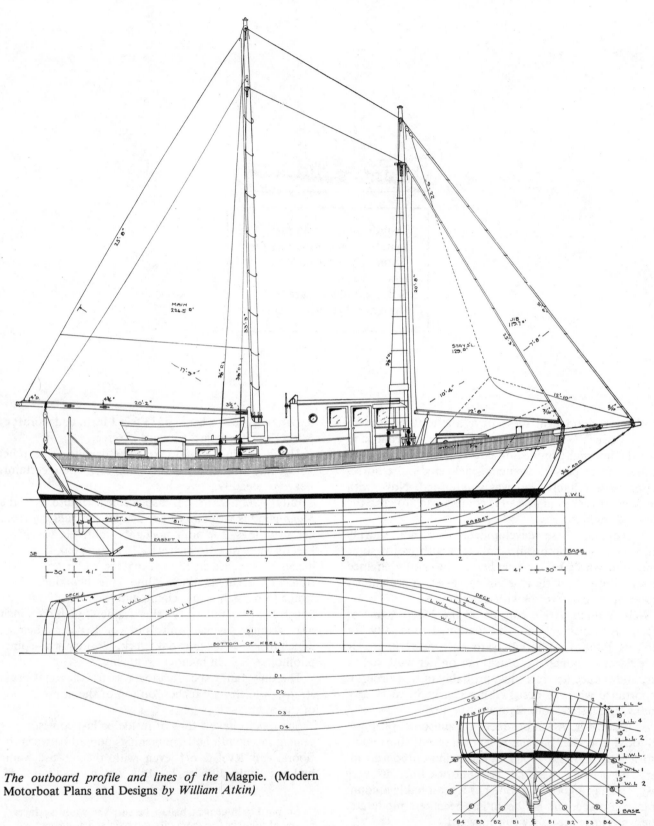

The outboard profile and lines of the Magpie. *(Modern Motorboat Plans and Designs by William Atkin)*

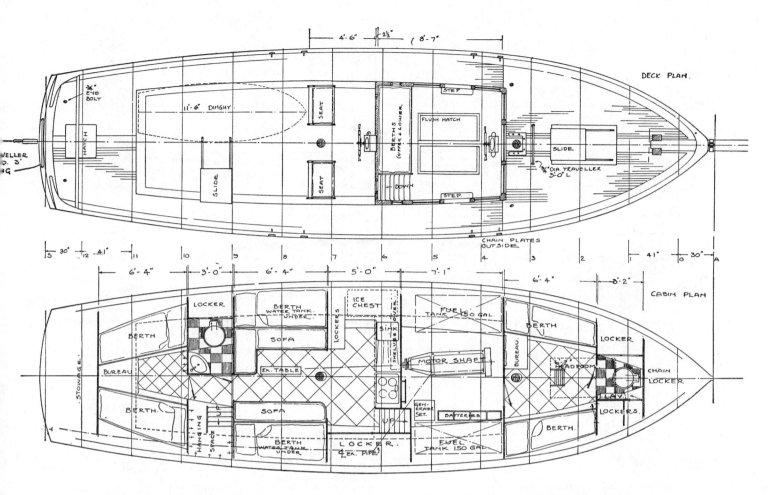

Her deck and accommodations plans. (Modern Motorboat Plans and Designs *by William Atkin*)

decay; in fact the cement will preserve the wood. I should put in the cement before the floor beams have been fitted and before the boat has been launched. Smooth off the top surface, and after the cement is perfectly dry, paint thoroughly with good deck paint. The bilge can be kept beautifully clean if it is cemented as described above. I do not know of a better way to treat the bilge of any boat that requires inside ballast.

Mr. Atkin estimated the *Magpie*'s cost at $9,000-$16,000 (pre-World-War-II dollars), depending on whether she were built plain or fancy.

The auxiliary rig spreads a mere 580 square feet of sail: 330 in the mainsail, 130 in the forestaysail, and 120 in the jib. She has no foresail, because her house and steering station are in the way.

Her rig has been kept simple. Her deadeyes and lanyards are cheap and reliable. Her leg-o'-mutton mainsail is held to the mast with mast hoops.

I'd have to rattle down the main shrouds and put a crow's nest up on the forward side of the mainmast, since there is no fore gaff to bang into it. And this is a boat on which I'd be tempted to rig a roller-furling jib, even though I'd want a plank on top of the bowsprit and a swordfishing pulpit on its end.

The thing to do with all that nice space between her masts is fill it with a fisherman staysail, with its head snugged up under the lower springstay and its foot coming down about even with the reef in the mainsail. With that beauty added to her sailplan on a reach in any kind of breeze, the fuel bill would be reduced to zero.

Another worthwhile sail in the *Magpie* would be a balloon forestaysail to pole out when running, because then, of course, the fisherman staysail would have to be handed.

On deck, she has a stout gallows frame to take the main boom; space for an 11½-foot dinghy on top of the house, as shown, ready to be hoisted out by the main halyard; a couple of nice seats beside the mainmast; and a high steering station amidships. I'd want to fence that steering station in, I think, and put a low wind deflector across the after end of the pilothouse roof to shoot the breeze up over your head.

The power schooner's inside steering station gives good visibility (unlike some you see these days). The wheelhouse windows drop into pockets. There are only two 6-inch portholes in the after bulkhead; I'd want windows back there too, so when I hear the whine of an outboard motor astern, I can tell right away whether or

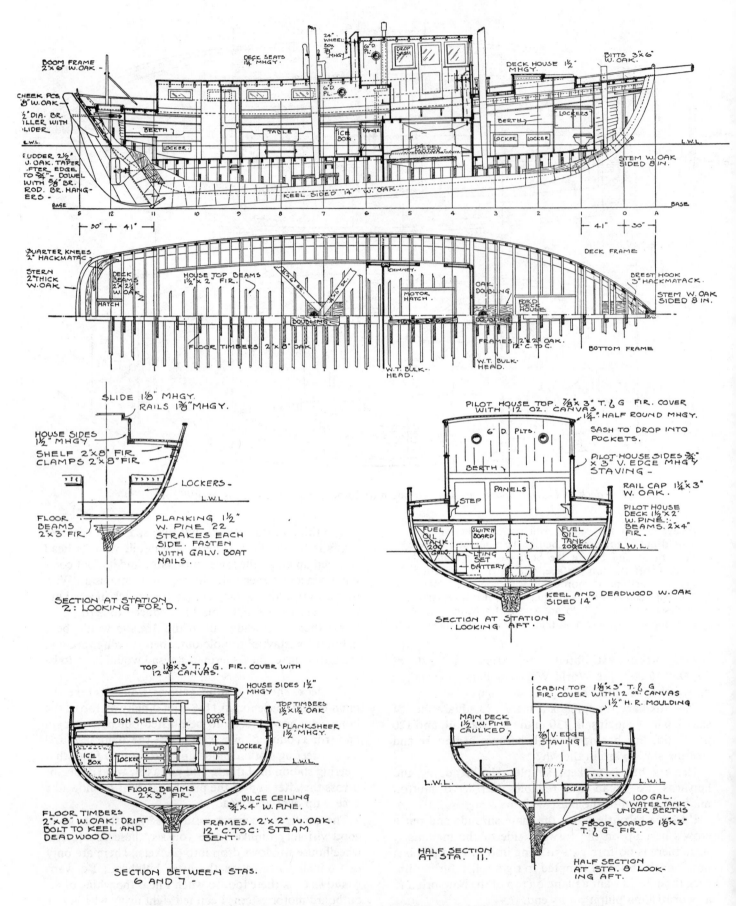

The Magpie's *construction drawings.* (Modern Motorboat Plans and Designs *by William Atkin*)

not I need to run outside and screech at the guy to get his attention before he hits me. I'd want a chart table on each side of the wheel. Happiness is rolling along on a cool fall day steering behind glass in the sun with the lee wheelhouse door open.

The deck of the wheelhouse has a pair of big flush hatches so you can open the engine room right up; there's also a door into the place from the fo'c's'le. In any case, you have plenty of space around the big machine. (Mr. Atkin specified a six-cylinder diesel in the 65- to 100-horsepower range, such as a Redwing-Waukesha 80-90 Hesselman.) Her long shaft is nearly level. She has a separate generator set and plenty of batteries. I have always been intrigued, however, with the idea of starting a big engine like this with air and having a compressor that you start by hand. Then if you can keep the air system tight, you can start the engine. She'd go very easily at 8 knots.

There's a watertight bulkhead at each end of the engine room and a pair of 150-gallon fuel tanks in the wings. She has a 100-gallon water tank under each bunk in the saloon.

I don't know about those sideways companionways that used to be all the rage on powerboats. Great on the port tack, but what happens when wind and spray are coming over the starboard rail? I'd rather just put a hatch in the top of the house and climb up and over.

Her layout below is straightforward. The galley, saloon, and a couple of bunks are right amidships. She has a raised deck over the fo'c's'le, and there is over 6 feet of headroom under the fo'c's'le hatch.

She has no fewer than 8 bunks, including an upper and lower in the wheelhouse, so she could accommodate 8 souls.

Robert C. Leslie talked about this "soul" business in his wonderful book *A Waterbiography.*

> We were, to speak nautically, seven souls all told on board; though why sea-faring people should be thus spiritualized has always puzzled me. No one calls railway or omnibus passengers souls; they are always persons, bodily filling places or seats.
>
> It might, however, often be well if people, especially passengers, could leave their bodies ashore when taking a voyage — souls, we are taught, being so easily provided for in every way; while this would do away with that mortal dread of the sea so trying to some people. No one in a storm fidgets about his soul; it is his bothering body he always wants either to save himself, or someone else to save alive for him; and except in the case of a body too seasick to care, I have observed that the greater the real or fancied danger at sea, the less people trouble about their souls. This is, however, a digression . . . ."

Anyway, however many souls were on board the *Magpie,* I'll bet they'd have a fine time of it.

The Magpie, *fully modified for daydreaming.*

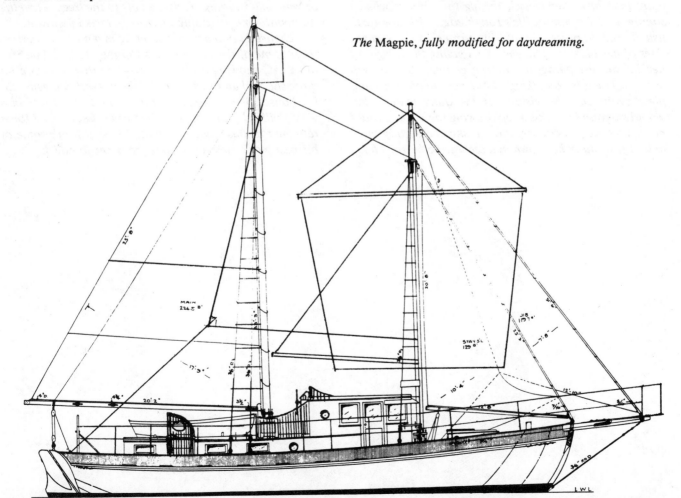

Chapter 29

The *Retreat*

The Retreat *has been my imaginary refuge, I think, more than any other vessel, during those times when I simply have to smooth life's rough edges. I know I can usually secure peace of mind by turning to the straight lines of her plans and maybe by rereading the images of her in the last paragraph of the chapter. She is well named. There is something about her simple yet complete cabin and the visions of the quiet waters that would surround her that keep drawing me back. I find I never take her on cruises, though she is certainly movable. I just plunk her down in a secluded cove on a lake,* or in a saltwater pond behind a sheltering barrier beach, or way up a winding creek, tied off to the trees. Then life on board—mostly doing nothing—starts in earnest.

I chanced upon a lovely painting in a museum that reminded me of the Retreat. *It is Claude Monet's* The Studio Boat, *showing a black scow—admittedly with a bit more shape than the* Retreat *displays—with a green, tallish house. She is lying against a couple of stakes in a very civilized-looking, tree-lined river. I suppose Monet retreated to this vessel to paint. I like to think some of his best work may have come from her foredeck.*

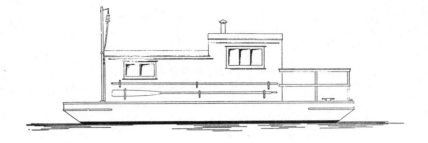

Length on deck: **18 feet**
Length on waterline: **14 feet**
Beam: **7 feet**
Draft: **5 inches**
Displacement: **1 ton**
Designer: **William Atkin**

One of my favorite boats to watch, growing up on the Pawcatuck River, was the handsomest little 30-foot western-rigged dragger you'd ever want to see. Her owner, when I knew her, had taken her over as pretty much of a wreck from his father and had rebuilt her completely into a fine, serviceable vessel. The old boat had been named for the son who later saved her from dying — she was called the *Bobby D.* — which seemed fair enough. She lived in the cove next to ours, so we could see her moving majestically down the river plenty of times.

I lost track of the *Bobby D.* for some years and feared she'd been sold away. Then one fall she showed up again in the tiny, secluded cove right off our cove, where she tied up for the winter. She was acting as tender to a houseboat alongside, a nice 20-foot scow with a well-proportioned dwelling on it. The two vessels were round the corner where you couldn't see them except from a certain angle, and they were snuggled right up against the shore. Some fun, it looked like.

William Atkin had a similar experience of seeing a fine little houseboat in an idyllic setting in a cove on Long Island, which inspired him to design a similar vessel for *Motor Boating* magazine. The design jumped off the page at me when, with these visions of the *Bobby D.*'s charge somewhere in the back of my mind, I was thumbing through a copy of *40 Designs for Postwar Boats* (Volume 20 in *Motor Boating*'s Ideal Series, published in 1944), kindly loaned to me for an entirely different purpose by Mr. R.G. Bailey of North Fort Myers, Florida.

Billy Atkin's inspiration had been named the *Retreat,* so that's what he named his design, which he also labeled a "shantyboat deluxe." *Retreat* is a good name for a vessel to be so used. A minister friend of mine calls his cruising boat the *Retreat.* When you call him up in the summer with some burning theological question, the person at the church who answers the phone says, "Oh, I'm afraid the minister's not here. He's on *Retreat.*"

I see Mr. Atkin's *Retreat* moored in a quiet cove on a lake, long bow and stern lines to trees ashore keeping her just out of reach of the lily pads. There are dragon flies, a straw hat, and shimmering water.

Of course she could be a river vessel, drifting her lazy way toward the sea, maybe with somebody helping her along a bit standing up on the front porch pushing on a pair of sweeps, and maybe even with a mate doing a bit of towing with a pulling boat.

Not to worry. We're not starting an imaginary river voyage. You can read a great account of a real one in Harlan Hubbard's book *Shantyboat: A River Way of Life,* published in 1953 and reprinted in 1977 by the

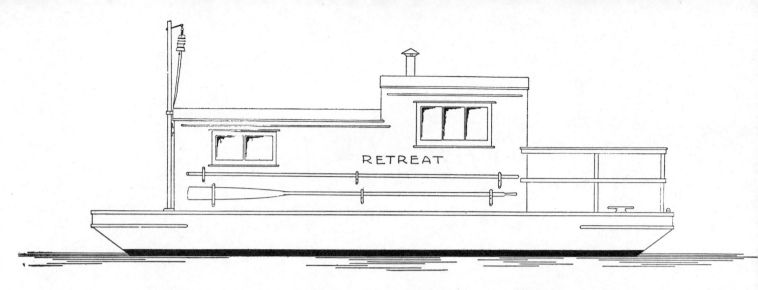

The outboard profile of the Retreat. *(40 Designs for Postwar Boats by William W. Atkin)*

University Press of Kentucky. Harlan and Anna Hubbard spent seven years easing down the Ohio and Mississippi Rivers from Brent, Kentucky, to New Orleans.

Billy Atkin envisioned moving the shantyboat *Retreat* over land if necessary to reach a particular watery objective:

> Fact is it would be no trick at all to fix a pair of automobile wheels each side at the middle point of the over-all length, making a trailer that at the same time would be a houseboat. Axle would not be required nor springs. Two front knuckles from a heavy car welded to suitable plates could be through bolted to the sides; then removed after the trailer had been wheeled down into the water.

My usual comments about the pretty curves in a boat's hull don't seem to apply to the *Retreat*. But she does have a snug, practical look, doesn't she?

The shantyboat is 18 feet long on deck, 14 feet on the bottom, with a beam of 7 feet and a draft of 5 inches, depending on loading. The depth of the hull is 2 feet, so if she drew 5 inches, she'd have left a freeboard of 1 foot 7 inches. She'd displace just about a ton, without books.

Mr. Atkin recommended keeping the scantlings of this shantyboat reasonably light. He specified side and bottom planking of ¾-inch white cedar, with end planking of a heavier wood, such as yellow pine or white oak. Chines to be ¾ inch by 1½ inches; frames, ¾ inch by 2 inches; and doubling pieces where the ends join the bottom, 1½ inches by 4 inches — all white oak.

He suggested 1½-inch by 1¾-inch oak stringers to stiffen the bottom. Shelf, ¾-inch by 2¾-inch fir. Deck beams, ¾-inch by 2-inch fir. Deck, two layers of ¼-inch plywood, covered with canvas. (I suppose it would be tempting to build the whole vessel out of plywood today and use plenty of the high-class sealants.) Cabin floor, ¾-inch tongue-and-groove fir, laid right on the stringers.

Studs for the house, 1⅛-inch by 1¾-inch fir. House sides and ends, ½-inch Homosote. Housetop beams, ¾ inch by 2 inches. Housetop, ¼-inch plywood, canvas covered.

The designer estimated the cost of all materials for this vessel — in 1944 — to be $200. She'd be relatively cheap to build today.

And she's so simple with most everything square that most any of us can visualize ourselves building this little home afloat. Well, at least I can visualize myself painting her: red copper bottom, dark green hull and house with black and dark red trim. You wouldn't want her to stand out too much against the shore.

Her front porch (complete with porch railing) is 4 feet 6 inches long. The back porch is only 2 feet 6 inches long. I think I'd have to extend the back porch a bit; you need room for a good chair back there out of the wind when anchored by the bow.

You can tippy-toe round the outside of the house on the narrow side decks holding onto the grab rails under the eaves. There's a 10-foot oar and a 10-foot pole stowed in brackets on each side of the house.

If you were doing much moving and anchoring, you'd want heavy ground tackle handled by an anchor davit at each end of the vessel. Once her anchors were down, you wouldn't want to have to come outside for anything.

You could anchor her bow and stern or plant her with an anchor off either bow with the rodes crossed to keep her from sailing around. You could let her lie to an endless line run through blocks on two anchors so you could shift her position at will without disturbing the

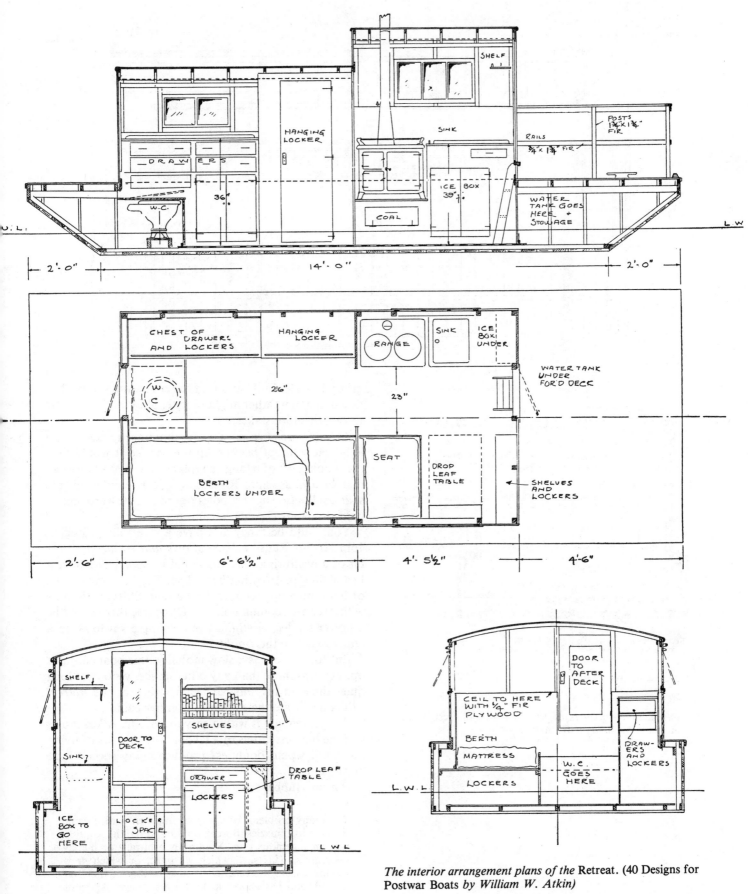

The interior arrangement plans of the Retreat. *(40 Designs for Postwar Boats by William W. Atkin)*

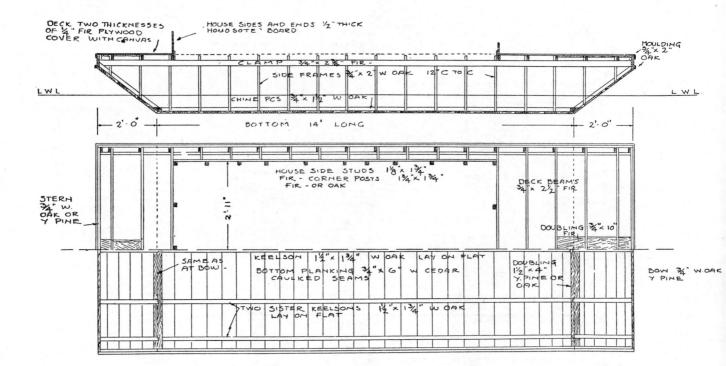

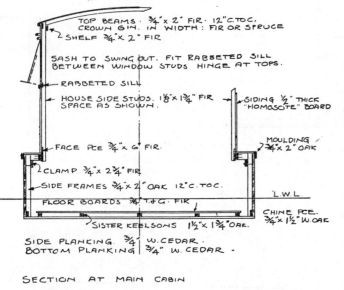

The construction drawings of the Retreat. (40 Designs for Postwar Boats *by William W. Atkin)*

ground tackle. Pull her out of the cove a ways or back in as whim and weather might dictate. She could be tied up to one or more stakes.

At any rate, her mast is for holding up her riding light. How about beefing up the spar so it would take the topping lift of a long gangplank, lowered ashore like that of a Mississippi River boat? So strengthened, the spar could also support poles rigged out athwartships to hold the boats clear on a calm night.

You could be fancy and have a nice sailing dinghy. Join Arthur Ransome's *Swallows and Amazons* for a bit of adventuring. Or, you could be sporty and have a fast sliding-seat rowing boat. I see flat-bottomed boats of handsome line tending the *Retreat*. Skiffs and punts with oversize sculling notches. Of course there could be a power tender, anything from a simple yawlboat to a real vessel like the *Bobby D*.

But for all her easy, slow mobility, this boat conjures up, perhaps more than any other image, visions of long quiet times in her innards. Many who see the *Retreat* will concentrate their attention on her cabin.

Everything in it is within easy reach. Mr. Atkin shows you the bare essentials of a layout, but 10 years of living on board would doubtless produce many special little arrangements.

Harlan Hubbard wrote:

The many problems of space arrangement which came up were like puzzles to work out, and often the solution was an ingenious one. Nothing is arbitrary or merely decorative. This shell which we built, or which grew around us, has become as efficient as that of the river mussel, and has almost as little waste space. A visitor does not see how intensively the space is developed. Many innocent objects have unexpected uses, and our guests require some training and instruction in living with us. We sometimes think of our boat in the hands of a stranger. He would come upon puzzling contraptions and unexpected compartments one after another. The boat would fall apart with some of its secrets undiscovered.

The heart of the *Retreat* seems to be her iron range. You'd carry coal for it, but you'd gather and burn driftwood. She'd have kerosene lamps, with a mantle lantern for reading.

In the high part of the house there is 6 feet of headroom, and in the sleeping part, 4 feet 10 inches. The windows, hinged at the top, open out, You'd have sticks for different amounts of air.

The water tank is under the front porch. I'd want a roof over the back porch for rainy days. I suppose it's inevitable that canisters of bottled gas would find their way back there? Anyway, the back porch would be the base for the morning swim.

Some fine vessel, I call her. A good place to watch the early morning mists rising off the still water and the moonlight sparkling off the ripples of the night wind. Make sail in the skiff; reach out across the moon path and then reach back for that riding light showing where the little houseboat lies.

Chapter 30

The *Scrimshaw*

Jim Brown has a boat like the Scrimshaw *perhaps in part because people flock to him, attracted by his articulate expression of innovative ideas, so he needs a lot of deck space to accommodate the crowd. When the* Scrimshaw *is in port, she always seems to be swarming with folk.*

On the moonlit drift mentioned in the introduction to Chapter 21, there were certainly at least a dozen of us on board the Scrimshaw. *We were tied up to a float; there was a guitar and singing. When the moon rose, Jim slipped his lines.*

The next thing we knew, we were on a magic carpet floating among the anchored boats. Jim nudged her now and then with the outboard, but it was so quiet it didn't interrupt the low strains of song. A few voices were very good, and, for once, we amateurs knew enough to sit back and listen, and watch the moonbeams play.

Kathleen and I wanted to look at a Searunner as a potential vessel to live on board. We were particularly interested in the 34-footer but couldn't find one for sale on the East Coast. We did go on board a couple of 37-footers that were on the market. I was tempted chiefly by the acreage of deck space; I could envision turning one of

these vessels into a cruising boatyard, with the space to haul a fleet of small craft. Unfortunately, the builders of both these trimarans had installed cabin joinery that reminded us of a sixties motel.

Jim Brown believes that the multihull is the boat of the future. I agree with him, but with Jim I never know whether I agree with him because I think he's right or because he's charmed me into it. He is a Pied Piper.

He also has a case. The multihull has speed, tremendous deck space, and a rare combination of shoal draft and seaworthiness. You can argue that a multihull can be capsized and that she will then stay upside down, but you can also argue that in the same conditions, a monohull can be knocked down and sunk. Multihulls are short on cabin space (at least trimarans are) and carrying capacity, but Searunners have enough of each for many of us. The biggest drawback in a multihull for me would be that instead of the easy motion of a good boat in a seaway that I love, I would get the frisky motion that goes with sailing fast over every wave.

One good-boat quality that multihulls don't have yet is beauty. Maybe if multihull designers add good looks to their boats, multihulls will become the good boats of the future.

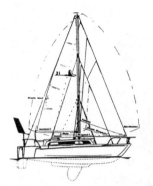

Length on deck: 31 feet 2 inches
Beam: 18 feet 8 inches
Draft: 2 feet 9 inches
Sail area: 453 square feet
Displacement: 5,600 pounds
Designer: Jim Brown

On my office bulletin board is a cartoon, clipped out for me by one of my colleagues, showing a guy at a big desk absolutely covered with little bits of paper with notes on them. He is saying to the person across the desk, "Let me just make a little note of that. I never seem to get anything done around here unless I make little notes." My colleague gave me the cartoon because that's the way I am, always making little notes of things that I hope someday to get done.

Somewhere in the midst of working on Jim Brown's book *The Case for the Cruising Trimaran,* I pulled out an index card and made a little note on it: "Get a sail in a Searunner."

I kept that little note handy for over a year before I was able to crease the card and heave it one October day. It was the day Jim and Jo Anna Brown took a small group of us sailing in their Searunner 31, the *Scrimshaw.*

Jim's book was the first thing I had read on multihulls that made seamanlike sense to me. He designs trimarans for cruising, not for racing. He is attracted to the type for its high performance, among other things, but rather than go all out for speed he goes all out for safety and comfort, and then takes what speed is left over, which is considerable. His Searunners can carry a half-decent cruising payload, and he keeps that payload down in the middle of the center hull to give his vessels maximum stability. He tries to create safe, comfortable, fast vessels — not record-breakers — in which to keep the sea.

I was excited to be going sailing in a real multihull, my only previous experience with the type being a dismasting in a 17-foot catamaran in a flat calm. A cotter pin dropped out of the pin of the shackle holding the forestay to the mast, and the whole rig fell aft, neatly bisecting the craft. Fortunately, one of us was perched on each hull at the time, so the spar fell harmlessly between us. We left it right there and paddled home.

Jim Brown calls the Searunner 31 the "klutz" of the series. She is not the smallest; there is a 25-footer. Then there's a 34, a 37, and a 40.

Jim built the *Scrimshaw* eight years ago. He and his family use her as a way of traveling. Jim and Jo Anna had come to Camden, Maine, in her from their home in Virginia, via Nova Scotia. Their idea of cruising is to get somewhere that appeals to them and stay a while. To them the best part of cruising is getting to know people in different places. With their two sons they made a three-year odyssey from California to Virginia through the Panama Canal.

Soon after we were all on board, Jim pulled his little dinghy up alongside the port ama, politely waved

Left: *Jim Brown. (Jim Sollers).* **Below:** *The sailplan of the Searunner 31.* (Searunner Construction Manual *by Jim Brown)*

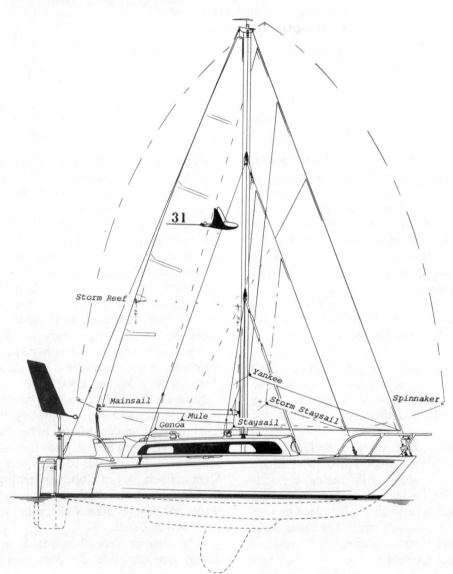

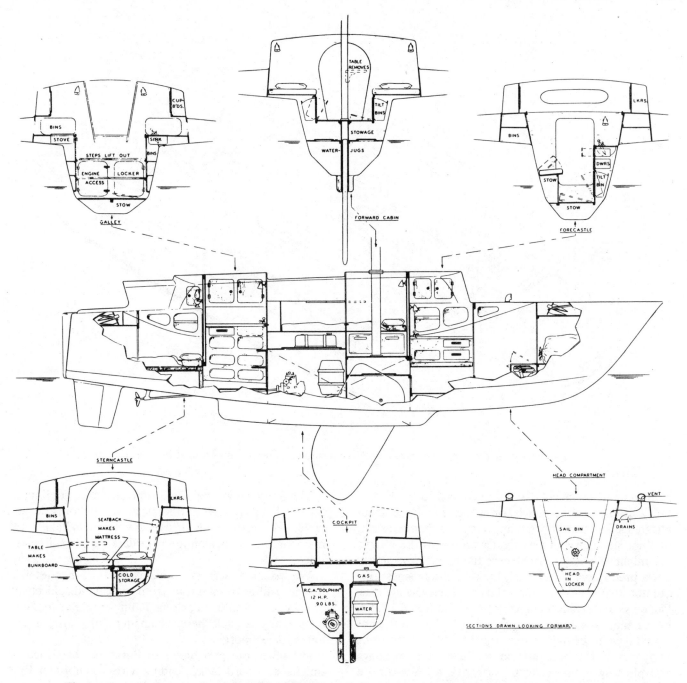

The interior arrangement drawings of the Searunner 31. (Searunner Construction Manual *by Jim Brown)*

would-be helpers out of the way, hauled the little boat easily up on board, and swiveled her fore and aft. It wasn't blowing much, so he didn't even need to lash her down. In three seconds he had brought her on board and she was all nestled in the netting between the main hull and the ama. When at sea, Jim stows her atop the house, back aft.

We were tied to the lee side of a moored float, wind abeam. Jim and Jo Anna cast her off, let her slide off sideways a few feet, ran up and trimmed a genoa jib, and then set the mainsail at their leisure. Off we went, as smoothly as you please.

The *Scrimshaw* consists of a lot of hulls. There are three of them, and the amas are nearly as long as the

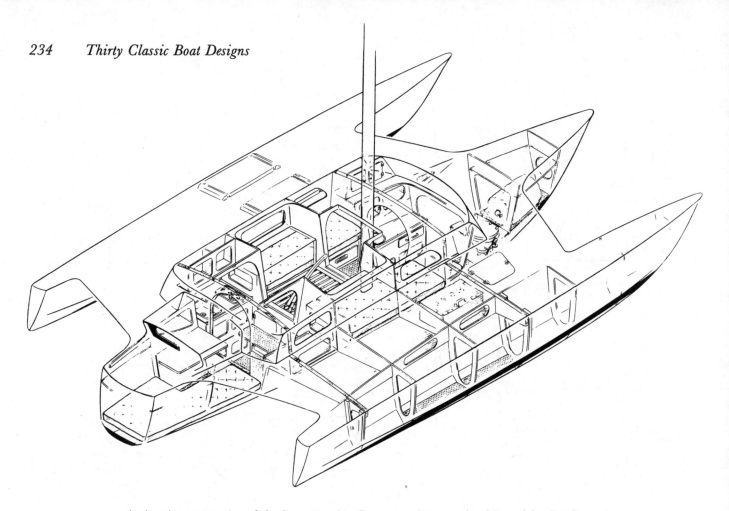

An interior perspective of the Searunner 31. (Searunner Construction Manual *by Jim Brown)*

main hull. It seems as if you are embarked in either a fairly sizable fleet of vessels, or at least in a large, complicated ship. Another first impression is that this fleet, or ship, sits high and very lightly on top of the water.

I might as well say right here that the *Scrimshaw* is not a pretty boat. Interesting-looking and businesslike, but not pretty. Why couldn't she have lovely whaleboat-like bows and sterns to all her hulls and at least a gentle, rather than absolutely flat, sheerline? The pretty ends would have to be higher and longer to achieve the same buoyancy in the hulls and so would increase windage and pitching moment, to be sure. It's a trade-off I'd gladly make.

Without my presumptuous modifications, the *Scrimshaw* measures 31 feet 2 inches long on deck, with a beam of 18 feet 8 inches and a draft of 2 feet 9 inches, board up. The main hull has a beam of 5 feet. The amas are 27 feet 2 inches long on deck with beams of 2 feet 5 inches. Provisioned for short-range cruising, she displaces 5,600 pounds. She can carry another 1,400 pounds of gear and stores for long cruises. Her sail area is 453 square feet.

The *Scrimshaw*'s hulls and superstructure are built of plywood covered with fiberglass on the outside and sealed with resin on the inside. Each ama is held to the main hull by two aluminum girders running athwartships.

We reached across Camden Harbor in the light breeze, sailing right away from a heavy-displacement cruising boat wallowing along in our wake. She looked a bit precarious back there, balancing along without any amas for support.

We sailed out past Sherman Point and hardened up on the starboard tack, heading across Penobscot Bay. Watching her go from the cockpit, the *Scrimshaw* appears rather clumsy. There's a lot of structure spread out in all directions; you're on a big raft. But then you look at the water rushing by and you realize that this great raft is sailing along very nicely, thank you.

Peering down through the netting on the weather side, you see that the windward ama is flying. Not touching the water at all. Just flying along over it. You climb out onto this flying platform to see what she looks like from there. Now this is fantastic, you've gotten

The Scrimshaw *in Penobscot Bay. (Jim Sollers)*

You can get "right off the boat" and watch her go from the weather ama. (Jim Sollers)

right off the boat and are looking back at her, watching her knife along through the water. Who says you never get to see your own boat sail? Anytime you want that thrill in a trimaran, you just walk out onto the weather ama and watch her go to your heart's content.

You can also watch the lee ama from the main hull. It's a very long skinny boat indeed, and is charging along through the waves under the pressing burden of the heeling force of the rig of a bigger hull locked to it to windward. You feel kind of sorry for the little ama thrashing along down there. "Hey, big shot. Try carrying your own rig for a while."

Stability there is plenty of. Jim Brown says that when the lee ama starts to dive through the seas it is time to reef. He says he actually shortens sail with the first dollop of spray. "We reef her a lot." This is conservative, high-speed sailing, not going for broke.

The *Scrimshaw* has a snug cutter rig. Her shrouds attach at the sides of the house, giving her rig what might be considered average monohull spread. This arrangement allows normal sheeting of a genoa jib on the wind. Preventer backstays can be set up to the amas, giving an enviable angle of pull.

The *Scrimshaw* has steps on her mast so you can climb up to clear a fouled halyard or whatever. (Of course, you have to watch out that the halyards don't foul on the steps themselves.) All her sheets are right in the cockpit.

Out in the middle of the bay we ran into a little lump of a head sea, and she seemed a bit pitchy. Do two or three skinny bows (the number depends on whether or not the head sea reaches the weather ama) pitch more than one fat one? (I'd still be willing to try my nicely curved bows and sterns.)

How fast does she go? Well, as a Dark Ages sailor who is used to sailing around in relatively heavy, fat craft without those slavish side helpers to keep the boat sailing relatively level, I must say her speed is impressive. The breeze increased to moderate for a while, so we saw her in light, gentle, and moderate conditions; and though I wouldn't describe her speed as phenomenal, it was certainly impressive. My 32-foot Herreshoff, the *Aria,* described in Chapter 17, couldn't have stayed with her. And, of course, off the wind in a breeze these trimarans move up onto a whole 'nother speed range.

The only direct comparison we had to the *Scrimshaw*'s sailing ability that day was the husky cruising sloop we outdistanced rapidly leaving the harbor. Of course, that vessel, of about the same length, was carrying around a lot more accommodations and could carry a much bigger payload.

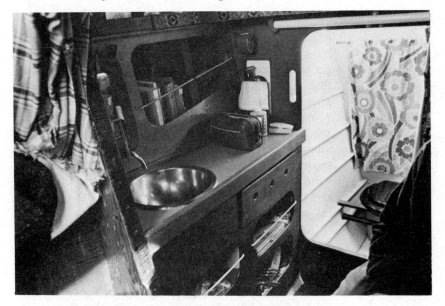

The washroom with the WC beyond. (Jim Sollers)

The main saloon (with table pushed back), movie playing. (Jim Sollers)

The *Scrimshaw* seemed sensitive to the vagaries of wind and wave, like any light-displacement boat. She accelerates like mad.

The *Scrimshaw* steers differently from any other boat I have sailed. In an overall sense, she is steady on her helm. She is nicely balanced and isn't trying to suddenly change course 45 degrees. She tacks majestically but surely. Yet on a small scale, she yaws around and has to be steered like a dinghy or an IOR boat. She has an outboard rudder, and Jim has a good wind-vane self-steerer on her.

After you have spent a bit of time in one of these trimaran contraptions, you begin to appreciate a few of the advantages of having three hulls sailing along side by side. You can handle the vessel entirely from the main hull, and if you should fall off it in so doing, you probably will fall into a nice netting or something instead of the ocean (a good reason to make these nettings very strong). There are even lifelines on the outboard sides of the amas to remind those with exceptionally strong wanderlust that there is, after all, some limit to the distance you can walk safely in a straight line.

Outboard of the house and cockpit structure, running fore and aft on each side is a heavy plank like a running board on an old-fashioned car. I found these contrivances a delightful contrast to the smooth, slick, modern-looking construction of the rest of the vessel. Climbing out of the cockpit for a stroll on one of those long heavy planks is like leaving the city for a visit to a farm.

And out there on the wings of the vessel you can lash down all sorts of ungainly stuff like spinnaker poles, boat hooks, and sounding poles. In the amas themselves there is plenty of space for light gear to be put away.

At the ends of the amas you can have fittings for great widespread bridles, a rigger's delight whether working with ground tackle at the forward end of the vessel or, say, a drogue at the after end.

When we got out near the islands in the bay, the idea was to put Jim Sollers, his cameras around his neck, out in the little dinghy to take pictures of the *Scrimshaw* as she circled around him and sailed by. We tacked her, left the genoa jib aback, hove-to, launched the dinghy, and sent Jim on his mission. He looked a bit lonely, even in the small sea. Discovered that a weather spreader had poked a hole in the poor old genoa, so we shifted to forestaysail and Yankee jib. The sail drill was performed by Jim and Jo Anna Brown, obviously a competent cruising team. We helped by staying out of the way. Then we steered various courses past the dinghy trying to look photogenic.

As a local, I was asked to explain the meaning of a massive dark cloud bank building up in the northwest. Since the breeze was steady from the southwest, I said not to worry. In fifteen minutes it was raining, and in thirty minutes it was a flat calm. We brought Jim Sollers back on board, followed by the dinghy. He was quite impressed with the difference between the small-boat feeling of the diminutive rowing boat and the big-ship feeling of the high, wide trimaran.

We all got out of the wet and let her drift. It was a benign little shower. Otherwise, Jim could have rigged his dodger over the forward end of the cockpit and even his canvas seat that goes into the forward companionway giving him a comfortable place from which to conn in comfort.

The breeze seemed to have taken off for good, so Jim lowered his 4-horsepower long-shaft outboard that was mounted on the stern and lighted her off. We headed back for Camden Harbor at a steady 4 knots. Jim says the Searunner 31 will do about six with his maximum recommended engine of 20 horsepower. Standard tankage for the design is not great: fuel, 20 gallons; water, 25 gallons.

It was a lovely evening as we plodded across a now-glassy bay. There was spectacular fall color on the Camden Hills. Well-defined, dense clouds slowly changed their immense sculptures overhead. All at once they left a long tunnel to the light of the low sun — it was just the right size for a giant to throw a medicine ball through — and the brightness from that cloudy shaft shone on the gray water like moonlight.

We tied up the *Scrimshaw* to her float just about dark, and then huddled out of the chill in the sterncastle. Jo Anna kept filling up mugs with hot cider. It's a tiny, snug little saloon back there with just room for four people to sit at the table playing kneesies. It may be a bit cramped physically, but never mentally, for your eyes are close to the wide stern window overlooking the harbor lights. You just can't keep from doing what one Searunner builder called "watching the movie."

The accommodations in the narrow main hull of the *Scrimshaw* are laid out in an exceedingly clever way to make use of what space there is. Away forward is stowage space. Next aft is the head compartment with sitting headroom. Then there is a stand-up washroom and wetroom. Next, in way of the mast, a sleeping area with two berths tucked away in the wings. Stowage for heavy gear is under this compartment and under the high center cockpit.

Go down the after companionway and you're in the stand-up galley. And right aft is the sterncastle with its narrow seats and table, or, when converted, a double berth and its free movie, playing continuously.

Since I disapprove of broadcasters telling you who won the election with less than two percent of the vote counted, I'm not going to pronounce any great conclusions with regard to trimarans. The *Scrimshaw* certainly captured my attention. I want to sail a lot more in these vessels, and the feeling is so strong I haven't even had to make a little note about it.

Index